India Becoming a Global Power in the Twenty-first Century

Rising Challenges and Newer Opportunities

Edited by
Raj Kumar Kothari
Eyasin Khan

ATLANTIC
PUBLISHERS & DISTRIBUTORS (P) LTD

Published by
ATLANTIC
PUBLISHERS & DISTRIBUTORS (P) LTD
7/22, Ansari Road, Darya Ganj, New Delhi-110002
Phones : +91-11-40775252, 23273880, 23275880, 23280451
Fax : +91-11-23285873
Web : www.atlanticbooks.com
E-mail : orders@atlanticbooks.com

Branch Office
5, Nallathambi Street, Wallajah Road, Chennai-600002
Phones : +91-44-64611085, 32413319
E-mail : chennai@atlanticbooks.com

Printed in India at Nice Printing Press, A-33/3A, Site-IV, Industrial Area, Sahibabad, Ghaziabad, U.P.

Dedicated to

Prof. B.N. Mehrish

Foreword

In the previous two books edited by him, *India's Foreign Policy in the New Millennium* (2010) and *Emerging India as a Global Power: Growing Ties and Challenges* (2012), Dr. Kothari has probed India's great power aspirations as reflected and mirrored in her foreign policy. The objective of the present volume, edited by Raj Kumar Kothari and Eyasin Khan, is to assess if India is at least on the threshold of gaining global power status, and to use India's foreign policy again as its touchstone.

For clarifying what is really meant by the term 'global power' when applied to a nation, and when India started being taken seriously as a claimant of this status, one cannot fall into the historically established trap of ascribing the term only to those possessed by irresistible expansionist urges. Prince Alexander Mikhail Gorchakov, the *bête noire* of Western Russianists, pointed out in 1864 that "The United States in America, France in Algeria, Holland in her colonies, England in India—all have been irresistibly forced, less by ambition than by imperious necessity, into this onward movement where the greatest difficulty is knowing where to stop." A historian searches for evidences of this 'imperious necessity' in the 'forward movement in the foreign policy of the great powers' in the first half of the twentieth century [Anthony D'Agostino, *The Rise of Global Powers: International Politics in the Era of Global Wars*, Cambridge University Press, 2011: 1].

Since, in today's decolonized and postcolonial world this criterion of global power status is anachronistic, one has to search for other criteria, and here structural realism helps. Waltz sees test of a state's global power capability lying in its capacity to impose polarity on an otherwise anarchic international system, i.e., in the capacity of powers to turn themselves into 'poles'. After showing how 'well-known theories', while referring to 'numbers of great powers or polarities', variously and imprecisely define polarity 'in terms of countries or blocs', "sometimes according to the physical capabilities of nations or of alliances, sometimes by looking at the pattern or national interrelations, and sometimes by awarding or denying top status to those who get or fail to get their ways", Waltz shuns such confused, vague, and fluctuating definitions of poles [Kenneth N. Waltz, *Theory of International Politics*, Addison-Wesley, 1979: 15], to define them in terms of 'combined capabilities'. Though living in a self-help system, states have to use their combined capabilities in order to serve their interests, still pole status of the system will depend less on the will or compulsions of individual states in the system than on how they "score on all of the following items: size of population and territory, resource endowment, economic capability, military strength, political stability, and competence" [Waltz 131]. Since counted on the basis of these criteria, the "barriers to entering the superpower club have never been higher and more numerous" than in 1979, Waltz predicted that the club "will long remain the world's most exclusive one" and the system will stay bipolar [Waltz 183].

So, conceptually 'great power', 'superpower', and 'global power' are contextually specific concepts, and to that extent do not covey identical meanings. The five great powers which dominated the balance of power system during the eighteenth, nineteenth, and the first two decades of the twentieth century, have not survived the First World War. Of the two superpowers, the only members of the exclusive 'superpower club' whom Waltz banked on so much, one has disappeared after 1992. A person no less than Barry Buzan has raised this point when reflecting on the shape of the world that was to succeed bipolarity. Distancing himself from "the prevailing mode of polarity theory in neorealism", Buzan bases his "argument on a distinction between *great powers* and *superpowers*, with *regional powers* as the most useful way of designating the next rank down". While superpowers 'operate globally', "great powers typically have their main influences in two or more regions". Regional powers are not unimportant however. Conceptually, more precise than *middle powers*, regional powers signify "much larger and, in international security terms, much more significant category of states that define the power structure of their local region", a term applicable to "India and Pakistan in South Asia; South Africa in southern Africa; Iran, Iraq, and Saudi Arabia in the Gulf; Egypt, Israel, and Syria in Levant; and so forth".

Even as recently as in 2005, Buzan did not consider India as anything more than a regional power and did not think that the current polarity status of the international system, i.e., one superpower plus four great powers (China, EU, Japan, Russia), was going to change in the foreseeable future. It may become 1 + x, where x = 3, 4, or 5, with the US continuing to be the lone superpower, and the number of great powers either staying the same, or rising or falling negligibly, with, for example, India making the grade of great powers and Russia dropping out. But, that is not going to affect the polarity status of the international system significantly. For, at the systemic or global level changes in the number of superpowers is causally far more decisive than changes in the number of great powers. A 1 + 3 system may not be all that different from a 1 + 5 one, but 2 + 3 will be quite different from 1 + 4. The key exception is when the number of superpowers falls to zero, and this is significant because there is a historical trend for the number of superpowers to decline [Barry Buzan, 'The Security Dynamics of a 1 + 4 World', in Ersel Aydinli, James N. Rosenau (Eds.), *Globalization, Security, and the Nation State: Paradigms in Transition*, SUNY Press, 2005: 177-98].

There are many others who have not considered India a potential global power before and after 2010. Friedman, a gifted writer of two huge *New York Times* bestsellers and founder-cum-CEO of intelligence unit, SRATFOR (the Strategic Forecasting, Inc.), argues that it is in the nature of international politics to spring unpredictable surprises in the rise and fall of great or global actors. Just as nobody could have imagined in 1900 that the global interdependence led by a 'peaceful and prosperous Europe', making war seems almost impossible, would be shattered by a global war in one decade and a half; in 1920 that a Europe in tatters sustained only by the heartening thought that the irritant of a fledgling communist Russia notwithstanding, the Versailles treaty guaranteed that Germany 'would not soon reemerge', would see the bogey reappearing fully in 1940, allying with the Soviets, and going to seal Europe's fate for at least the next hundred years; in 1960 that with a defeated and crushed Germany in just another five years, the occupation and splitting of Europe 'down the middle' by the United States and the Soviet Union, both vying for global supremacy and making calculations about Maoist China to complete it, the US would find itself vanquished in a seven-year war, not by the Soviet Union but by an unlikely communist Vietnam; that by 1980 a harassed US would conclude an alliance with Maoist China, finding it hard to contain an increasingly aggressive Soviet Union; and in 2000 that after the complete collapse of the Soviet Union, transformation of communist China into a capitalist superpower complete in all but name, advance of NATO not only into Eastern Europe but in Russia as well, in a world the US thought 'prosperous and peaceful', all geopolitical considerations being eclipsed by economic ones in a steadily globalizing world, four such strikes on September 11, 2001 will again turn the world 'on its head'. Arguing that "things that appear so permanent and dominant in any given time of history can change with stunning rapidity", and in "international relations, the way the world looks right now is not at all how it will look in twenty years or even less", Friedman draws up an improbable list of global powers in the middle of the 21st century based on their *innenpolitik* and external contextual imperatives. The list begins with Japan (the second largest economy in 2010) to meander through Turkey (the seventeenth largest), through Poland, and even Mexico towards the end of this century [George Friedman, *America's Secret War*, St. Portland, US, Broadway Books, 2004 and *The Next 100 Years: A Forecast for the 21st Century*, New York, London, Toronto, Sydney and Auckland: Doubleday, 2010: 1-10]. But, India is just not mentioned!

Among the doubting Thomases, there are many who recognize the signs and factors conducive to India's arrival, but question its ability to translate these conditions to her benefit. What are these factors? For one thing, it is for the 'first time in history' that "transpacific trade equaled transatlantic trade" (Friedman 2010: 4). While along with trade, the global balance of power is also shifting from the Atlantic to the Pacific. Observers are feeling that with her "vast size and population, resilient democracy, rapidly growing economy, booming information technology sector, scientific and technological sophistication, fast-expanding middle class, nuclear and conventional military strength", leadership in global governance, and its geostrategic position on the Indian Ocean and its littoral and sea lanes, the rise of India together with China as great or at least major regional power is an inevitability and only partially realized. Hagerty predicts that 'from a neorealist perspective', India is finely "poised to become a global great power within the next decade". With an expected GDP growth rate of 7.5% over the next five years, India's economy is projected to world's third largest after those of the US and China. The dimensions of this rise and its strategic payoffs have been calculated by the US National Intelligence Council Report ('Mapping the Global Future'), the CIA, Goldman Sachs, and others, where the international political community is being asked to prepare itself for the military, political, and economic impacts of the rise of China and India, their growing ascendance being compared with that of Germany in the 19th and America in the 20th centuries. By 2040, China, US, India, and Japan are projected to be the four largest economies in that order. India is predicted to surpass the G-6 economies before the predicted time, with its economy hopefully surpassing that of the US by 2050 [Harsh V. Pant (Ed.), *Indian Foreign Policy in a Unipolar World*, 2015: 1-2; Devin T. Hagerty, "India and the Global Balance of Power: A Neorealist Snapshot", in Harsh V. Pant, *Indian Foreign Policy in a Unipolar World*, London, New York: Routledge, 2009: 23, 41-42].

Enthusiasts, as contrasted with the detractors, gloat over the manifestations of India's 'rise', like the ascension from G-20 to G-8 summits, the condescending speeches from US Secretaries of State, etc. But, do these signs of recognition, ask who are finical about political grammar, directly lead to signify causal polarity? There are many reasons apart from GDP growth why the economic rise of India together with China is taken notice of, one being the "overwhelming influence of China and India on trends in global inequality change" between 1980 and 2005, where one key to the question whether "true global income inequality is likely to reverse its course of reduction and start increasing again in the next quarter century", is if "the phenomenal rise of China and India is exceptional or if it is a harbinger of rapid growth in other populous, developing economies" (Ho-fung Hung and Jaime Kucinskas, 'Globalization and Global Inequality: Assessing the Impact of the Rise of China and India, 1980-2005', *American Journal of Sociology*, Vol. 116, No. 5, 2011: 1478-1513). It is difficult for the G-8 and its leader not to take notice of India's economic rise.

But the translatability of this economic rise into acceptance in the ranks of global powers is beset by many problems, because the enhanced attention to India by the US and other great powers has been "aided by some fortuitous global and internal developments, while harmed by others". First, the increased focus and attention is linked to India's economic power rather than to military or even soft power (this in spite of the present Prime Minister's diplomacy of bear hugs). Secondly, the attention has not been gained by India only on her own, but has drawn notice as part of a group of rising powers that also includes Brazil, China, and Russia. Thirdly, the attention has come from external factors not of India's making. While the global changes resulting from the collapse of the Soviet Union, the sudden unipolarity the US started enjoying, the dramatic emergence of China, the ongoing economic crisis starting in the West, and India's nuclear tests produced certain basic realignments that took the long bitterness away from India-US relations; the attention has found India somewhat unprepared. Thus, Sinha and Dorshner point out that while a source of India's power is internally driven (economic) and aspirational (people-oriented), exogenous developments of the types mentioned above have projected more power to India than it has the capacity to digest or translate. It is possible that some gestures and steps of the US and the EU have had an unintended effect in propelling India to a status of world power before India is itself ready for a global role. If contextual imperatives and factors, rather than internal ones, "institutional factors, or strategic planning" have catapulted India to its present exalted international status, the question remains if India herself has "articulated a coherent strategic vision of what it wants to achieve" with this exalted status [Aseema Sinha and Jon P. Dorshner. 'India: Rising Power or a Mere Revolution of Rising Expectations?' *Polity*, Vol. 42, No. 1, January 2010: 74-99].

The need for such a coherent vision arises from the fact that while India shares some problems with her competitors for global attention, China and Brazil, she also has some unique problems of her own. Like them India has to match her global aspirations with the transformed international system, while simultaneously ensure that its emergence as a rising power keeps in step with its domestic dilemmas and constraints, and not allow the former to run athwart the latter. But, in a more urgent way than any of the other BRICs, India's chaotic democratic system demands a linkage between its global strategy and its domestic politics. And unlike Brazil and China, India must manage its regional context with great skill, faced as it is with serious challenges from internal developments in Pakistan, Afghanistan, and Sri

Lanka, each of which poses an external challenge to India that spills over into internal security risks [Sinha and Dorshner, 75].

A coherent vision is important also because, in spite of the wide consensus about the greater potential impact of China on the twenty-first century international political and economic system, in many senses the reverberations of India's claim to great power status and its potential contributions to the nature of an Eastphalian world, would possibly be much more intriguing. Kim, the originator of the term 'Eastphalia' with Ganguly and Fidler, its famous joint users, employed it to assess the impact of the rise of Asia on international law and politics [Sung Won Kim, David P. Fidler and Sumit Ganguly. '*Eastphalia* Rising? Asian Influence and the Fate of Human Security', *World Policy Journal* 26:2 (Summer 2009): 53-64]. Ganguly and Fidler suggest that in spite of its democratic and secular credentials, India equally embraces principles that stand in opposition to the Western-led push for global democratization and its attendant human rights, namely the principles of sovereignty and nonintervention in the domestic affairs of other states. To this extent India remains "much more of an enigma" than China "in the emergence of an Eastphalian world" [David P. Fidler and Sumit Ganguly, 'India and Eastphalia', *Indiana Journal of Global Legal Studies* 17:1 (Winter 2010): 147-64].

I hope that the sundry papers in this volume hammer all this out on the anvil of Indian foreign policy to help editors catch all the gyrations and steps of the Indian elephant's *Bharatanatyam* on the world stage.

Amartya Mukhopadhyay
Professor of Political Science
University of Calcutta

Preface

The idea of editing this volume—*India Becoming a Global Power in the Twenty-first Century: Rising Challenges and Newer Opportunities* occurred during early 2015 when the Department of Political Science with Rural Administration, Vidyasagar University, West Bengal organised a two-day UGC sponsored national seminar on "India: An Emerging Global Power" held on March 11-12, 2015. Eminent intellectuals and subject experts representing several institutions located in various parts of the country took part and presented papers on various aspects on the seminar theme. They emphasized on India's meteoric rise in the economic field since early 1990s and its implications on security, politics, culture, environment, defence, and many other related fields. The core part of the seminar focused on numerous multidimensional challenges and newer opportunities presented before India in the backdrop of globalization. The present volume includes papers presented by most of the seminar participants as well as some others who could not take part in the program but merit inclusion for their scholarly contributions in the field.

We express our sincere gratitude to all the contributors of this volume who despite their hectic schedule favorably responded to our request for writing a piece in this volume. We are highly indebted to all our former and present colleagues in the Department—Prof. Tarun Kumar Bannerji, Prof. Anil Kumar Jana, Prof. Ambarish Mukherjee, and Sri Suratha Malik—for their active support in this regard without which timely publication of this volume would not have been possible. We also owe sincere thanks to Prof. Sibaji Pratim Bose who has joined the department very recently but still extended moral support into this present editorial endeavour.

Special thanks are due to Sukanya Mukherjee, currently the UGC sponsored major research project fellow in the department, who has made extra efforts to assist us in editing this volume. Also, we are extremely grateful to Prof. B.N. Mehrish of the University of Mumbai and Prof. Purusottam Bhattacharya of Jadavpur University, who were kind enough in giving valuable support and guidance in all possible ways in completing this work. We express our sincere gratitude to Prof. Amartya Mukhopadhyay for having kindly agreeing to write a foreword for this edited volume. Last but not the least, we thank each one of our family members and friends for their moral support and constant encouragement in this venture.

Raj Kumar Kothari
Eyasin Khan

Contents

Section Two

Section Three

Contributors

Ambarish Mukhopadhyay. Professor and Head, Department of Political Science, Vidyasagar University, Midnapore, West Bengal.

Anindya Batabyal. Assistant Professor, Department of Political Science, University of Kalyani, West Bengal.

Anindya Jyoti Majumdar. Professor of International Relations and Director of the School of International Relations and Strategic Studies, Jadavpur University, Kolkata, West Bengal.

Ankhi Sen Sanyal. Assistant Professor, Basantidevi College, Kolkata, West Bengal.

Badruddin. Associate Professor, Department of Political Science, PES College of Arts and Science, Goa University, Ponda, Goa.

Budh Bahadur Lama. Assistant Professor, Department of Political Science, Sikkim Central University, Gangtok, Sikkim.

B.N. Mehrish. Professor (Retired), Department of Politics, University of Mumbai, Mumbai.

Chandrima Chaudhuri. Research Scholar, Centre for Indo-Pacific Studies, School of International Studies, Jawaharlal Nehru University, New Delhi.

Debasish Nandy. Assistant Professor, Department of Political Science, Kanchrapara College, 24 Parganas (N); Guest Faculty in the Department of Political Science, Rabindra Bharati University, Kolkata, West Bengal.

Jayita Mukhopadhyay. Assistant Professor, Department of Political Science, Women's Christian College, Kolkata, West Bengal.

Peu Ghosh: Assistant Professor, Department of Political Science, Lady Brabourne College, Kolkata, West Bengal.

Prosenjit Pal. Assistant Professor of Political Science, University of Burdwan, West Bengal.

Purusottam Bhattacharya. Professor (Retired) and Former Head of Department of International Relations; Former Director, School of International Relations and Strategic Studies, Jadavpur University, Kolkata, West Bengal.

Raj Kumar Kothari. Professor of Political Science, Vidyasagar University, Midnapore, West Bengal.

Rashmi Bhure. Associate Professor and Head of the Department of Politics, SIES College, Sion, West, Mumbai.

Shibashis Chatterjee. Professor, Department of International Relations, Jadavpur University, Kolkata, West Bengal.

Smriti Singh. Research Scholar in Political Science, Mumbai.

Sreya Maitra Roychoudhury. Guest Faculty, Department of Political Science, Bhawanipur Education Society College, Kolkata, West Bengal.

Sukanya Mukherjee. Research Scholar and UGC sponsored major research project fellow in the Department of Political Science, Vidyasagar University, West Bengal.

Suratha Kumar Malik. Assistant Professor, Department of Political Science, Vidyasagar University, Midnapore, West Bengal.

Swatilekha Bhattacharya. ICSSR Doctoral Fellow, Centre for International Politics, Organization and Disarmament, School of International Studies, Jawaharlal Nehru University, New Delhi.

Introduction

Raj Kumar Kothari

'Power' is one of the key concepts in the discipline of international relations which has been defined from different perspectives. Modern discourse of power generally speaks in terms of state power that includes both economic and military power. Sovereign states in the present international system have been referred to as middle power, regional power, great power, superpower or hegemons. There is however no standard concept for what defines a powerful state. Entities other than sovereign states—international organisation, regional organisations, military alliances, multinational corporations, non-governmental organisations, etc.—can also be relevant in power acquisition in international relations which are however beyond the purview of this edited volume.

Niccolo Machiavelli and Hans Morgenthau were the two noted theoreticians who advocated the usage of 'power' as a goal in international relations. To classical Realist thinkers power is an inherent goal of mankind of states. It is used when actors have achieved military victories or security for their state in the international system. In other words, power is the capacity to direct the decisions and actions of other states. Power is derived from strength and will of the states. Strength comes from the transformation of resources into capabilities. Will infuses objectives that guides the ways the state deploys and applies its power abroad. Thus, power is used to describe the resources and capabilities of a state.

Academicians and experts on the subject have devoted adequate amount of time and energy to understand the status of 'power' and how they could be measured. The findings are mixed. There are several categories of power, and the inclusion of a state in one category or another is fraught with difficulty. Paul Kennedy in his book *The Rise and Fall of the Great Powers* charts the relative status of various powers from 1500 to 2000 AD. Kennedy develops working definition of great power for different era.

In the discipline of international relations, a number of terms are used to describe various types of powers—'superpower', 'great power', 'middle power', 'small power', 'regional power', 'cultural superpower', 'energy superpower', 'hard power', 'soft power', 'smart power' and so on.

According to *Encyclopaedia Britannica*, 'superpower' is a state that possesses military or economic might or both and influence vastly to that of other states. Their influence and impact cannot be ignored on the world stage. Kenneth Waltz stated that the number of superpowers determines the stability of the international order, as well as the prospects of war and peace. Britain during the Victorian era and the USA and the USSR after World War II belonged to this category. The term 'great power' was first used to represent the most important powers in Europe during the post-Napoleonic era. It refers to the states that have strong political, cultural and economic influence over nations around the world. Today, China, France, Germany, Japan, Russia and India belong to this category. They play important role in the United Nations and other international organisations such as WTO, IMF, World Bank and many such institutions. Scholars are however not in agreement about the definition. The present international system is for the most part made up by small powers, whose existence cannot be ignored for the simple reason that all the above stated hierarchical categories of states need their support on major issues of world politics and economics. 'Regional power' is used to describe a nation that exercises influence and power within a region but their support is also important in the functioning of the United Nations and other international organisations. Combination of hard power (military power/nuclear arsenals, etc.) and soft power, which includes culture, technology and so on, makes smart power that takes a country forward in its own way. Hard power refers to coercive tactics, the threat or use of armed forces or economic sanctions. Realists and neo-realists such as John Mearsheimer, are advocates of the use of such power for the balancing of the international system. Joseph Nye, in contrast, is the leading advocate of soft power that is used to achieve political ends. It includes diplomacy, dissemination of information, propaganda, cultural programming and so on. In view of the above-stated concepts of power, it would be suffice to say that global power means a state is powerful enough to influence events throughout the world. Global power is an overarching concept that relates to the concepts of great power, major power and even super-power. It is however a matter of debate whether India could be classified into the category of global power. The fact is that today in the twenty-first century India well fits into the category of smart power that corresponds to the concepts of various classified categories of power.

For a very long time, since independence to till the late 1980s, India was positioned on the periphery of global politics resulting in minimal or no influence on major issues affecting the international system. New Delhi only used issues like Third World solidarity through non-alignment movement and complete nuclear disarmament to make its presence felt on the international stage. The arena of international politics was largely dominated, guided and controlled by the major powers that determined the trajectory of global politics. Today because of its meteoric rise in economic strength and military capability, India has moved to the centre of global politics.

In view of the fact that India has emerged as one of the powerful economies in the world, New Delhi's clout on the global stage could only be matched by a handful of states. Today, India's economic and military rise has the potential to decisively shift the global balance of power. It is therefore necessary to comprehend not only India's 'power' capabilities but also the potentialities and limits of that power.

In the above-stated backdrop, the present volume entitled *India Becoming a Global Power in the Twenty-first Century: Rising Challenges and Newer Opportunities* extensively focuses on the conceptual and theoretical aspects centring on the myth and reality of India's rise as a global power. As India moves on in the twenty-first century, because of its path-breaking economic growth record over a period of last two and half decades—for which it is now considered as the fastest growing economic power in the world—and a vertical rise in its military might, it is in a relatively much better position to assert its power and influence at the global level. At the same time, many new challenges, right from energy security, terrorism, air pollution, water crisis, food security, to a host of various other issues have hindered its growth and advancement.

The present volume—though not thoroughly inclusive—attempts to address major topics and wide ranging issues relevant to the title. The focus of the volume is multi-faceted, and the arguments rest on subtle distinctions. Introduction apart, the present volume has been divided into three parts based on conceptual, theoretical and strategic considerations. Section One deals with conceptual and theoretical issues that explain the very nature of India's rise in the direction of becoming a global power since early 1990s that is in the post-cold war years. The very first article entitled "Theorizing India's 'Rise': Levels, Structures and Agency in India's Foreign Policy" by Shibashis Chatterjee and Sreya Maitra Roychoudhury provides a theoretical audit of India's rise from normative perspective as well as on the basis of its evolving material capabilities and power since the immediate post-independence period. In the post-Cold War years, Indian foreign policy shows a persistent effort to graduate India into a major power and to obviate the structural challenges issuing from the global system. But the claim to this kind of great power status and its recognition in the region has always been contested. This is partly due to Pakistan's adroitness and ability to engage extra-regional actors, the United States and China frustrated India's attempts to unite the subcontinent through its own vision of strategic autonomy. This apart, Chatterjee and Maitra very aptly argue that the claim to being a great power has been closely related to notions of legitimacy and authority and not about the possession of crude material power. Despite India's meteoric rise in the post-

1998 period, it has not succeeded in translating its material preponderance into either strategic consensus or even general leadership of the subcontinent. In other words, the foreign policy of states is invariably structured by the complex interaction of systemic forces on one hand, and agential actions on the other. India serves as a test-case to this theoretical observation.

India achieved independence in 1947, at a time when the world politics was heavily motivated by the ongoing tussle of power ushered by the Bloc politics between United States and Soviet Union. The predominant notion guiding the states was to devise ways to survive in a system of hostile environment where the states were suspicious of one another which remains valid even today. Security has become the prime mover of foreign policy formulations in the present global order. Swatilekha Bhattacharya's paper on "India's Foreign Policy and the Notion of 'Security': Disengagement and Linkages" seeks to identify the sharp divide that exists between domestic and external imperatives of foreign policy formulations. In fact, the concept of security enjoys a supreme position when it comes to articulating aims and goals of foreign policy. However, the very idea of security kept changing and expanding for India with each marginal increase in her capabilities and the necessity to respond to the ever-changing global security environment. As its security concerns expand beyond the region of South Asia and make forays into areas where other actors are present, the themes of Rising China and Emerging India become interweaved. It is aptly emphasized that while other major states in Asia are not unduly concerned or distressed with India's rise, China however views India's rise with growing concern. Thus, the security implications of the story of Rising China remains incomplete without the story of Emerging India taken into consideration, and in the same fashion, the Emerging India story would have little value if it left out the security implications of the Rising China which have been aptly dealt by Anindya Jyoti Majumdar in his article "Innate Security Contest in the Emerging India Theme". The paper seeks to ascertain the major props on which the very theme of Emerging India is based and accordingly derives India's security challenges in the contemporary period corresponding to these basic props. In the process, it makes an attempt to explore India's non-committal balancing act as a response to emerging security environment and advocates an expanding and firm security reach combining both traditional and non-traditional aspects.

Nuclear strategy is another important area that has direct bearing on India's global power ambition. India's peaceful nuclear test of 1974 made Western nations conscious of the existing loopholes in the non-proliferation regime and heightened their 'atomic dilemma'. It was alleged that India diverted the nuclear technologies intended for civilian purposes under the Canada-India-Reactor-US (CIRUS) agreement with Canada and the US. Thus, in the post-1974 period, India was regarded as a 'nuclear pariah'. The US Congress passed the Nuclear Non-Proliferation Act of 1978 (NNPA), which barred nuclear exports unless the non-nuclear weapon state accepted comprehensive International Atomic Energy Agency (IAEA) safeguards. India was internationally isolated, yet it refused to accede to the NPT and pursued an ambiguous policy on nuclear weapons. In 1998, India conducted a series of nuclear weapons explosions and declared it a nuclear weapon state. In the aftermath of the 1998 nuclear tests, the Clinton administration along with couple of other Western nations imposed sanctions as per the Glenn Amendment, thereby restricting bilateral and multilateral economic assistance to India. In addition, the non-statutory measures also curtailed high-level visits and military-to-military contacts. Suratha Kumar Malik's article "Analyzing India's Nuclear Strategy: Making Debates on the Issues and Problems" extensively focuses on how India successfully countered the trade embargo and went ahead with its nuclear programme without succumbing to any untoward pressure. The signing of Indo-US nuclear deal was indeed a landmark development having wide ranging impact upon the nuclear non-proliferation regime that gave a major boost to India's 'global' power image.

In fact, India's role as a 'global' power needs to be examined with reference to both internal determinants—such as domestic politics, economic reforms, conventional and non-conventional security threats—and the global factors. Hailed as the world's largest democracy, more than sixty years of democratic governance in India has failed to be 'inclusive' in nature. It had to tackle a number of daunting challenges within the framework of a democratic order. Ambarish Mukhopadhyay in his article entitled "The Problem of Food Security in 'Emerging' India: Some Reflections" very pertinently argues that despite her mounting ambitions, India is still very much a developing nation on many indicators of human development. Some persistent problems that our country faces include poverty, rampant corruption and crime, caste war and communal violence, terrorist insurgency, resource depletion and environmental degradation, conventional and non-conventional security threats and so on. India's great power ambition coexists with extreme inequality and social vulnerability in the domestic front. Of the myriad problems faced by our country, challenges to human security are a major one. Food security is one of the essential components of human security. Problems of human security are major impediments to India's development and serious threats to the welfare and very survival of millions of Indian people.

Energy security is another important aspect of human security that has drawn immense attention to India's foreign policymakers. India co-relates energy security with the issue of economic development. Ankhi Sen Sanyal in her article "Energy Security: The Strategic Outlook of the UPA Government" very rightly argues that the Indian economy is at a critical stage of development where energy requirement is increasing at a phenomenal pace. India is the fourth largest energy consumer in the world after USA, China and Russia. The domestic availability of oil and gas constitutes 40% of the energy basket and India imports over 75% of its domestic requirement and is subjected to the vagaries of the volatile international price scenario. In order to achieve 8% projected GDP growth during Twelfth Plan period (2012-17), oil and gas sector needs to grow in tandem with economy at a faster pace. Therefore, the challenge is to ensure supply of oil and gas on a sustainable basis and at affordable prices.

Section Two of the present volume focuses on the strategically important areas from the perspective of India becoming a potential global power in the twenty-first century. While dealing with BJP's foreign policy strategy, Rashmi Bhure and Smriti Singh focused on the role of Indian diaspora in taking the country forward in the direction of India becoming a global power. Badruddin however in his paper "Indian Diaspora in the USA: Issues and Challenges" has confined his study on the role of Indian diaspora in the United States. India and the US, being economically strong, socially well connected and professionally well qualified, Indian diaspora have been instrumental in the development of infrastructure including IT, skill transfer, circular migration habits and transnational investment opportunities. Preservation of Indian culture through naturalization, inter ethnic engagements and Indo-US Ties have been significantly valued by the Americans.

In fact, diasporas have a long history of migration across the world but the group of population or their kin who are now recognized as a part of Indian diaspora have mainly migrated during the colonial and the postcolonial period. During British rule, many Indians migrated as temporary labourers under indentured labour system and kangani/maistry system particularly, on sugar and rubber plantation to British colonies in Africa, Asia, and Caribbean. British could easily transport the Indians as labourers to other countries mainly due to two reasons—one, the growing poverty in India and secondly, the forcefully inbuilt existence of slave mentality among the Indians towards their British masters. Though in the initial years there were lot of restrictions that were imposed upon the migration of Indians starting with the Passport Act of 1917 by the British Government followed by the restriction based on racial discrimination imposed by various host country on the entry of Indians in their respective country, all this led to the decline of the Indians migrating to the other country. But those who migrated under the British rule formed an inseparable part of the Indian diaspora, which mainly consist of unskilled labourers. However, for a long time various initiatives that were taken by the Indian Government were inadequate to instill confidence among the Indian diaspora towards New Delhi. The major shift in the Indian Government's diaspora policy was seen only after 90s when the country's economic policy was liberalized due to grave financial crisis and further gained momentum under the present BJP-led NDA Government.

Sukanya Mukherjee turns our focus on to a relatively new area that is extremely important from India's geo-strategic and economic point of view. To strengthen its foothold in Central Asia, India has been extremely keen to promote strategic partnership with the region. In view of the fact that the Central Asian countries are endowed with tremendous reserve of crude oil and natural gas, the region has attracted attention of major powers around the globe. India, though late comer in the field, has been working hard to make its presence felt in Central Asia. Sukanya's article on "India's Central Asia Policy: Quest for Strategic Partnership" elaborately deals with India's 'Connect Central Asia' Policy launched in the year 2012 which has got a major boost during Prime Minister Narendra Modi's visit to the region in July 2015.

Peu Ghosh also focuses our attention to another extremely important area from India's foreign policy and strategic interests' points of view. In the paper entitled "Political and Economic Review of Indian Ocean Region (IOR): Positioning India in the IOR", she attempts to highlight the fact that the Indian Ocean Region (IOR) commands a significant position in India's ambitious 'global' power framework. The presence of some extra-regional powers—most importantly the USA—in the IOR has made the region a hotbed of tension. The world is witnessing a game of checks and balances in the IOR because of the presence of important powers like the USA, China, India, and Pakistan. India has been working hard to further its economic and security interests. Peu Ghosh focuses on the tricky game that is on by making a comprehensive political and economic review and future prospects of IOR.

Apart from the geo-strategic importance of the Indian Ocean, 'water' itself has emerged as a key strategic resource that would determine the future course of strategic cooperation or conflict among the Asian giants. The risk of water becoming a trigger for war or diplomatic strong-arming is especially high in Asia, which is home to three-fifths of the human population, yet has the lowest per-capita freshwater availability among all continents. Asia's per capita fresh water availability is less than half the global average. By 2025, two-third of the global population is likely to be living in water scarce or water-stressed conditions. And the majority of the world's people living in water-related despair will be in Asia.

The moot point is that there is undeniable shortage of water in Asia, particularly South Asia, precipitated by the changing climate and a tendency of water wastage in the region, and this shortage has the potential to create a major water crisis in the region. Unfortunately, India is caught up in the vortex of such water disputes with almost all its neighbouring states some of which dates back to the period of India's birth as a free nation. Jayita Mukhopadhyay's paper on "India's Water Sharing Disputes with Its Neighbours: A Challenge to Its Regional Ascendancy" begins with an attempt to highlight why the water disputes are major concerns for all the stakeholders, i.e. governments and people alike. The author very cogently puts forward her views about what could be done to grapple with this difficult issue so that it does not create obstacles to promotion of friendly relations between India and her neighbours. Further to what extent India, as an emerging big power should actually walk the extra mile to eliminate chances of friction among neighbours on water sharing.

The Third and Final Section attempts to show how far or to what extent New Delhi's march towards global power status has been practiced into reality through assessing India's bilateral relations with some of the major powers like China and Japan and few strategically important neighbours—Pakistan, Bangladesh, Nepal and Myanmar.

Anindya Batabyal's article entitled "The Tibetan Enigma and the Sino-Indian Boundary Dispute in the Twenty-first Century" very pertinently focuses on the unsettled frontier between India and China that provides Beijing the much needed strategic leverage over New Delhi. The author further argues that the issue of Sino-Indian boundary dispute is inseparably tied with the issue of Tibet. In fact, Sino-Indian boundary dispute is intimately tied with the issue of Tibet and it is impossible to discuss the former without making a reference to the latter. The very basis of China's policy towards India regarding Tibet has been to exercise pressure in order to force the Indian Government to refrain from adopting policies and pursuing actions that might endanger Chinese Government's control over Tibet. In recent years, China has hardened its position in settling the boundary dispute with India and incidents of incursions by Chinese P.L.A. troops into territories claimed by India all along the Line of Actual Control have increased significantly. In other words, a thorough understanding of the intractable nature of the India-China boundary dispute cannot be done without analyzing the issue of Tibet, which remains a core issue in Sino-Indian bilateral ties.

China apart, Japan is another important Asian country with which India aims to promote stronger strategic partnership which is extremely relevant in respect of the title of this volume. In 2006, the Indian Prime Minister Manmohan Singh stated at the Joint Session of the *Diet* that India and Japan needs to build a strong global and strategic partnership that will have a greater significance for Asia and the world as a whole. With the new government coming to power in New Delhi, the shift from 'Look East Policy' to 'Act East Policy' was announced. The tenure of Prime Minister Modi also coincides with India's third decade of 'Look East Policy'. This was in reaction to the criticism that India in the past decades did not have a consistent policy towards this region. Thus in the last two decades there has been a shift from a low key relationship to strategic relationship between India and Japan. The relationship is on an all-time high with large number of diplomatic exchanges taking place. Since historical times, both these countries had showed no real sign of friction and thus they have carried forward their friendship till date. Chandrima Chaudhuri in her paper "India and Japan: Strategic Partners in the New Era" argues that India-Japan bilateral relations is based on mutual respect and shared values on democracy, rule of law and human rights. The bilateral ties are expected to get a major leap forward from the personal camaraderie between Japan's Shinzo Abe and India's Narendra Modi.

After China and Japan, South Asian countries draw maximum attention from India's perspective. As the largest and the most dominant country, India attracts the maximum attention among the eight states in the region. With its location in the middle of South Asia India shares land and maritime borders with all the other countries of the region with the exception of Afghanistan. The Indo-centric nature of the region has been a source of discord between India and its South Asian neighbours for the past seven decades. The size, resources and capabilities of India have given rise to an asymmetry which has caused feelings of insecurity among the smaller states of the region. Besides India also has contentious issues at stake which characterize, to a considerable extent, its bilateral relations with its neighbours.

Relations between India and Pakistan have been marked by hostility and bitterness since 1947. The descending curve of Indo-Pak relations reflected the bilateral antagonism. During last seven decades, India-Pakistan relations have not gone beyond the framework of mutual suspicion and discord. Both are concerns of each other's foreign and security policies. Islamabad and New Delhi have developed adversarial relationship with each other from the beginning. Debasish Nandy in his article on "Recent Trends in India-Pakistan Relations: Track II Diplomacy as an Alternative" rightly argues that the strings of wars and crises that have erupted between India and Pakistan have left little room for optimism about its future prospects. The paper focuses on the complexities of Indo-Pak relations and sheds light about the effectiveness of Track II diplomacy between them. Prosenjit Pal's article "Security Imperative in Contemporary India-Pakistan Relations: Terrorism as a Factor" deals with the Kashmir issue that remains the bone of contention between the two countries since independence resulting in massive upsurge of terrorist activities in the region. In other words, terrorism has become an important factor that not only affects bilateral relations between India and Pakistan, but also security of the entire South Asia and even beyond.

Geopolitics has been a major factor in conditioning India-Bangladesh relations. Bangladesh is often referred to as 'India-locked' because 90 per cent of its border is shared with India. Its access to the Bay of Bengal is also problematic due to a robust naval presence of India. On the other hand, India's North-East is 'Bangladesh-locked' prompting her to seek transit rights through Bangladesh in order to "open up the region to trade and economic activity, and in particular, to bring it closer both physically and psychologically to the rest of the country".

The irritants which have bedevilled India-Bangladesh relations over the years comprise longstanding issues like illegal migration, sharing of water of 54 common rivers, energy resources, access to seaports, maritime and land border disputes, presence of anti-social and anti-national elements in both countries. Purusottam Bhattacharya in his article "India and Bangladesh: Can the Asymmetry in Bilateral Relations be Overcome?" argues that any improvements in India-Bangladesh relations depend considerably on the resolution or at least partial progress in several contested areas.

As far as geostrategic location of Nepal is concerned, it is extremely important from India's security point of view. India-Nepal relations are 'distinctive' for many reasons ranging from geographical proximity to close cultural ties, and wide institutional and social relationships. Socio-cultural, political, economic and geographical factors along with the common bond of a shared religion have had a great impact on their bilateral relations. In spite of some turbulence in the recent past, India-Nepal relations have remained close, stable and mutually beneficial to each other. However, domestic and systemic factors are instrumental for creating disturbances in their bilateral ties which could be seen in the recent movements (in the year 2015) launched by the Madeshi groups against the newly drafted constitution of Nepal in Terai regions. The article entitled "Emerging Trends in India-Nepal Relations: Select Issues" by Budh Bahadur Lama analyzes the recent political developments in Nepal and their impact on New Delhi-Kathmandu relations. The author very rightly points out that the new constitution—adopted in 2015—has sharply polarised Nepal along ethnic and regional lines that would affect India's security and strategic interests in the long run.

Myanmar is another important country that has drawn attention of the whole world in recent years. The spirit of democracy is in the air in Myanmar. India's efforts to stabilise its Northeast region with the help of Myanmar combined with the economic benefits of trade and transport links across the Indo-Myanmar border is an important determinant in its policy towards Myanmar. New Delhi's Look East policy has largely focused on a stretch running from Bangkok to Jakarta and in the process left Myanmar out of its framework. China and India, two of Myanmar's giant neighbours, as for long have showered the military junta with investments, aid and sale of armaments. China's active support is not surprising at all as it has its own record of suppressing democratic movements at home. India has also helped the military junta with arms and training. For strategic reasons, India needs a stable and self-confident Myanmar that can keep China at bay. B.N. Mehrish's article "India and Myanmar: Implications of New Democratic Forces' Victory in 2015 Elections for New Delhi" highlights the recent political developments in Myanmar relating to the process of democratization and its implications on national security.

Finally, in view of the above-stated theoretical and conceptual developments, it could be stated that the image of India as an emerging power in world politics and a contender to 'global' power status has become very common one in recent times, thanks to print and electronic media. "Shining India", "Incredible India" has become the buzzwords. Such imagery has been boosted by India's economic growth, demographic trends and increasing military capabilities and interests. These factors have been instrumental for India's options to play an increasingly important role in Asia and beyond. India's vision in the contemporary world order is linked with its aspirations to play an even greater role in global politics, economy and security issues.

We are living in a globalized multi-polar world order in which every sovereign country faces challenges from within and from outside. In order to be a global power, India will have to travel a long path. There are numerous domestic challenges like poverty, under/uneven development, illiteracy, malnutrition, lack of health care facilities, widening rich-poor disparity and so on. Fundamentalist elements are also gaining ground day by day. In the international arena, India seeks reforms in the structural set up of international institutions to reflect global reality of the contemporary world. In view of these developments, the volume makes a very modest attempt to assess realistically the feasibility of India becoming a global power in the twenty first century, if at all, taking into account the major internal and systemic challenges and new opportunities that have come up in the backdrop of globalization.

Section One

1

Theorizing India's 'Rise': Levels, Structures and Agency in India's Foreign Policy

Shibashis Chatterjee and *Sreya Maitra Roychoudhury*

India's significance is unambiguous in world politics today. Emerging from the depths of colonial servitude, it has come a long way in establishing its stakes as a global player, with considerable influence in power equations involving the traditional major powers. However, a theoretical audit of India's rise to this stature would reflect not only on its evolving material capabilities and power, but also on the normative and ideational registers since the immediate post-independence period. A structure-agency reading argues that it is the setting or the systemic context that conditions a state's foreign policy which in turn elicits responses from the structure, notwithstanding the ideational, political and cultural factors which often qualify these structural signals. When a state's capabilities alter, the foreign policy would also change in response. But there is always a gap between structural causation and agential response. Adopting this perspective in India's context, structural factors and agential responses can both be located and linked to the overall approach in general, and foreign policy formations in particular. This is because, since the very beginning of its journey as a sovereign state, India thought of itself as a great power, regardless of her material weaknesses, absence of strategic reach and depth, manifest lack of an international recognition of its great power potential, and the many constraints created by the existing body of great powers to prevent India from breaking into the rank of great powers. In the post-Cold War years, Indian foreign policy shows a persistent effort to graduate India into a major power and to obviate the structural challenges issuing from the global system. But the claim to this kind of great power status and its recognition in the region has always been contested. Partly due to Pakistan's adroitness and ability to engage extra-regional actors, the United States and China frustrated India's attempts to unite the subcontinent through its own vision of strategic autonomy. Moreover, the claim to being a great power has been closely related to notions of legitimacy and authority and not about the possession of crude material power. Despite India's meteoric rise in the post-1998 period, it has not succeeded in translating its material preponderance into either strategic consensus or even general leadership of the subcontinent. The chief argument of this paper is that the foreign policy of states is invariably structured by the complex interaction of systemic forces on one hand, and agential actions on the other (Rose 1998: 144-72; Schweller 2006; Zakaria 1998; Wohlforth 1993). A state, no matter how powerful it is, cannot determine its policies in spite of or going completely against the global pattern of distribution of power. The lesser the power of the state the more constraining or disposing is the effect of the international system. Middle level powers aspiring to a great power status, struggle to articulate policies in the light of their sovereign intent since existing great powers tend to curb their ambitions. While some states manage to prevail against such systemic constraints in the long run, others capitulate. India serves as a test-case to this theoretical observation.

To trace India's qualified and often contested rise and audit its foreign policy assertions, we must examine the levels, structures and agency exhibited and coveted by the country. The paper is divided into the following sections; it first traces India's interaction as a middle level power with great powers, and the almost unending influences of structural and systemic constraints. The regional dynamics and constraints are discussed in the next section to highlight India's power negotiations in its immediate neighbourhood. Finally, India's own agency in manoeuvring through structural shackles to assert its claim to major power status is discussed. The paper concludes with a theoretical discussion on prospects and limitations of India's rise.

Levels and Structures: A Theoretical Reading

Most Indian officials regard their country as a middle level power with the potential to become a major power and seek greater international recognition of this status (Travis 1992: 243). India as a middle level power interacts constantly with great powers and lesser states. In vein with the theoretical approach of this paper, structural explanation of the relations can be provided, arguing that it is the structure that determines the schedule of interests for states and no state can therefore pursue policies vis-à-vis another state that go against the logic of the given structure (Rajgopalan and Sahni 2008: 12-13). To quote Rajgopalan and Sahni:

> Thus, our focus should be on the state of global balance of power and the nature of the international system that it gives rise to. The nature of their systems exerts a certain amount of influence on the strategic policy choices of the states in that particular system. Examining such (international systemic) pressures on national policies and on the outcomes of inter-state relations is different from examining the foreign policies of great powers or the policies of regional actors. (Rajgopalan and Sahni 2008: 13)

However, it cannot be glossed over that pure structural theories cannot efficiently explain foreign policy approaches of states, and its changes over time. Structural theories employ the concept of polarity to define a system; poles are defined by concentrations of power at the unit level. They change when the number of states (units) inhabiting a system having the power to inflict unacceptable damage on their adversaries vary. But how does power accumulate in a state? A pure structural theory of world politics is unable to account for this.

It would be prudent to argue that unless interaction capacity as a process variable is interposed between the structure and the units neither the so-called structural effect—that shoves and pushes the units—nor the variations in the distribution of power can be properly explained.

To get to the matter more directly, it is necessary to look at the debates between structural realists and neo-classical realists a bit closely. Waltz (1979/1996) contrasts this theory of international politics from foreign policy theories by saying that they are different in purpose. A structural theory of world policies explains why different states behave similarly; while foreign policy theory reasons out why similarly placed states behave differently. This is simple enough from Waltz's view point. As oligopolistic firm cannot wish away the fact of a competitive market but can manipulate the latter to advance its cause, so similarly, powerful states cannot be immense to structural (systemic) effects though they can work their ways through them.

If we analyze this distinction closely, we find that it is true that all kinds of states, regardless of their domestic composition, are primarily interested in physical survival. But beyond recognizing their cardinal interest in survival, states do differ on other things, primarily; the choice of strategy and the means of survival. Hence, realists must introduce secondary assumptions having crucial bearings on motives, costs and presumptions of behaviour. A few analytical illustrations are instructive at this stage. Faced with a threatening environment, states can balance, bandwagon, hide or even seek to transcend the setting. Again, for a state, security might mean either holding on to their positions or seek domination over their adversaries (hegemony). Further, in a multipolar system, states might either chain gain or buck pass. These forms of state behaviour are apparently all sanctioned by structural realism (neorealism) but they are definitely not the same. This seems to suggest that beyond establishing the universal desire of states to obtain security/survival through self-help means, which includes internal balancing as well as alliances (external balancing), structural realism will say little about what actually a state will do in its foreign policy behaviour. Structural realists could still defend their parsimony in the face of such ambiguity and multiple findings. They can argue that such under-specification or indeterminacy is nothing peculiar to their theory. Great powers are expected to balance and maintain the stability of the system. If some great powers refrain from doing this, the explanation will have to be sought at lower (domestic) levels. Similarly, weaker or lesser powers are supposed to be susceptible to the constraints imposed by the system structure. If they leave their security to chance, they are only abandoning their primary responsibility whose outcome may indeed be catastrophic for them. Such inability, however, is an exceptional condition, and requires explanation at the domestic level. If anything, it is not for a systemic theory to explain such deviations.

Yet, deviations happen and irregularities occur in foreign affairs, and unless one were to concede more ground to non-systemic factors, no proper explanation of such behaviour is possible. Two fundamental points beg consideration in the light of this tension. First, the systemic or structural effects are not free-standing; as Alexander Wendt had shown so clearly, the structure and the units constitute each other (Wendt 1999). Therefore, there is hardly a *pure* structural effect. The distribution of power is never automatic; and no structural realist has provided a convincing explanation why it should be treated as a system level variable at all. A large number of intervening factors are involved here. To dump them on to the unit level is most unhelpful as a theoretical move. The nature of the global structure is vital; but this global entity has multiple modes of working; which leverage the units diversely. Secondly, the constraints and opportunities of the system structure are invariably filtered and mediated through domestic level variables. The fact that states often do not behave the way structural realists predict is because of the role played by domestic variables. What is distinctive about the contemporary global system is brilliantly brought out by Ashley Tellis (Tellis 2007: 118-30). He says that in the last one millennium, the motives of states have not changed. Survival remains the unique leitmotif of all states. Again the modes of survival have also not undergone any radical transformation: states either produce the deterrence capacity themselves through internal mobilization of resources, or join with other states in alliance for that purpose. The nature of the global system decides the choice of strategies. In the Cold War, bipolar system the warring camps were close-unit universes; they were not required to communicate with their rivals or adversaries for economic growth and prosperity. In the present system, globalization has altered the logic of relations between adversaries. The adversaries now compete in connection with each other for mutual economic development and prosperity. Unlike the past, they do not have the luxury to cut off themselves into autocratic camps. The resulting gains from such economic exchanges are however fed into the rivalry itself. This complex dynamics of the present global order is the structure within which major powers strategize vis-à-vis each other. Just as the US faces competition from China in a condition of extremely high mutual economic interdependence, so must India and China manage their competitions in the days ahead. Even if relations were to deteriorate for political/power reasons, the states in each other's economy would continue to condition the overall dynamics of their ties (Tellis 2007: 127-29).

Post-Cold War Changes in the International Structure

The collapse of the Soviet Union has fundamentally altered the international system from bipolarity to unipolarity. Though many structural realists doubted this transformation, the nature of world politics witnessed during the period from 1991/92 to 2005 clearly validates the unipolar character of the system. This is best illustrated by a quick glance into the major movements of crisis of this period which may be briefly considered. In 1991, the First Gulf War took place which saw Iraq being pitted against a multi-national coalition led by the United States. It is instructive to note that all prospective great powers of this era; Germany, Japan, Russia and China either supported the war or stayed neutral, which tantamount to tacit consent. There was no veto exercised by the four great powers: Russia, China, UK and France against George Bush's decision to take military action against Saddam Hussein. This does not mean that the American action received wide legitimacy. The opposite seems be to true inasmuch as though the American action did not enjoy widespread legitimacy, there was no manifest great power action against it.

The second case was the Afghanistan war of 2001, which once again saw an Atlantic coalition by-passing the United Nation's

Security Council mechanism and launching a disproportionate military strike against Afghanistan. The reasons of this crisis are too well-known to merit a recital. The point is that once more, American allies did not approve of the entire set of American justifications offered and actions taken in the course of the war, and many neutral states criticized the character of the US primitive measures. But there was no military counter to the American offensive from any quarter and the existing great powers, expected to challenge the hegemon's military activities, did not join with the weaker side or condemned the United States for its actions. On the contrary, the Afghanistan war was largely supported by the other great powers on the ground that it was symptomatic of the hegemon's willingness to engage in desirable collective action meant to eliminate a common threat. The international isolation of the Taliban regime and the widely shared belief in its complicity with Al-Qaeda forces responsible for the destruction of the Twin Towers united the major powers behind the American lead. The standard balance of power would explain this behaviour by the persistence of unipolarity, although the durability of unipolarity goes against the prediction of the theory. For, if the international system was multipolar, this kind of behaviour would have been extremely remote. The balance of threat variant would say that countervailing coalitions to the American preponderance did not form as the American role seemed benevolent for the other great powers, regardless of the strategic consequences of a comprehensive American victory.

The final test-case for the unipolar international system was the unprovoked American military expedition against Iraq in 2003, which led to the collapse of the Saddam regime. The US conduct in this case was nothing short of outrageous, since the justification offered for the war, the evidence that Iraq was actively building and hiding weapons of mass destruction, turned out to be utterly false and baseless by both credible international sources and a number of American agencies themselves. This crisis saw the fracture of the Western alliance as never before in the post-1991 period, with the EU as a group and France and Germany as member states, openly criticizing the American action. Russia and China also preferred a policy of moderation and Security Council involvement in place of unilateral American action. Despite these oppositions, pleas, protestations and criticisms, the United States *prevailed upon a course of unilateral military action* by completely bypassing the United Nations. Second, the great powers other than the United States evidently did not militarily oppose the United States as they lacked any meaningful capability or intent to deter the American offensive. It can thus be asserted that the present international system is truly unipolar because the dominant power is able to exercise power over and above other great powers in the system. China apparently has the assets to turn into a superpower in future, if it can sustain its economic performance and military modernization. The experts are, however, divided over the challenge that China throws up at present. Moreover, China's neighbourhood remains unsettled and provocative. But China's capabilities are on the up, and she is engaged in unprecedented investments in a strategy of vigorous diplomacy not only in Asia but in the energy-intensive states of the African continent that is clearly indicative of an evolving grand strategy of a superpower in the making, which, in the long run, might transform the present unipolar system into a bipolar one.

For India, unipolarity levelled a major structural threat to the imperatives of foreign policy. Security scenario was jeopardized not only by the loss of Soviet support but also with the waning of India's relations with the Clinton administration and Washington's ties with Pakistan and China becoming better. Inder Kumar Gujral, then the Indian ambassador to Moscow, summarized the Indian response in the following way:

> Perestroika and the new Soviet foreign policy...offers us the prospects of dealing with both East and West without affecting our close and purposeful relations with the USSR. The strategy and nuances of these dealings have to be worked out carefully with one point in mind: our policy must, under no circumstances, smack of opportunism or dilute our time-tested friendship with the USSR. (quoted in Chari *et al.* 2003: 15)

Constrained by the logic of structural unipolarity, India sought to carve a new power imagination through a curious mixture of bandwagoning and balancing vis-à-vis the United States. During the Iraq war of 1991 India supported the US-led coalition in broad terms. It allowed US planes to refuel from its air bases despite domestic dissent. Post-9/11, once again India supported the US action in Afghanistan. After 2001, India's difference with the P-5 states over its positions on CTBT and the NPT also became narrower. It began to signal its willingness to sign these instruments if the P-5 states were willing to accept it within their ranks, with similar prestige and responsibilities. Most conspicuous of bandwagoning behaviour has been its vote against Iran on the nuclear issue. However, on other issues it continued to differ with the US-led West. It did not support the US war against Iraq in 2003, although it did not openly demonstrate any hostility either. There still remain problems over the issue of obtaining a permanent seat in the United Nations Security Council, and over the ambit or scope of its nuclear programme. As Kanti Bajpai notes, India seems to prefer a strategy of internal balances to become militarily strong enough to resist entanglements (Bajpai 1998: 178).

Though India understands that this new-forged partnership with the US is a means to preserve American dominance in the Asian balance of power, open greater opportunities for American companies eager to exploit the vast potential of a rapidly growing Indian economy, and lend evidence to the American version of a partnership of democratic states, its ultimate value is that it helps New Delhi to expand its national power. Although this growth in capabilities leads India inexorably to formally demand a "multipolar world, the leadership in New Delhi is realistic enough to understand that American primacy is unlikely to be dethroned any time soon and certainly not as a result of the growth in Indian power" (Tellis 2005: 8). It is felt that issues and areas where India would want to project this power are consistent with US interests or, definitely would not contradict them.[1]

The post-Cold War period has also lent a renewed garb to India's relationship with China. While their power competition is inevitable, this rivalry would have to be managed in a world of myriad interdependent ties and economic linkages, where the spoils would have to be carefully invested into the relationship to ensure that none of the players succeed in leveraging the benefits unilaterally. This is an exceedingly complex challenge for both the states and India's great power potential would hinge significantly on how she manages her relations with her sprawling and powerful northern neighbour. India's power imagination in foreign policy strategy needs to thus, be mindful of both structural constraints and an explicit great power ambition that invests the agency with significant autonomy often at variance with its actual capability or the degree of external opposition. As Bajpai puts it, "Indian decision-makers do not appear relentlessly preoccupied with power and its deployment. Indeed, they repeatedly turn to other resources and methods" (Bajpai 1998: 194).

South Asian Regional Sub-systemic Structure

At the regional level, the Cold War trends apparently continued, with India having major conflicts, leading to a series of crises, with Pakistan, and having major difficulties in its foreign relations with Bangladesh, Nepal and, to a somewhat lesser degree, with Sri Lanka. India's conflicts with Pakistan centred primarily on Kashmir, but also involved other territorial issues, like the Siachin Glacier, and military rivalry that included a distinct nuclear and missile component. The bitter contestation over Kashmir in the forms of India's accusation of Pakistan's involvement and support of terrorist movements in the Kashmir valley, Pakistan's counter narrative of Kashmir being strangulated by the Indian army, a spiraling political rivalry in Pakistan between Nawaz Sharif and Benazir Bhutto that continuously utilized the anti-India rhetoric, leading to further escalation of the problem, a spate of border crossing and exchanges of firing between India and Pakistani troops, and the deterioration of the communal situation in India, led to the collapse of diplomatic activity between the two rivals during 1994-97 (Buzan and Waever 2003: 108).

The regional politics of South Asia assumed a new dimension with the nuclear tests of 1998 and a series of conflicts that unfolded in the shadow of nuclear arms. The nuclear and missile competition of the region was not limited to India and Pakistan inasmuch as the latter's missile capability was systematically developed by China (with North Korea contributing through Beijing), and India, arguably receiving assistance from Israel. Russian technological partnership was crucial for India in her defence modernization drive that included the development of a range of surface-to-surface missiles (Buzan and Waever 2003: 109).

The inter-regional level saw both continuity and change. India-China-Pakistan relations evolved roughly along the Cold War pattern, with China using its relations with Pakistan to balance India, and India using the Chinese threat as its primary security rationale to acquire nuclear and missiles capability. The 1990s in that sense witnessed continuous Chinese assistance, though clandestine, to develop Pakistan's nuclear and missile capability and the continuation of strategic partnership with a clear anti-India orientation. However, the same period also saw several other trends. First, the 1990s witnessed rapid improvement in Sino-Indian relations despite the Pakistani factor, and although the border dispute between India and China could not be resolved, tension subsided continuously as differences got reduced through active diplomatic means. Second, the partnership between China and Pakistan reached its limit, for neither the Chinese got drawn into any of South Asian crises, nor did they necessarily take Pakistan's side on the Kashmir dispute. The rise of Islamic fundamentalism and terrorism as global phenomena furthered widened the gap between Pakistan and China while narrowed the same between New Delhi and Beijing.

Limits of Structure and India's Agential Autonomy

Despite such tectonic shifts in the international structure and India's need to respond to them while seeking to attain its great power status, India has manoeuvred its *locus standi* in the unipolar international affairs through its own agency. This is clearly brought to fore by several factors. Broadly, these are evidenced in the continuing idea of nonalignment under the guise of 'strategic autonomy', the poverty of imagination arising out of its paucity of trained international affairs specialists, uncertainties induced by the political compulsions of coalition politics, modalities of dealing with Iran's quest for nuclear weapons, and India's firm resistance to any "unilateral exercise of US military power against recalcitrant regimes" (Ganguly 2012: 6).

The problem for India in gaining sufficient autonomy under unipolarity is directly related to its mode of exercising autonomy in the international sphere, which has largely been negative in the sense of staying away from superpower entanglements and from for a dominated by the powerful. The post-Cold War reality has forced India to articulate a sense of positive autonomy, and work out a conception of power in alignment with such a view. It pursues multilateralism through institutions such as the non-aligned movement, the UNCTAD, the UN General Assembly and the WTO though unipolarity impinges critically on the workings of these institutions. The logic of the system-transformation, in terms of polarity, has already turned some of them merely ornamental. India seeks to delicately balance by engaging the support of the United States where their vital interests have conveyed, and exploring alternative modes to push her interests where they clash with American priorities. Of course there have been instances when India has bandwagoned with the US for its own security concerns, particularly in the crusade against terrorism. Motivated by the need for a stable Pakistan as a front-line state in the battle against terror, the concern that Pakistan's nuclear arsenals must never reach the hands of the terrorists, and India's own experience on terrorism, coupled with its ambition to break into the ranks of an extra-regional power, India joined with the American initiative, despite strong pressures to the contrary.

It would not be wrong to argue that Indo-US relations today constitutes the single most crucial foreign policy cleavage of domestic politics in India and this gravely shapes the foreign policy trajectory despite the compulsions of unipolarity. While the two mainstream parties, the Congress and the Bhartiya Janata Party (BJP) do not have fundamentally divergent orientations, political compulsions prevent a bipartisan and united front on the issue. The left parties are seriously opposed to any grand partnership with the United States, and their electoral strength in future may decide the extent to which they can alter the contemporary dynamic. The regional parties that dominate India's political landscape at present do not have a principled stand on the issue. But their electoral performance may be decisive in not so much perhaps in tilting relations in one way or the other, but rather in controlling the depth and spread of the relationship. If the immediate past is any indicator, Indo-US relations have deepened in all aspects as never before. Strategic, commercial, ideational and political factors have all contributed to this new found partnership. The perceived common threat of terrorism, the rise of China, the attractions of India's growing market and mutual investment opportunities, the long democratic traditions, the need for expanded energy sources, the strengthening of the Indian diaspora in the US, add up to explain this transformation. It seems rather absurd that the contemporary tendency would be reversed quickly from India's end. The structural factors that undergird all major bilateral ties seem to obviate such a possibility.

There is a belief that the two sides can create a grand partnership and achieve collaborative gains, though each might emphasize rather different aspects of the quest. Thus, India understands that this new-forged partnership is a means to preserve American dominance in the Asian balance of power, open greater opportunities for American companies eager to exploit the vast potential of a rapidly growing Indian economy, and lend evidence to the American version of a partnership of democratic states united by a common purpose by incorporating the world's largest functional democracy outside the Western world (Tellis 2004: 241-42). From the Indian side, the chief attraction is the transition to a great power status, which the mainstream believes to be impossible without the blessings of the world's most dominant power. There is undoubtedly some theoretical discomfort here; for great powers are expected to prefer multipolarity than unipolarity in terms of their opportunities for accumulating more power. But this distress melts in the face of a more abiding recognition of the durability of American predominance which makes the attraction of joining with the source of power, rather than opposing it, far higher [and less costly] for an aspiring great power like India. It is felt that issues and areas where India would want to project this power are consistent with US interests or, definitely would not contradict them.

While the power competition between India and China seems inevitable given their geopolitical assets and the unresolved territorial disputes, this rivalry would have to be managed in a world of interdependent ties and economic linkages of a myriad kind, where the spoils would have to be carefully invested into the relationship to ensure that none of the players succeed in leverages the benefits unilaterally. This is an exceedingly complex challenge for both the states and the great power potential of India would hinge significantly on how she manages her relations with her sprawling and powerful northern neighbour. The increase in India's power is likely to fuel multi-dimensional competition with China, and an alliance with the United States is widely believed to be the most effective ploy to prevail in these areas of competition in the long run. Common discomfiture with China, a strong belief that militant Islamic fundamentalism threatens the security of both states, a mutual desire to prevent the benefits of nuclear weapons passing on to other states and non-state actors, and an unwillingness to allow multilateral institutions to discipline their nuclear weapons, further cement the partnership (Tellis 2004: 241-42). This explains the idea of India being a natural ally of the United States, a partnership that is based not only on common geopolitical interests, but resting more fundamentally on shared socio-economic preferences, particularly in the ideas of the vast majority of Indian immigrants, who are increasingly becoming vital to the economic development of their homeland.

This has resulted in a number of writings on Indian foreign policy regarding the branching of different approaches to secure India's interests both in the immediate neighbourhood and beyond. The dominant forms of the post-Cold War paradigms of India's foreign policy subscribe to either pragmatic or maximalist varieties of realism. It is not that these approaches do not share anything in common. Their economic strategy is broadly similar: Both support neo-liberal policies as the only panacea to India's developmental needs. They also betray a clear perception of faith in India's ability to develop as a great power, or being almost there, and a bold recognition of the tasks ahead to make that aspiration real. The proximate stimulus to the great power ambition remains the international system, and India's strident moves to develop her military and economic capabilities are a clear response to systemic pressures. But there are a number of critical differences between the pragmatists and the maximalists. Firstly, the more common pragmatic variant advocates foreign-policy choices primarily in terms of systemic needs. It supports a strong defensive capability consistent with the nature of external threats. The maximalists in contrast harp on offensive capabilities that would increase the fire power of the state. Secondly, the pragmatists favour policy expediency and flexibility, eschewing dogmatism of all kinds. It is receptive to the idea of regional and international organizations, but does not advocate overt dependence on them. The maximalists prefer policy realignments in line with India's new capabilities and commitments. They prefer tighter and regular alliances based on the pre-eminence of India's strategic interests. Maximalists are non-committal so far as regional organizations are concerned; they approve regionalism and international organizations if these serve as conveyor belts of India's dominance and help in more effective power projections. Thirdly, the pragmatists emphasize mutual gains in diplomatic bargains, which are claimed as consistent with the realities of the new globalized, interdependent world. It recognizes the dual aims of a state's external policy—national security and sound economic well-being, and considers the management of the complex relation between these two goals to be the most vital test of strategy. Although maximalists are not fundamentally opposed to this line of thinking, they are visibly opposed to diplomatic concessions to vital security interests that betray the weakness of the state. Moreover, they are opposed to long drawn diplomatic efforts that tend to tie down the state to moderate commitments at variance with the unexceptional long-term goal of power maximization. While the maximalists recognize the urgency of economic well-being, they invariably prioritize the needs of security over economic development should they come to a contradiction. The maximum emphasis, however, is given to the successful implementation of growth-oriented, market reforms to explode the vicious cycle of destitution, ethnic violence and alienation.

Conclusion

For a rising power, the structural constraints inherent to the international system are critical. The established powers tend to prevent the new aspirants from becoming powerful states. In an extended unipolar system as the present epoch, the role of transformation of a middle level power to a major power critically hinges on the relationship of the state with the hegemon. Under the present system, India's diverse ties with the US are an effort to grapple with the structural dynamics of the unipolar international system. It seems India perceives a mixed strategy of bandwagoning, hiding and soft balancing with the US to gain more prominence within the system. India's anticipated power status however depends more critically on two other factors. First, it depends on how she manages her relations with China in the days ahead. Once again, no unilateral strategy is in sight. India prefers a strategy of balancing and engaging China both strategically and economically, depending on the nature of the issue at hand. While the cost of this complex strategy is somewhat subsidized by the hegemonic role of the US as holding the ring for both the Asian powers, there is a possibility that the hegemon might withdraw from this role in future. But Indian policy would still straddle between pragmatist and maximalist postures, since the operational costs of a unilateralist strategy is very high. The second issue concerns India's challenges in the South Asian subcontinent. India's major challenge in the neighbourhood remains facing up to the menace of terrorism that emanates from both Afghanistan and Pakistan. While the Hamid Karzai Government in Afghanistan is faltering against a resurgent Taliban in the south, Pakistan is in the cusp of becoming a failed state with rising terrorism, fundamentalism and a massive economic crisis. India's record of managing her immediate neighbourhood is poor. And until she conceives a strategy of optimal returns vis-à-vis her immediate neighbours, her potential of becoming a big power will remain seriously constrained. Externally sponsored terrorism sustained by local or domestic roots eats into the vitals of the Indian state and seriously detracts from her power potential.

If recent empirical trends are any indicator, there does not seem to be a possibility of a major deviation from the pragmatist or maximalist versions of realism in Indian foreign policy. In the last ten years both the National Democratic Alliance and the United Progressive Alliance governments have sought to push the agenda of turning India into a big power in world politics. Accordingly, they have invested in discreet power capabilities of the state. The basic consensus underlying the approach translates in attempts to raise India's power projection capabilities by augmenting her economic strength. This is nothing unique to India. All major powers have followed a similar trajectory in the past. In fact, the possibility of power transformation hinges critically on the relation between economic performance and strategic assets. Their relationship, however, is never direct. Economic capability provides the foundation to strategic depth. But the conversion of economic gains to strategic assets requires conscious policy choices. Those choices in turn depend on how external and domestic constraints are negotiated.

The major challenge in the theoretical prisms hereto forth adopted on Indian foreign policy, whether the pragmatist or the realist versions, is that there is a lack of serious engagement with the issue of terrorism, primarily because it so graphically challenges the conventional levels of analysis in foreign policy studies. In a wider sense, the weakness of India's foreign policy remains the insufficiency of its grand strategic imagination, particularly with regard to the domestic basis of order including internal security. As a rising power, India's foreign policy is more concerned with structural issues and great powers at present. While this is fair and understandable from the standpoint of the foreign policy elite, the lack of attention to the domestic is a serious deficiency on the part of the academia since scholars have the luxury of a much larger time frame to work with in comparison with the much shorter duration of their policy counterparts. It can be hoped that with time the pragmatists and the maximalists would be more attentive to India's domestic bases of grand strategy in their theorizations of India's rise, cognitive explanations and corresponding policy recommendations.

Note

1. The structural inspiration of this transformation is well captured by many scholars. Tellis writes, "In this context, augmenting Indian power is judged to be essential to US interests because it permits Washington to 'pursue a balance-of power strategy among those major rising powers and key regional states in Asia which are not part of the existing U.S. alliance structure—including China, India, and a currently weakened Russia,' a strategy that 'seeks to prevent any one of these [countries] from effectively threatening the security of another [or that of the United States] while simultaneously preventing any combination of these [entities] from 'bandwagoning' to undercut critical US strategic interests in Asia'." (Khalilzad et al. 2001: 47 cited in Tellis 2005: 54-55)

References

Bajpai, Kanti (1998). India: Modified Structuralism. In Muttiah Alagappa (Ed.). *Asian Security Practice, Material and Ideational Influences* (157-97). Stanford and California: Stanford University Press.

Buzan, Barry and Ole Waever (2003). *Regions and Powers: The Structure of International Security*. Cambridge: Cambridge University Press.

Chari, P.R., Cheema, Pervaiz Iqbal and Cohen, Stephen Philip (2003). *Perception, Politics and Security in South Asia*. London and New York: Routledge-Curzon.

Ganguly, Sumit (2012, July 5). Think Again: India's Rise. *Foreign Policy*, Washington DC, accessed at http://www.foreignpolicy.com/articles/2012/07/05/think_again_india_s_rise?page=0,6 on 16 July 2012.

Khalilzad, Zalmay, Orletsky, David, Pollack, Jonathan, Pollpeter, Kevin, Rabasa, Angel, Shlapak, David, Shulsky, Abram and Tellis, Ashley J. (2001). *The United States and Asia: Toward a New U.S. Strategy and Force Posture*, Santa Monica, Calif.: RAND.

Mastanduno, Michael, David A. Lake and John G. Ikenberry (1989, December). Toward a Realist Theory of State Action. *International Studies Quarterly*, Vol. 33, No. 4: 457-74.

Rajgopalan, Rajesh and Sahni, Varun (2008). "India and the Great Powers: Strategic Imperatives, Normative Necessities". *South Asian Survey*, Vol. 15(1). New Delhi: Sage Publications.

Rose, Gideon (1998). Review: Neoclassical realism and theories of foreign policy. *World Politics*, 51(1).

Schweller, Randall L. (2006). *Unanswered Threats: Political Constraints on the Balance of Power.* Princeton, NJ: Princeton University Press.

Tellis, Ashley J. (2004). "China and India in Asia". In Francine R. Frankel and Harry Harding (Eds.). *The India-China Relationship: Rivalry and Engagement* (134-77). New Delhi: Oxford University Press.

———. (2005). India as a New Global Power: An Action Agenda for the United States (11-59). Washington D.C.: Carnegie Endowment for International Peace.

———. (2007). "India in Asian Geopolitics", in Prakash Nanda (ed.), *Rising India: Friends and Foes.* New Delhi: Lancer.

Travis, Thom A. (1992). "United States-India Relations: Obstacles and Opportunities" in Verinder Grover (Ed.). *USA and India's Foreign Policy* (236-47). New Delhi: Deep & Deep Publications.

Waltz, Kenneth N. (1996). "International Politics is not Foreign Policy". *Security Studies.* 6(1): 54-57.

Wendt, Alexander (1999). *Social Theory of International Politics.* London: Cambridge University Press.

Wohlforth, William C. (1993). *The Elusive Balance: Power and Perceptions during the Cold War.* Ithaca, NY: Cornell University Press.

Zakaria, Fareed (1998). *From Wealth to Power: The Unusual Origins of America's World Role.* Princeton, NJ: Princeton University Press.

2

India's Foreign Policy and the Notion of 'Security': Disengagement and Linkages

Swatilekha Bhattacharya

The purpose of my paper is to critique the concept of notion of security as it has been projected by the prevailing paradigms of foreign policy thinking in India. The paper seeks to point towards the sharp divide that exists between domestic and external imperatives of foreign policy formulations. The concept of security enjoys a supreme position when it comes to articulating aims and goals of foreign policy. Yet Indian foreign policy thinking is preoccupied with concerns of 'high politics'. Thus, there is a lack of debate on many issues which are simplistically categorised as 'domestic issue'. Many are considered fit to be discussed at various international forums or noted at the sidelines of bilateral and multilateral summits. Consequently, this paper makes a case for human security, as opposed to state-centric concept of security, as proposed and promoted by several works related to sustainable development. The paper includes the initiatives on advancing the cause of Farmer's rights as highlighted by the Food and Agricultural Organisation that adopted International Treaty on Plant Genetic Resources for Food and Agriculture (ITPGRFA) to substantiate the argument.

Foreign policy thinking, as it started in case of India, was a mix of balance of power and idealism. Being a country free from the clutches of colonial power, still nascent in the process of state consolidation, India, like other developing countries was also influenced by its geographical position and history. India achieved independence in 1947, a time when the world politics was heavily motivated by the ongoing tussle of power ushered by the Bloc politics between United States and Soviet Union. The predominant notion guiding the states was to devise ways to survive in a system of hostile environment where the states were suspicious of one another. It still has remained that way. Security has become the prime mover of foreign policy formulations in such a scenario. However, security is taken as synonymous with 'national security'. National security is itself an 'ambiguous symbol', what it means in totality is debatable (Wolfers 1952: 483). Broadly, national security is meant as the safeguarding of the territorial integrity of a state, military strategies aimed at achieving that and issues of deterrence. The concerns of foreign policy thinking are then ought to be described in terms of 'vital' interests. States like to invest time, resources in and attribute importance to issues which elevate their position in the global politics and ensure the safeguarding of their interests in terms of investments and trade.

This tradition of thinking in foreign policy is positivist in attitude and defined in terms of attainment of relative gains. Cooperation is sought but to the extent of achieving one's gains. The power relations in the global politics are to be preserved in such a system. Changes on a global scale and facilitating development of socio-economic nature are rarely seen. In this way, there is not much difference in foreign policy thinking of the developing states and the colonising powers from whom many developing states fought for freedom. The state has long been theorised as political unit with ambitions narrowly defined in territorial terms. The states that fought war successfully are seen as a strong unit politically. Realist tradition paints a state-centric account of the world seeing state as the product of war and conflicts. Conveniently, it was the Treaty of Westphalia which is credited with the creation of the modern state system which ended the Thirty Years War in 1648. An exhibitionist approach taken towards showing of power and technological advancement being ushered in by the end of the War ensured the successful reproduction of the state system. Political units characterised by territorial identity and having legal sovereignty is the key feature of state. Yet, this is a system where a state recognises the presence of similarly composed sovereign units. In the state-centric International Relations, foreign policy of a state is essentially considered an extension of its 'statecraft'. The state possesses a monopoly on the processes of governance in the 'domestic' life within its territory. There remains a sharp divide between what is considered as 'domestic' and 'foreign'. However, this gives rise to conceptual riddle that accompanies such strict characterisation of what constitutes 'foreign policy' of a state, in this case India. Foreign policy is all about security and devising ways to ensure that. National security as mentioned above is an ambiguous term. The realist account talks about threats concerned with brute force. However, threats come from not only traditional sources but non-traditional sources as well. People are concerned about other issues in their daily lives which are of utmost importance to them. Security for common people constitutes freedom from wants and needs, ensuring employment, protection from crimes, political instability and environmental hazards.

For them, security has a human face. Every initiative for security must be taken to help the people. Importance is to be given to human life. Sustaining physical environment is only a means, not an end, towards achieving human security. Development patterns that perpetuate today's inequities are neither sustainable nor worth sustaining. A major restructuring of the World's income and consumption pattern is a necessary precondition for any viable strategy of sustainable development. Poor people and poor countries depend on the soil for food, the rivers for water and the forests for fuel. A sustainable concept of development talks about equity also which in turn ensures human security. The cost of environmental degradation would have to be paid by the poor section of the population. The more environment is destroyed the more people will have to face problems. Because they need these resources desperately, they have little choice but to destroy their natural environment to survive. Sustainable development puts human beings at the centre of the environmental debate and the larger debate on what constitutes security.

Sustainable Development and Human Security: 'Low Politics'

Sustainable development is one of the hallmarks of the consolidated efforts at dealing with climate changes developed and put into practice by world community. By world community what we mean is the numerous environmental negotiations and summits. It is the aim of the paper to look into the various efforts that these environmental negotiations have taken in the name of promoting sustainable development and also how far they have gone to implement what they promised. The broad concept of sustainable development is often attributed to the Brundtland Commission Report commonly known as UN-sponsored World Commission on Environment and Development (WCED) report published in 1987 titled *Our Common Future* which states that

> 'we must ensure that development meets the needs of the present generation without compromising the ability of future generation to meet their own needs' and adds 'sustainable development is not a fixed state of harmony, but rather a process of change in which the exploitation of resources, the direction of investments, the orientation of technological development and institutional change are made consistent with both future and present needs'. (WCED 1987: 17)

The developed states are not willing to let other states go ahead in the race of development. The call for sustainable development requires that the developed countries come forward and take adequate measures to eliminate poverty from the developing world. As Schmidheiny points out in the following way:

> When politicians, industrialists, and environmentalists run out of practical advice, they often take refuge in appeals for a new vision, new values, a new commitment, and a new ethic. Such calls often ring hollow and rhetorical. This is the crux of the problem of sustainable development, and perhaps the main reason why there has been acceptance in principle, but less concrete actions to put into practice. (Schmidheiny 1992: 11)

The structures of multilateral environmental agreements are designed in such a way that the question of enforcement can be easily evaded. The example of Kyoto Protocol can be taken into account.

> For several Countries, fulfilling their targets entail significant costs. Indeed, the expected damage to its economy is one major reason why the United States declined to ratify. (Hovi 2009: 32)

Sustainable Development promises something for everyone. It is a concept that unites everybody—from farmers to bureaucrats. These characteristics attract a wide array of supporters but they also make Sustainable Development a highly contestable concept. Even in case of Millennium Development Goals, the implementation of which is crucial if sustainable development is to maintain its relevance in policy formulation circle, there is a condition of despair. The Millennium Development Goals (MDG) require much more than money, but they cannot be achieved in low-income countries without adequate money since the nurses, medicines, bed nets, fertilizer bags, safe water points and so forth all come with a price tag attached (UN Millennium Project 2005). Moreover, money that is allocated for such services rarely reaches its intended recipients. There is no plan in place to enforce accountability also. Thus, the pessimism of the people can be explained where sustainable development is concerned.

The current system of international trade is deeply inequitable: it exposes developing countries to unfair competition, and discourages diversification of their economies. Changes in politics are not enough. There is a need for a more fundamental change of the dominant development paradigm. The current crises reflect a model of development that is oriented on a modernisation approach, blind to environmental and human rights issues and confusing economic growth with progress in society.

Brundtland Commission report came into existence in 1987. More than two decades have passed. Still the world community is struggling to give a proper a shape to the term and concept of sustainable development. One summit after other is being organised but there is no change in the real picture. The word Sustainable Development has become a 'catchphrase' (Lele 1991: 607). And the blame is to be placed on the failure of numerous environmental negotiations and summits to and countries that gives them leadership.

ITPGRFA and the Question of 'Sovereignty'

India signed and ratified the ITPGRFA in June 2002. The main stakeholders for the implementation of the Treaty are the Ministry of Agriculture (Department of Agriculture and Cooperation), Indian Council of Agriculture Research (ICAR), Ministry of Environment and Forest (MoEF), National Biodiversity Authority (NBA), and Protection of Plant Varieties and Farmers' Rights Authority (PPV & FRA).

The paper deals with an endeavour to delve deeper into loopholes of the current theory of sustainable development as developed by the environmental negotiations and summits through the working of the ITPGRFA as a whole and in India, the latter claims to ensure sustainable development. Subsequent to the adoption of Food and Agricultural Organisation (FAO) Resolution 5/89 (1989), Agenda 21 called on the United Nations and regional organisations to 'strengthen the global system on the conservation and sustainable use by Plant Genetic Resources for Food and Agriculture by...taking further steps to realise farmers' rights. In November 2001, the FAO conference adopted the International Treaty on Plant Genetic Resources for Food and Agriculture. "Although it transfers responsibility for ensuring farmers' rights from the international community to the national state, it also—for the first time—specifically outlines the basic measures necessary to promote and protect farmers' rights" (Zerbe 2007: 104).

In 2001, the International Treaty on Plant Genetic Resources for Food and Agriculture (FAO International Treaty, ITPGRFA) was adopted by the FAO. It provides for the recognition and realisation of Farmers' Rights. The FAO International Treaty recognises past, present and future contributions of farmers in all regions of the world in conserving, improving and making available plant genetic resources for food and agriculture as the basis of Farmers' Rights. Its preamble highlights the necessity of promoting Farmers' Rights at the national as well as international levels. The FAO International Treaty does not define the concept, but states explicitly that the responsibility for implementing its provision on Farmers' Rights rests with national governments. Governments are free to choose the measures they deem appropriate, according to their needs and priorities. Each country will determine the specific content and substance of Farmers' Rights, according to national needs. However, specific attention should be given to the protection of traditional knowledge, fair and equitable distribution of benefits derived from the use of plant genetic resources and participation in decision-making processes, when addressing development of the substantial contents of Farmers' Rights. Finally, the FAO International Treaty states that none of these provisions should be interpreted to limit any rights that farmers have to save, use, exchange and sell farm-saved seeds, subject to national law and as appropriate. Plant genetic resources are essential to a sustainable agriculture and food security. FAO estimates, of the myriad of varieties of these crops developed by farmers over millennia, which form an important part of agricultural biodiversity, more than 75% have been lost in the past 100 years.

At the heart of the treaty is an attempt at explaining 'Farmers Rights' (Art. 9.2). 'The demand for Farmers' Rights was voiced in the FAO negotiations on plant genetic resources for the first time in 1986, as an attempt to counterbalance the demand for the recognition of plant breeders' rights. Intensive negotiations ensued, leading to the understanding of Farmers' Rights as a precondition for the maintenance of agro-biodiversity (FAO Conference Resolution 5/89). Not least, the findings from the Farmers' Rights Project reveal that Farmers' Rights are regarded among the majority of the respondents as a central means in the fight against poverty (Andersen 2006). These 'rights' are limited by the countries 'needs and priorities' and are 'subject to national legislation'. Even the age-old right of farmers to save and exchange farm-saved seed is not clearly guaranteed, but made subject to 'national law and as appropriate'.

Convention on Biological Diversity (CBD) through its 42 Articles establishes commitments on conservation and sovereign rights of nation on biological resources, suggests a method of access and transfer of genetic resources with prior informed consent. On a principle of benefit sharing (Articles 15, 16, 19, 20, 21) CBD establishes the foundation to link conservation and utilisation with sustainable development (Articles 6, 10, 14). Developed countries of the north have made huge investments in the field of biotechnology. The provision of CBD on the application of biotechnology (Article 19) calls for profit sharing between the country modifying and the country providing biological material for application in biotechnology.

There is a conception that farmers rights or privilege is granting of rights in actuality. Under plant variety protection law saving seeds is a right of the breeder. The farmers are not allowed to that. If they do this they breach the rights of the breeders. They will have to bear economic and legal consequences. The farmers' privilege is an important issue because the seed industry wants to control who produces seeds as has been highlighted in the following way:

> A substantial part of world food production is based on farm-saved seed—as much as 90% in sub-Saharan Africa or 70% in India. Even in industrialised countries, farmers also save seed rather than buy a fresh batch, if it makes sense for them and they can.... It's also a hot issue because the seed industry is working hard to secure legal systems that restrict seed saving by farmers, be it through the World Trade Organization (WTO), bilateral trade agreements or direct lobbying of governments. PVP or plant breeders' rights legislation is all about taking power away from farmers to produce and reproduce seeds. And these laws are gaining ground. (Grain 2003)

The tussle for institutional control over genetic resources is for a simple reason. The developed world has the technological tools needed to convert genes to products. It does not have the raw materials, which are concentrated in the tropical, developing countries. In order to overcome this limitation, a harmonised IPR regime for genetic resources has been introduced into the WTO, with its threats of trade sanctions against countries that do not comply.

The International Undertaking on Plant Genetic Resources for Food and Agriculture (IU) was adopted by governments at the FAO in 1981. It was meant to counteract privatisation of genetic resources by making it a 'common heritage of mankind'. A clash was in the making between the North and South. The main concern for the North was to accumulate profit and to deprive south of any profit. In the late 1980s, the drafting of the Convention on Biological Diversity (CBD) started. This is where the trouble started. The convention changed the status of genetic resources from common heritage to a subject under 'national sovereignty'. Genetic resources were thus reduced to a commodity to be bought and sold under the authority of individual governments.

India was once under the colonial rule. Then, every form of resources was under the control of the government. The process of privatisation had already started when Indian Forest Act was passed in 1865 by the Supreme Legislative Council. Forests and wastelands were formalised as state properties. Thus, what Convention on Biological Diversity had started was already present in some form or the other in many countries. One of them would be India. With the advent of the system of Intellectual Property Rights, the rights of the community and their indigenous knowledge are being eroded and are being taken over by private corporations who have law on their side. Monopoly on the forest and the production of farming materials like seeds means replacing the renewable seed produced by the farmers with the hybrid or genetically engineered seeds rendering high costs of seeds which have to be bought every year. This also entails that the farmers have to more pesticides and chemicals too as the newer varieties of seeds are vulnerable to diseases and pests. In contrast Convention on Biological Diversity and ITPGRFA are of the opinion that, traditional small-scale farmers maintain the yields and quality of their crop varieties by saving and exchanging seeds and seedlings. Without genetic renewal, yields will decrease and quality deteriorates. Plant genetic diversity is vital in marginal environments in order to have plants that can adapt to difficult conditions.

Multinational corporations have laid siege on the indigenous innovations and techniques developed by people. The need to safeguard and promote plant genetic resources is brought under the guidance and decision of states and subject to 'national sovereignty'. However, such dictum was not arrived at by democratic negotiations between countries and concerned public interest groups. Transnational Corporations headed by few industrial giants like General Motors, DuPont, General Electric, Monsanto, IBM, Pfizer, Hewlett Packard and Bristol Myers, Union of Industrial and Employees Confederation (UNICE) and Japanese economic organisations to name a few stakeholders who had vested interests in pushing forward the intellectual property rights (IPR) regime through the TRIPS agreement of World Trade Organisations (WTO). Biodiversity was to be preserved but at a cost. Any consideration of potential ethical and social fallouts of the said treaty arrangements were dispensed with. Several countries were and are still being coerced into modifying their own patenting laws to toe the line prescribed by the international IPR regimes as dictated by the Multinational Corporation and the developed countries driven WTO. India has also not been given respite which was dragged to the Dispute Settlement Mechanism court of the WTO and was forced to amend its patent laws. Life forms are dehumanised and being treated as mere 'products'. The state acts as mediator or in some cases, acts as a silent bystander against the onslaught of the transnational corporations acting in collusion with the multilateral treaty arrangements.

In this era of globalisation, the concept of unilateral state authority in the form of 'sovereignty' is somewhat a misnomer. Likewise, foreign policies are dictated by trade considerations. Bilateral relations with countries are dependent with favourable trade relations as well. Moreover, it is beneficial for the countries to project itself as a potential market conducive to trade and investments. India is no exception. The multinational corporations engage in bio piracy but are sometimes not looked at stringently as it allows the developed states where these corporations are based to maintain dominance over the developing and underdeveloped states where they act as source of employment and as buyer of raw materials. This does apply in case of India. There are several reports as well as news replete with the plight of Indian farmers. Hordes of them are committing suicides for rising prices of seeds and chemicals. Monsanto has pushed Bt. Cotton into the Indian market signifying an attempt at capturing India's farming market. India's foreign policy formulations do not talk about combating various forms of attempts at preserving biodiversity that are engineered by these Multinational Corporations. Private corporations wrecking havoc in the lives of the common masses are not new in India. History witnessed the disaster that was caused in Bhopal in 1984 at the Union Carbide plant. ITPGRFA talks about safeguarding the farmers' rights. India signed and ratified ITPGRFA in 2002 signalling its obligations towards checking bio piracy, strengthening intellectual property rights regime with keeping the farmers' interests in mind and a commitment towards ensuring sustainable development. As food, medicine, two square meals and livelihood that is sustainable—these are basic rights of an individual.

Conclusion

There has to be a realisation that the people belonging to the farming community are poor. But they are contributing immensely to the production of food. By denying the profit that they deserve is to betray the goals of sustainable development. Robbing the farmers of their means of subsistence falsifies one basic claim of sustainable development—human beings are at the centre of the environmental debate. Every development initiative must have a human face. Cost of farming is high yet the profit is not there. Profit from economic venture is needed. But it must be realised that economic development must not be the end. It should be considered as the means to an end, the end being development and progress of the mankind. If people are left out of the development debates then one basic question remains unanswered—Development for whom? Sustainable Development provides answers to these questions.

However a look at the Human Development Index (HDI) reports gives an idea how much discrepancies exist between the interpretations of different development paradigms. The late Mahbub ul Haq, former Finance Minister of Pakistan and consultant for United National Development Programme (UNDP), prepared HDI as well as Human Governance Index (HGI) which was outlined in his paper 'New Imperatives of Human Security' (Haq 1994). Human Development Index is measured by taking into account 3 factors—life expectancy at birth, access to knowledge as measured by adult literacy rate and combined enrolment ratio, a decent standard of living measured in terms of Purchasing Power Parity (PPP). Many countries have high GDP (Gross Domestic Products) growth rate while rate very poorly in terms of HDI, e.g. India.

The core of the current sustainable development agenda reflects new thinking among the environmental and the developmental communities about the linkages between key issues on the international agenda. Some critics contend that this new agenda threatens to divert attention from the fundamental goals of fighting poverty, reducing military expenditure, increasing respect for human rights, and promoting democracy. International agreements are negotiated in an isolated manner. Specific regimes are taken into account while negotiating. The treaty making process is also extremely time-consuming. It typically takes over a decade to advance from the agenda setting stage, *via* a framework agreement, to the negotiation of the first operational protocol for collective action. The result is that treaties overlap. These shortcomings affecting the progress of environmental regimes affect the progress of the process of sustainable development. The problems which the mankind faced twenty years ago are still there. But there are new problems also. The disparity between the developed and developing states is growing in terms of national income. There are many states which are struggling to bring into existence legitimate, accountable governments. To enable a strong national environmental regime to work, a strong government is needed. Moreover the people at the grass root level must be given a voice while formulating policies surrounding sustainable development. Merely following a development paradigm which has worked in other countries is not desirable. There is a need for the environmental agreements to recognise these factors. Consequently, foreign policy formulations needs to be linked with basic rights and needs of people, i.e. ensuring security that has a human face to it. The concept of 'national security' needs to co-opt a notion of security that talks about basic needs of people within its fold, and not merely security of territories.

Foreign policy ought not to be a zero sum game. It is not. The era of globalisation has ensured and reinforced the need to reach out to other countries all the more. Countries are suspicious and wary of each other but that has not stopped them from keeping lines of communication open as with changing times issues change, newer forms of threats change and they threaten many countries at a time. Cooperation has to be there in order to manage such issues. Similarly, national interests also change with changing times and circumstances. However, national interests are always to be devised and modified while keeping the security of the country intact. The paper would conclude by reiterating that as the concept of national interests change so is the need to see the concept of security in new light by doing away with the divide that exist between 'high politics' and 'low politics'. A policy is effective and necessary to the extent it serves the people. Thus, this paper highlights that in the Indian context a reinvention of the terms like 'foreign policy' and 'security' is necessary.

References

Andersen, Regine (2006). *Realising Farmers' Rights under the International Treaty on Plant Genetic Resources for Food and Agriculture.* Norway: The Fridtjof Nansen Institute.

Grain (2003). *Farmers' Privilege Under Attack.* From: <https://www.grain.org/article/entries/103-farmers-privilege-under-attack> [Accessed on August 26, 2015].

Haq, Mahbub ul (1994). *New Imperatives of Human Security*, Rajiv Gandhi Institute for Contemporary Studies. New Delhi: Rajiv Gandhi Foundation.

Hovi, J., Spinz, D.F. and Underlal, A. (2009). Implementing Long-term Climate Policy: Time Inconsistency, Domestic Politics, International Anarchy. *Global Environmental Politics*, Vol. 9(3): 20-39.

Lele, Sharachchandra M. (1991). Sustainable Development: A Critical Review. *World Development*, Vol. 19 (6): 607-21.

Schmidheiny, S. (1992). *Changing Course: A Global Business Perspective on Development and the Environment*. Cambridge: MIT Press.

United Nations (1992). *Convention on Biological Diversity*. [pdf] United Nations, from: <https://www.cbd.int/doc/legal/cbd-en.pdf> [Accessed on August 26, 2015].

UN Millennium Project (2005). *Investing in Development: A Practical Plan to Achieve the Millennium Development Goals*. New York.

World Commission on Environment and Development (1987). *Our Common Future*. London: Oxford University Press.

Wolfers, A. (1952). National Security as an Ambiguous Symbol. *Political Science Quarterly*, Vol. 67(4): 481-502.

Zerbe, Noah (2007). "Contesting Privatization: NGO's and Farmers' Rights in the African Model Law". *Global Environmental Politics*. Vol. 79(1): 97-119.

3

Innate Security Contest in the Emerging India Theme

Anindya Jyoti Majumdar

For some time now, through the turbulences of everyday global politics and its twists and turns, a consistent theme recurrently appears in any projection of power hierarchy of the coming decades. It is the theme of Rising China—economically robust and militarily potent—pushing its way through the Western dominance to establish itself as a power pole. Beyond the immediate predicaments of human displacement and refugee crisis, acts of terror and war on terror, climate change or nuclear proliferation—issues that demand instantaneous response, a general systemic change in the existing international order is usually predicted. These predictions portray a security scenario where an assertive China greatly reduces the reach and the extent of influence of a supposedly declining United States. Whether a new set of rules based on a new power order is forthcoming or not, such a theme includes a very compelling sub-theme as well. The compelling sub-theme is of an Emerging India with growing economic muscles and military clout paving its way towards a greater say in international affairs. Being an immediate neighbour of the Rising China India becomes thereby a party to the unfolding global security arrangements of the future.

The growth story of India over the last seven decades in itself is an exciting case study of experiments with political and economic attitudes and policies that went beyond mere survival strategies and strove for a greater role in the world arena. The growth has not been meteoric or spectacular but despite all the constraints and setbacks, it shows a resilient but incremental advancement over a period of time. However, an effective departure from the established patterns in the early 1990s in terms of economic reforms and an upbeat foreign policy was the result of a combination of compelling and inducing factors that enhanced the speed and extent of India's progress. It is interesting to note that independent India's security and foreign policy grew with the task of grappling with the vagaries of Cold War which determined many of her choices for almost five decades and began a journey afresh on a new path when Cold War ended.

The very idea of security kept changing and expanding for India with each marginal increase in her capabilities and the necessity to respond to the ever-changing global security environment. Emerging India's growth story can be independently told as well but as its security concerns expand beyond the region of South Asia and make forays into areas where other actors are present, the themes of Rising China and Emerging India become interweaved. It is aptly emphasized that while other major states in Asia are not unduly concerned or distressed with India's rise, China however views India's rise with growing concern (Ganguly 2008: 150-64). The security implications of the story of Rising China remains incomplete without the story of Emerging India taken into consideration, and in the same fashion, the Emerging India story would have little value if it left out the security implications of the Rising China.

This paper seeks to ascertain the major props on which the very theme of Emerging India is based and accordingly derives India's security challenges in the contemporary period corresponding to these basic props. In the process, it makes an attempt to explore India's non-committal balancing act as a response to emerging security environment and advocates an expanding and firm security reach combining both traditional and non-traditional aspects.

The Four Props of Emerging India

Since the theme of Emerging India effectively began resonating by the turn of this century, it is to be seen what India acquired by this time that was not present before. On four major counts, Emerging India is different from her previous incarnation, i.e. independent India of yesteryears. These are: (1) steady economic growth and her emergence as a huge market and a suitable investment destination; (2) major shift towards a policy of fostering economic and strategic partnerships with the major actors and willingness to act on less ideational but more pragmatic considerations using international platforms; (3) expansion of military power beyond the land borders and the coastlines with a nuclear weapons strategy a part thereof—a policy that can be best described as peace through strength; and (4) despite many divisive factors, differences and inequalities, and somewhat limited success in delivering collective goods, India remains united as a territorial entity—the very idea of 'unity in diversity' progressively becoming a reality with new generations gradually moving out of primordial and ethnic considerations. These are the issues—reducible to four major dimensions of state policy: economic gains, alliance formation, military clout and domestic cohesion and stability—that major powers have always been concerned with (albeit in different forms at different points of time) and not really with a normative, ideational world order that India had preached during the Cold War days. In other words, as India begins to think and behave like the other major powers who have already set the rules of the game, and backs this attitude up with material gains, India transforms herself into another major power in the making.

These four props on which the very idea of Emerging India is based needs greater elaboration to dispel the view that India's rise would essentially herald a multipolar world order where soft power would play the primary role. Expanding on Joseph Nye's ideas of soft power[1] (Nye 2002: 176), Tharoor observed that "a country's soft power...emerges from the world's perception of what the country is all about. The associations and attitudes conjured up in the global imagination by the mere mention of a country's name is often a more accurate gauge of its soft power than a dispassionate analysis of its foreign policies" (Tharoor 2012: 277-78). He proceeds to argue that "...India's claims to a significant leadership role in the world of the twenty-first century lie in the aspects and products of Indian society and culture that the world finds attractive" (Tharoor 2012: 279) and makes a case for Indian pluralist civilization and cultural resilience, he agrees that "soft power becomes credible when there is hard power behind it" (Tharoor 2012: 286). We may say that Emerging India's image is not based on its civilization and culture (a pre-existing variable that was available prior to India's rise), though a renewed interest in re-exploring India's civilizational attributes as a consequence of India's rise would definitely contribute to its soft power. In effect, the new image is based on traditional understanding of hard power.

However, beyond the debate on the respective utility of hard power and soft power, it may be argued that both coercive and co-optive measures become necessary as a means of strategy formulation to match ends, ways and means. State capacity would determine the achievable ends and state capacity once again would determine the ways to achieve those ends where a judicious mixture of hard power and soft power would prove effective. Expansion of the very idea of security to include issues hitherto neglected in traditional defence doctrines too determines the kinds of ways a state would employ to achieve new and non-traditional security objectives. Security is best viewed as a comprehensive whole and not in its prismatic elements of different bands of colours. The very theme of Emerging India is based on a combination of interacting variables necessitating application of both hard and soft power techniques in traditional and non-traditional areas.

If macroeconomic projections are to be believed, the US Department of Agriculture predicted in its April 2015 report that India is going to be the third largest economy surpassing Japan by 2030 (*Indian Express*). It was at the 10th spot in 2013, at 9th spot in 2014 and at the 7th spot in 2015 (Money.cnn.com...). In these projections, in 2030, US maintains the lead ($24.8 trillion), China is a close second ($22.2 trillion) and India comes a distant third with a $6.6 trillion economy. A World Bank report released in April 2014 informed that India had already displaced Japan to be the third largest economy in terms of purchasing power parity (*Economic Times* 2014) with an $8 trillion plus economy. In terms of growth rate, it topped the list in 2015 and a 7-8% growth rate was predicted to continue. Increasingly, it is assumed that the three-way relationship among these states will have a profound impact on global politics. There could be many unforeseen uncertainties capable of derailing the projections, but despite occasional hiccups or temporary downturns, the steady growth rate encourages ambitious forecasts.

In terms of policy goals, the action plans are clearly cut out. The very first priority has always been economic development as India after years of colonial exploitation was a poor and backward state at the time of independence. Raising the standard of living of the people, eradication of poverty, mobilizing resources for industrialization, job-creation, rectifying trade imbalance, investing money in research and development—all depend and lead to accumulation of economic power and economic power only can sustain military power. India experimented with mixed measures where state would play a major role not only in nation-building but also in erecting a political structure and guiding the economy. Inward-looking protectionist measures however became untenable over time and as the end of Cold War heralded the victory of liberal democracy and market economy, India's economic reforms coincided. Post-1991, India became open to foreign capital, investment and technology. As the reforms to make India investment-friendly were initiated, a change in political attitude was necessary which was not readily forthcoming. And the process went on, slowly but progressively, in the following decades. Prime Minister Narendra Modi took the drive to a new high with his 'Make in India' campaign inviting foreign investment and as a corollary to it, he initiated skill development programmes at home for the youth. The Look East (now Act East) policy highlights the renewed emphasis on India's age-old priority. Modi highlights the dividends of democracy, demography and demand implying political stability, cheap labour and a suitable market.

A country that is bent upon accumulation of economic strength would not ordinarily disturb a stable environment suitable for incessant flow of trade and investment by getting into unnecessary wrangles. While infrastructural developments and creation of facilities for rapid economic growth would be of prime interest; armed conflicts, power struggle or instability would be needless distractions. This may explain India's increasing intent to solicit stable, cooperative, mutually beneficial relations with the neighbours (through bilateral accommodation and sub-regional initiatives) and other distant lands. Irritants in relations persist but there is a tendency to downplay the differences—even with Pakistan (though the last named being most unpredictable, can derail any normal projection).

Areas and issues that become important in consonance with these objectives are many. It highlights the issue of uninterrupted energy supply—fossil fuel or nuclear—to maintain high economic growth rate (a stiff competition with China is foretold in this respect). It further stipulates that protection of sea-lanes of communication would be necessary (to ensure free movement of goods and energy), protection from piracy and acts of terrorism on sea and to this end exercising legitimate influence over the Indian Ocean region in order to prevent adversarial encroachments inimical to India's commercial interests in this expanse.

As the very notion of non-alignment lost its edge as a viable strategy at the end of Cold War, India took a vigorous turn towards establishing strategic partnerships with every major power and regional groups like the Association of South East Asian Nations. While in broad terms, India went beyond the South Asian region with her much-publicized Look East policy (1992), followed by lesser-known Look West policy (2005) and Connect Central Asia policy (2012), neither all of these policy directions gathered equal momentum, nor all the partnerships experienced a similar rate of progress. For example, the Look East policy came to stay and expanded its range beyond Southeast Asia to strengthen relations with states in the Asia Pacific. Look West policy did not gain similar dynamism. Likewise, while the strategic partnership with the US (declared in 2001) moved towards the 'Next Steps in Strategic Partnership' in 2004 and included vital areas of cooperation; the strategic partnership with Russia (signed in 2000) was mostly rhetorically elevated to a 'Special and Privileged Strategic Partnership' (in 2010). As the strategic partnerships increase in number, the specificity of a strategic partnership is lost and it is but natural that a few of these arrangements would be redefined as priority partnerships.

At any rate, the attempts of India to connect with other states without the baggage of an ideational and normative attitude provided improved and increased prospects of interaction among them. Relations could be reinstated on the basis of new opportunities that were mutually beneficial and not on the basis of any abstract philosophy. No wonder, India's strategic partnerships are mainly with the states from the developed world and with the major or middle powers, and less with the developing states and the smaller nations. The new associations and intensity of increased interactions with the major states of the world help India grow in stature. It may be noted however that India continues to be a member of the Non-Aligned Movement and Group of 77, which is a cluster of developing countries but her focus is on multi-alignment and it is a member of G-20, a group of performing economies.

Opening up to the world meant opening up to the smaller neighbours as well. Independent India—as the successor state of British India—inherited also the British attitude that induced her to look to its South Asian neighbours not as equal peers but as subordinate sentries in security calculations. As a consequence, overarching presence of India as a factor in the domestic and external politics of small states hampered normal interstate relations in South Asia. The very process of nation-building in smaller states was further influenced by the propensity of the administrations to deliberately create a sense of anxiety of a hegemonic and inimical India in order to mobilize and ensure internal unity. Apparently, withdrawal of the British from the subcontinent did not bring much difference to them as India took over. This hyper-nationalist anti-India syndrome makes it easy for China to develop better relations with the smaller countries of South Asia. However, in the present period, as the focus shifts more towards economic gains and since the South Asian Association for Regional Cooperation continues to remain ineffective, India is increasingly willing to initiate sub-regional ventures of connectivity and economic ties with her neighbours leaving out a recalcitrant Pakistan. As Tharoor observes, "...a rising India has an obvious interest in the success of its neighbours, since a stable neighbourhood contributes to an enabling environment for India's own domestic objectives, while disturbances on India's borders can act as a constraint on India's continued rise" (Tharoor 2012: 87). The smaller states would like to derive benefits from an India-China competition, but India needs to integrate the neighbours more in a prosperous regional economy to prevent them from unwittingly falling prey to the so-called 'String of Pearls' design of China. Aiming at an encirclement of India the 'String of Pearls' strategy might jeopardize the security of the region as a whole to the detriment of security interests of the smaller states as well.

Greater involvement with states, collaborative ties and mutually beneficial relations should alleviate security risks. However, fruitful interactions require state capacities to deliver on promises made. As the reach extends, India would be required to provide security (like providing escort services to friendly ships in the region as it does), to offer aid and help in times of natural disaster (like she did after the Indonesian tsunami), to advance the search for resources (like oil exploration in far-flung areas), to bring Indians to safety from war zones if needed (like she did during the Gulf wars). India therefore needs to enhance the capacity to deliver and to expand its zone of legitimate interest accordingly. This corresponds to the third prop that contributes to the image of the Emerging India as her zone of interest expands beyond the coastlines and India perceives that from the Strait of Hormuz to the Strait of Malacca, with the Indian Ocean in between, as her legitimate area of interest. Traditionally, scholars viewed India as a 'self-contained empire' with a defensive orientation. But now, peace through strength is probably the guiding philosophy. India aspires to be a net provider of security in this region. There has been a sustained effort to increase its naval strength with two aircraft carriers, nuclear-powered submarines and a fleet of other vessels which in effect means a possible naval power competition in the region for dominance. India for the last few years has been the world's largest arms importer till Saudi Arab overtook India in 2014.

Many of the scholars are of the view that India's nuclear programme was motivated not primarily by security considerations but by unrelated issues including the cravings for international status[2] (Frey 2006: 197) and leadership choices. It has been stated by some that Prime Minister Mrs. Gandhi—a believer in 'sportsmanlike nationalism'—made a distinction in 1974 between the development of nuclear capacity and the weaponization of that capacity but the outsiders failed to see that distinction. On the other hand, Prime Minister A.V. Vajpayee unlike his predecessors was an oppositional nationalist vis-à-vis Pakistan[3] (Hymans 2006: 171-203). He personally pushed the agenda to make India a nuclear weapons state in 1998. One can however place the 1998 nuclear tests in the context of a renewed nuclear non-proliferation drive by the Clinton Administration in the mid-1990s that not only extended the Nuclear Non-Proliferation Treaty indefinitely in 1995 but also spearheaded the Comprehensive Nuclear Test Ban Treaty in 1996. As the last bastion of resistance, India actually vetoed the Comprehensive Test Ban Treaty and the 1998 nuclear tests followed as a sequel to escape the tightening dragnet of non-proliferation. Then came a doctrine that focused on 'no first use' and a self-imposed moratorium on tests. Despite the immediate response from Pakistan in the same fashion and debate on the efficacy of a regional India-Pakistan deterrence, Prime Minister Vajpayee's letter to President Bill Clinton referred to deterioration in the security environment in a nuclear neighbourhood where an overt nuclear weapon state (China) was materially helping another to become a covert nuclear weapon state (Pakistan) (*New York Times* 1998). In all her postures, India has tried to project the image of a responsible nuclear weapon state that does not encourage proliferation and believes in a credible minimum deterrence.

Despite the initial setback in Indo-US relations, the tests led to a year-long nine rounds of talks between India and the

US and a steady flow of high-level bilateral visits followed. Within two years sanctions were lifted. In 2004, both agreed to work together in the fields of civilian nuclear technology, space programme, high tech trade and missile defence. Initiated in 2005, the Indo-US nuclear deal was approved in 2008 which is essentially a commercial contract by which the US agreed to provide nuclear fuel and other facilities for the civilian nuclear programme in India operating under India-specific IAEA safeguards. This means a formal acceptance of a division between India's civilian and military nuclear facilities. While the US declared that at least more than half of India's nuclear programme was under inspection now, domestic opinion in India was against the deal and the government justified the deal by emphasizing the point that at least half of India's nuclear programme was not under any kind of inspection.

Nuclear deterrence in the strategic triangle comprising China, India and Pakistan is being nurtured and updated every day. While general and approximate estimates put Chinese nuclear warheads at 240-250, Pakistan's at 100-120, and India's at 90-110 (*Bulletin of the Atomic Scientists* and *SIPRI Yearbook*); it is to be noted again that India's nuclear doctrine advocates a credible minimum deterrence and no first use. India's second strike capability depends on land-based short-range missiles (intended to deter Pakistan) and long-range variants of Agni missile and submarine-launched long-range missiles (to deter China) that are now under an increased pace of development. As it happens with nuclear deterrence, security at the top allows flexibility at lower levels and a conventional deterrence becomes necessary to raise the threshold of nuclear weapon use, India would have to nurture and manage its deterrence abilities—both conventional and nuclear—to avoid inadvertent warfare based on adversary's miscalculations.

The fourth prop—domestic cohesion and stability—has been an area of great concern in India and it is doubtful whether national cohesion is stronger in contemporary India than it was any time before. It has always been a matter of debate for the India-analysts whether the country would be able keep itself together since the divisive factors were far too many and nation-building with the idea of 'unity in diversity' progressed haltingly. Despite religious, linguistic, cultural, caste-based, class-based and ethnic differences leading to violent manifestations at regular intervals and sub-national sentiments challenging state authority, India could pull itself together. This achievement of staying together does not mean that the days of ethnic, religious, secessionist or class-based insurgency are over in India, rather these disorders continue to be a serious threat to India's internal security. Terrorism adds a new dimension to the existing security threats.

However, the prevalent culture of democracy and pluralism (with active participation of the civil society, free media, independent judiciary and interest groups) ensures opportunities for individual upward mobility to a significant extent. India being a land of billion-plus people of different shades and natures living under a non-authoritarian democratic regime defies stereotypes of any kind. A great many individual success stories in different fields transcending group identities are frequently told in the midst of economic deprivation or social inequalities. Growth in telecommunication and physical mobility along with rapidly growing economic activities within the country consistently bring one in touch of another—breaking narrow confines of perceived regional identities on the one hand and creating a new problem of accommodation on the other. While each disturbing story is highlighted to its fullest, countless stories of bonding —unreported and ignored—among individuals superseding the structural barriers in India who have been the silent agents of change—override the much-hyped diversity of people and the resultant fractured pattern of politics and help project a complex but cohesive functioning system.

When this fractured politics is taken as a determining variable, scholars are inclined to argue that political fragmentation and diffusion of power lead to ideological incoherence and under the circumstances, the most expeditious policy is that which is predicted on interests rather than ideology (Malone and Mukherjee 2010: 161-62). In other words, with fragmentation of political space, India's ideological coherence diminished and it has become reactive in nature without a vision (Malone and

Mukherjee 2010: 163). An explanation is thus provided as to why India's foreign policy would be pragmatic in its response. However, this is an area that is full of security challenges of both traditional and non-traditional varieties necessitating application of both coercive and co-optive measures. State security in the long run depends on ensuring human security. While human security is no security in a weak state, alienated citizens are a threat for the state from within. Good governance becomes an indispensable element of healthy state-individual ties. It is to be noted however that great powers in history have not always been perfect states but they reached some form of domestic cohesion or discipline that allowed them to project power abroad. Insurgency and terrorism of various forms often with external links remain a serious security challenge for India's domestic cohesion as well.

The four props that distinguish India's growth have their respective security predicaments and challenges, and it goes without saying that almost in each case a competition with China is anticipated be it in and beyond the Indian Ocean region, the neighbourhood or the disputed border areas.

The Balancing Game of Rising India

There is a general perception that India (along with Japan) adopts a hedging strategy against China as both share some common concerns about probable outcomes of China's rise (Ganguly 2008: 160), India insists on a balanced approach that would carefully avoid the option of choosing sides. India would not be comfortable with a swing power status in a game of traditional balance of power as long as such a situation does not become inevitable and warrants so. One line of argument goes like this:

> New Delhi's aim is to act as it always has: to play both ends against the middle. Despite India's 'tilt' to the Soviet Union during the Cold War and its current 'tilt' to the US, this philosophy has been at the core of Indian strategy for many years. The strategy enables India to retain its swing-state status and also to garner support from both sides of the strategic equation. (Gordon 2012)

However, a word of caution is sounded too:

> ...In the final analysis, it may not be wholly up to New Delhi to decide whether to stick to its present policy of 'strategic independence' or whether to increase the current strategic 'tilt' to the US...that decision is likely to depend more on external factors than any Indian predilection.

And these external factors will be: how rapidly China rises to power...and how it chooses to rise to power and to assert its interests, especially in regard to India's own core interests, which are the border, South Asia and the Indian Ocean (Gordon 2012).

India would hardly prefer to consider itself as a 'card' in anyone's deck, observes Cossa, though others may dream of playing an 'India Card' in the East Asia geopolitical game (Cossa 2008: 324) or in other theatres. India would rather like to see herself as a bridge-builder between two rival camps gaining as much benefit such multi-track relationships might offer. One line of argument therefore goes like this:

> Because of its geographical location, India is the natural bridge between the West and the East, and between Europe and Asia. Through forward thinking and a dynamic foreign policy, India can truly play the role of a facilitator and soother between the East and the West, including serving as a link between the competing demands of the developed and the developing worlds. At a time of heightened geopolitical tensions, the world needs such a bridge-builder. (Chellaney 2014)

The bridge-building exercise is however not always viewed in the same light by all. The following observation underscores in a lighter vein the complex balancing approach that India adopts:

> It is not too much of an exaggeration that on Monday, Wednesday, and Friday, India seems intent on cooperating with the United States and on being part of an emerging alliance of democracies, promoting multilateral cooperation (including defense cooperation)

> with Japan, Australia and the United States, while on Tuesday, Thursday, and Saturday, New Delhi further enhances its strategic relations with Beijing and Moscow, aimed at preventing a unipolar world. (Cossa 2008: 324)

This quotation leaves out Sundays and we would see as outlined below that India remains somewhat busy on Sundays as well.

Often it is advised that "Unless the usual rules of state-craft are suspended, India will need to show cunning and the willingness to play the game—the cynical game—of great-power politics. So far, it seems reluctant to do so. Its insistence on not forging permanent alliances of interest is not how these games are generally won." India needs to learn "...to play a good hand of realism" (Starobin 2010: 175-76). These observations give birth to the following questions mostly unanswered: Does realism dictate premature alliance formation? Does maintenance of independent and mutually beneficial relations with competing coalitions in effect allow US hegemony to be gradually undermined while that of China being promoted? Would the efforts to maintain strategic autonomy by being everybody's friend at present result in strategic restrictions in the long run as contradictory demands are made by disparate strategic partners? Citing India's basic unwillingness to become a party to a balance of power game, Mehta argues:

> If one were to give a name to what Indian Foreign Policy is driven by, it is best described as a case of cautious prudence. It is cautious in the sense that it operates with an underlying sense of its incapacity and unwillingness to use force. It is also cautious in not putting its weight behind enduring alliances; it is driven to them, if at all, by necessity. It is cautious in recognizing a limit to its own ability to affect change elsewhere. (Mehta 2009: 231)

He further maintains that "It may turn out that India's caution will serve it better than the recklessness that comes with illusions of power" (Mehta 2009: 232). However, while being cautious and non-provocative can be a part of prudent diplomacy, being oblivious of legitimate security needs is not and therefore India has to adopt multi-dimensional measures to protect—its security interests.

There are two opposite views regarding China's possible course of action. The alarmist view regards China as an offensive realist and power transition makes major showdown inevitable. The other view focuses more on the East Asian model of development where export-oriented economy impacts on security relations and an outward orientation for market and greater economic opportunities form the basics of relations. This view regards China more as a system-supporter than a system-challenger, though it admits that China will push its weight around within the system (Uriu 2015). More economic interaction between China and other states in the region over a longer period of time might undermine the US dominance thereby making way for Chinese dominance.

Both China and India are involved in a process of economic uplift and success depends on international support, cooperation and a peaceful environment. Stability and mutual benefit would count more than confrontational postures and antagonism. Further, while trade between India and China has grown so much in the recent days that China has become India's largest single trading partner. In this trade relations, China enjoys the upper hand as the balance favours China and since Indians may be seen more as consumers than as enemies by China (Tharoor 2012: 138), prudence dictates that China would not ordinarily disturb the arrangements by initiating forceful settlement of disputes. India is an important partner of BRICS. It is known that the US intransigence at one point pushed India to the embrace of the Soviet Union. The Chinese inflexibility might similarly push India to an US-led coalition. The US and India enjoy a very close strategic partnership and the US views India as a potential ally. From a Chinese perspective, it would be self-defeating to pursue a militant posture with India.

However, China's maritime and airspace claims in the South China Sea not only push out the smaller states to a peripheral existence but invokes the US containment strategy. In October 2015, the US sent a destroyer near 12 miles of Chinese man-made islands in South China Sea to emphasize freedom of navigation principles refusing to accept China's territorial claims that provoked strong Chinese reactions. Since China shows tendencies to become assertive in one region, it might become assertive in other theatres too, including the Indian Ocean Region. An old Chinese proverb instructs that a crisis is always an opportunity. India and the US have made it an annual feature to have joint naval exercises in the Indo-Pacific region and in 2015, Japan too joined this Malabar Exercises.

It is generally expected that partnership with the United States might make it easier for India to increase its clout over the Indian Ocean while the US concentrates on the Pacific. Though in general the idea of a US-China rivalry in the coming days has become a matter of great speculation, some are concerned with the possibility of US accommodation of China much to the detriment of the interests of other powers in the Indo-Pacific region. China does not regard the smaller powers as legitimate equal partners and is more in favour of China-US condominium (G-2). US domestic policy, it is argued, might lead to gradual US withdrawal leaving greater space for Chinese assertion. This angle of argument suggests a middle power coalition—excluding both the US and China—but including India, Japan, Australia, Korea, Singapore, Malaysia, in fact, all the major states in the super-zone of Indo-Pacific Region (Medcalf and Rajamohan 2014). With reference to the quotation made earlier, we might say that this is what India does on Sundays.

The Expanding Security Prospects

As outlined above, the four factors that distinguish Emerging India from its previous standing carry with them specific security vulnerabilities, challenges and requirements. Maintaining a steady economic growth will require steady energy supply and protection of trade routes and sea lanes from inimical interests. Fostering friendship and greater connectivity with neighbours and distant lands require provision of necessary security services offered to friendly countries in areas close by ranging from escorting ships to swiftly provide relief in times of emergency. Reaching beyond the coastlines to tackle piracy and terrorism requires a capable navy with a vast and unrestricted range of operation. Maintaining an effective nuclear deterrence based on a nuclear triad necessitates sea/submarine-launched ballistic missiles under naval command. In fact, a large part of security dividends would flow from a heavy military presence in the Indian Ocean Region where naval bases and aircraft carriers would become a priority consideration. Emerging India has to be a net security provider in the Indian Ocean Region.

Rising capabilities of India and her oceanic networks with other powers in the region would not only contain any Chinese encirclement strategy but would also reduce any adverse security impact of China's naval presence and expansion in support of its proposed maritime silk route and its effort to link Africa and Europe in one big belt through the Indian Ocean. On the other hand, while the land-border security is to be spruced up, cross-border expeditionary operations might be necessary to prevent launch of illegal cross-border activities by insurgents and terrorists. Security is a matter of perception as well which depends on how the enemy perceives the probable range of responses emanating from India to an act of aggression. Fast and assured proportionate retaliation acts as a deterrent. A security doctrine to this end would be necessary.

Protection of interests in the region might require clear and specific articulation of expectations from the smaller neighbours to weed out suspicion on India's real intentions. As long as hyper-nationalist sentiment in the smaller states finds in the bogey of Indian threat a convenient tool to build national unity, it will be well-nigh impossible for India to reverse the situation by being apologetic for its size and strength. Attempts of backchannel diplomacy may backfire in the region and any attempt by India to retrieve a bad situation would be viewed as undue interference in internal affairs by the smaller states. While sub-regional connectivity and greater economic integration may result in mutual economic gains, it should translate into some sort of political understanding as well, which can happen only when the neighbours are clearly aware of India's major security requirements in the region and her declared ways to achieve those goals.

Security however is also closely linked with a healthy functioning polity. Good governance, rule of law, social welfare, protection of democratic rights coupled with economic prosperity and military power, enhance state capacity to a high level. Mere material gains in terms of GDP or a high growth rate might not suffice if acute economic inequalities and rural poverty continue to exist. Mere increase in number of weapons and improvement in weapon-systems would not be adequate if large sections of people within the country feel alienated from the state. Corruption and economic offences on the one hand, and parochial and unprincipled political operations on ethnic, religious, regional, caste-based, class-based divisions on the other, would slow down or completely derail the pace of development and prosperity. These are no less security threats and should be tackled by the state as a priority. To keep the state on the right track—the media, judiciary, bureaucracy and responsive human collectivities have the added responsibility to make Emerging India a movement for second freedom: freedom from the constraints and restrictions that have kept India hitherto shackled to a diminutive form of what it could actually become.

Endnotes

1. Nye observes that command power rests on coercion and inducement while co-optive power rests on attractiveness of one's culture and ideology. Soft power resources tend to be associated with co-optive power behaviour. See Joseph S. Nye, *The Paradox of American Power*, Oxford University Press, New York, 2002: 176 f.n.
2. For example, Karsten Frey argues that in contrast to security-seeking, status-seeking became a basic national interest in India's nuclear policy formulation. See Karsten Frey, *India's Nuclear Bomb and National Security*, Routledge, London and New York, 2006: 197.
3. For elaboration on Sportsmanlike Nationalism and Oppositional Nationalism, See "We have a big bomb now: India's nuclear U-turn" in Jacques E.C. Hymans, *The Psychology of Nuclear Proliferation: Identity, Emotions and Foreign Policy*, Cambridge University Press, UK, 2006: 171-203.

References

Bulletin of the Atomic Scientists and *SIPRI Yearbook* (n.d). All figures are approximate estimates and most common figures are quoted from the *Bulletin of the Atomic Scientists* and *SIPRI Yearbook*. Various Years.

Chellaney, Brahma (2014, December 25). A discerning friend to all. *India Today*. From http://indiatoday.intoday.in/story/narendra-modi-foreign-policy-geopolitical-tensions/1/408714.html (Accessed on September 7, 2015).

Cossa, Ralph A. (2008). Security Dynamics in East Asia: Geopolitics vs. Regional Institutions. In David Shambaugh and Michael Yahuda (Eds.), *International Relations of Asia* (317-40). Lanham, Maryland: Rowman and Littlefield Publishers.

Economic Times (2014, April 30). From http://articles.economictimes.indiatimes.com/2014-04-30/news/49523310_1_capita-income-third-largest-economy-world-gdp (Accessed on September 8, 2015).

Frey, Karsten (2006). *India's Nuclear Bomb and National Security*. London and New York: Routledge.

Ganguly, Sumit (2008). The Rise of India in Asia. In David Shambaugh and Michael Yahuda (eds.), *International Relations of Asia* (150-64). Lanham, Maryland: Rowman and Littlefield Publishers.

Gordon, Sandy (2012, June 24). India: Which way will the 'swing state' swing? *East Asia Forum*. From http://www.eastasiaforum.org/2012/06/24/india-which-way-will-the-swing-state-swing/ (Accessed on September 7, 2015).

Hymans, Jacques E.C. (2006). *The Psychology of Nuclear Proliferation: Identity, Emotions and Foreign Policy* (171-203). UK: Cambridge University Press.

Indian Express. From http://indianexpress.com/article/india/india-to-be-worlds-third-largest-economy-by-2030-study/(Accessed on September 8, 2015).

Malone, David and Mukherjee, Rohan (2010). Politics, Security, and Foreign Policy in Contemporary India. In T.V. Paul (Ed.), *South Asia's Weak States: Understanding the Regional Insecurity Predicament* (161-62). New Delhi: Oxford University Press.

Medcalf, Rory and Rajamohan, C. (2014, September 3). Looking beyond old alliances to forge a safer Indo-Pacific region. *The Australian*. From www.lowyinstitute.org/publications_(Accessed on November 4, 2015).

Mehta, Pratap Bhanu (2009). Still Under Nehru's Shadow? The Absence of Foreign Policy Frameworks in India. *India Review*, 8(3): 231.

Money.cnn.com/news/economy/world_economies_gdp/index.html (Accessed on November 4, 2015).

New York Times (1998, May 13). From www.nytimes.com/1998/05/13/world/nuclear-anxiety-indian-s-letter-to-clinton-on-the-nuclear-testing.html (Accessed on September 14, 2015).

Nye, Joseph S. (2002). *The Paradox of American Power*. New York: Oxford University Press.

Starobin, Paul (2010). *Five Roads to the Future: Power in the Next Global Age*. New York: Penguin Books.

Tharoor, Shashi (2012). *PaxIndica: India and the World of the 21st Century*. New Delhi: Allen Lane/Penguin.

Uriu, Robert (2015, October 3). The Security Environment in Northeast Asia: Overlapping Sources of Stability, paper presented in a Conference on 'Taiwan and the China Seas', University of South Carolina.

4

Analyzing India's Nuclear Strategy: Making Debates on the Issues and Problems

Suratha Kumar Malik

The Backdrop: From Nuclear Estrangement to Cooperation

India's peaceful nuclear test of 1974 made Western nations conscious of the existing loopholes in the non-proliferation regime and heightened their 'atomic dilemma'. It was alleged that India diverted the nuclear technologies intended for civilian purposes under the Canada-India-Reactor-US (CIRUS) agreement with Canada and the US. Thus, post-1974 India was regarded as a 'nuclear pariah' (Kux 1992: 123). The US Congress passed the Nuclear Non-Proliferation Act of 1978 (NNPA), which barred nuclear exports unless the non-nuclear weapon states accepted comprehensive International Atomic Energy Agency (IAEA) safeguards. India was internationally isolated, yet it refused to accede to the NPT and pursued an ambiguous policy on nuclear weapons. In 1998, India conducted a series of nuclear weapons explosions and declared it a nuclear weapon state. The then US President, Bill Clinton, immediately retorted that the "Indian government had put itself at odds with the international community" as well as "at the wrong side of history" (CNN News 1998). In the aftermath of the 1998 nuclear tests, the Clinton administration imposed sanctions as per the Glenn Amendment, thereby restricting bilateral and multilateral economic assistance (Chellaney 1994: 44). In addition, the non-statutory measures also curtailed high-level visits and military-to-military contacts.

Nonetheless, within seven years of the 1998 nuclear tests, in an extreme policy reversal, the successive George W. Bush administration offered nuclear cooperation to India. On 18 July 2005, US President George Bush and the Indian Prime Minister Manmohan Singh, issued a joint declaration envisaging full civil nuclear cooperation. Significantly, the US declared India "a responsible state with advanced nuclear technology". The declaration included path-breaking pledges on both sides (The Indo-U.S. Joint Statement...). The US committed, *inter alia*, to: (i) offer civilian nuclear technologies to alleviate Indian concerns regarding energy security; (ii) seek to adjust US laws and policies in order to realize the goals of nuclear cooperation; and (iii) encourage its [supplier] friends to alter existing international regimes in order to enable civil nuclear cooperation with India. In reciprocation, India committed itself to: (i) Segregate its civilian and military facilities and place its civilian facilities under IAEA safeguards; (ii) Honour the voluntary moratorium on nuclear testing; (iii) Sign and adhere to an IAEA additional protocol with respect to civilian nuclear facilities; (iv) Refrain from transfer of enrichment and reprocessing technologies to states that do not have them and support international efforts to limit their spread; and (v) Strengthen its export controls through comprehensive national legislation to curb proliferation of sensitive technologies and harmonize them as per Missile Technology Control Regime (MTCR) and Nuclear Suppliers Group (NSG) guidelines (The Indo-U.S. Joint Statement...).

Based on the July 2005 joint declaration, during President Bush's March 2006 visit to India, the two sides finalized a plan for the separation of Indian civilian and military facilities. They also mutually agreed to "limit the spread of enrichment and reprocessing technologies" and "support the conclusion of a Fissile Material Cut-off Treaty". Subsequently, on 18 December 2006, President Bush signed into law the Henry Hyde United States-India Peaceful Atomic Energy Cooperation Act (hereafter, the Henry Hyde Act) (Perkovich). Interestingly, it was passed with strong bipartisan support in the US Congress. The Henry Hyde Act was described as an 'enabling legislation' as it created legal space, hitherto blocked by the NNPA, for resuming nuclear trade with India—a non-signatory of the NPT and a *de facto* nuclear weapon state. Nonetheless, Congress did attach certain clauses to emphasize the non-proliferation measures: the President must annually certify that India is adhering to the terms of the agreement; and, most significantly, the deal will lapse if India conducts further nuclear tests (Perkovich).

Based on the earlier agreements (July 2005 and March 2006) and the Henry Hyde legislation, a separate technical agreement, popularly called the Indo-US 123 Agreement, was signed by the two countries. It was called the 123 Agreement as it refers to section 123 of the US Atomic Energy Act (http://www.state.gov/r/pa/prs/ps/2007/aug/90050.htm). It specified detailed responsibilities of, and conditions for, the two nations. There were certain requirements India needed to fulfill before the agreement could be operationalised—a safeguards agreement with the IAEA and approval from the NSG. On the fulfillment of the conditions by India, the 123 Agreement was introduced in the US Congress and it passed with an overwhelming majority in both the House of Representatives and the Senate. Finally, the US-India Nuclear Cooperation Bill was signed into law by President Bush in December 2008 (Perkovich 2010). There was widespread consensus among scholars that the Bush administration's neo-realist objective of forging a strategic partnership with India vis-à-vis China was the primary determinant of this nuclear pact (Perkovich 2010). It was believed that Bush's strategy was to "cultivate a partnership with India and enhance India's international power. A more powerful and collegial India will balance China's power in Asia" (Carranza 2007: 464-93).

The persistent US-India nuclear estrangement not only impinged on bilateral relations, it also kept the recalcitrant India outside the nuclear non-proliferation regime. On this account, scholars considered the nuclear rapprochement between the US and India to be a positive development (Carranza 2007: 464-93). Paul called it a 'radical initiative', as otherwise the nuclear estrangement between India and the US showed "no signs of ending" (Paul 2007). Ashok Kapur argued that the agreement "leveled the playing field in the sphere of nuclear negotiations between 'nuclear haves' and 'nuclear have-nots'" (Kapur 2007: 55). Some intellectuals expressed concerns regarding the implications of the deal for India's nuclear weapons programme. Arun Shourie thoroughly analyzed the terms of the US-India agreement and related US legislation, concluding that Washington desired that "India [be] drained of its strategic nuclear programme, and thus [become] a dependent India" (Shourie 2006). He warned that the US planned ultimately to "rollback and eventually eliminate the nuclear weapons capability of India" (Shourie 2006). Similarly, Bharat Karnad opined, "this deal amounts to death by stagnation for the Indian nuclear weapons programme" (Karnad 2008). He emphasized that for India to be treated as 'a country of consequence', it is important to have a thermonuclear deterrent—"the prime currency of power in the new millennium". The US has significant "test data from the 1,800 [sic] nuclear tests and a computing ability of 100 teraflops and a gigantic ICF (Inertial Confinement Fusion) facility to obtain miniature thermonuclear explosions; its belief that it can do without testing is well-founded" (Karnad 2008). Unlike the US, India cannot afford to give up the nuclear testing, as it has neither the data nor the technology to conduct simulated nuclear tests in order to develop a thermonuclear deterrent. In this context, R. Rajaraman pointed out that India only intended to build a minimum nuclear deterrent and a "minimal deterrence force does not call for a boundless open-ended nuclear arsenal" (Rajaraman 67-68). Allaying the fears of the critics, he argued, "There will be no effect on the strategic programme, there will be no deceleration in our three-stage nuclear power programme... and there will be no effect on our advanced R and D programme" (Rajaraman 2006).

The Response within India on Nuclear Issues

In the beginning of April 2014, Manmohan Singh was addressing a conference at the Institute for Defense Studies and Analyses (IDSA) titled "A Nuclear Weapon-Free World: From Conception to Reality", where he casually urged the creation of a global convention to forswear the first use of nuclear weapons. Following Singh's remarks, the then opposition Bharatiya Janata Party (BJP) instantly issued a rejoinder in its election manifesto, stating that the party "believes that the strategic gains acquired by India during the [earlier BJP-led] Atal Bihari Vajpayee regime on the nuclear programme have been frittered away by [Singh's]

Congress. Hence, the BJP pledged to study in detail India's nuclear doctrine, and revise and update it, to make it relevant to [the] challenges of current times" BJP spokespeople clarified that a review of India's no-first-use policy would be accorded priority if the party came to power. Modi's campaigning for the 2014 election, subsequently declared that there would be "no compromise" on no first use, which reflected India's "cultural inheritance" (whatever that means).

India's no-first-use policy was originally declared by the BJP and the National Democratic Alliance Government after it conducted the May 1998 nuclear tests. The prime minister at the time, Atal Bihari Vajpayee, stated thereafter that India would pursue a policy of no first use of nuclear weapons vis-à-vis other nuclear-armed states and would not use these weapons against non-nuclear countries. This restraint was also embedded in the BJP's draft nuclear doctrine, declared in August 1999, which took several years to be finalized. It was finally endorsed by the Cabinet Committee on Security and officially promulgated in January 2003. Consequently, India's no-first-use policy and its nuclear doctrine are BJP formulations. The Congress party adopted them and, with Singh's April speech, simply sought to extend no first use globally. This makes the BJP's concern with its own no-first-use policy and nuclear doctrine part of the mystery of Singh's proposal.

India's Nuclear Strategy: The Theoretical Debate

The past few years have produced considerable debate over India's nuclear strategy and posture (Basrur 2014). Much of it has revolved around the credibility of India's nuclear arsenal (Chari 2014). This is an important question because it goes to the heart of India's capacity to deter its adversaries. Is the Indian deterrent properly organised? Are its capabilities enough? What makes a deterrent credible? The ongoing debate has produced three broad positions: that India's nuclear weapons are inadequate for deterrence; that they are sufficient to meet the requirements of minimum deterrence; and that weapons development is reaching for excessive capabilities. But to resolve such a debate, it is first necessary to know: how does deterrence work? For all the differences aired, there is remarkably little or no disagreement on the meaning and fundamental requirements of minimum deterrence. Everyone seems to agree that the central principle of deterrence is "assured/secured second strike capability". From this flow the criteria for assessing the effectiveness of an arsenal: the survivability, reliability and accuracy of weapons, plus an efficient system of command control. To deter, so it went (and still goes), one has to survive a first strike and be sure to retaliate sufficiently well to create large-scale damage.

Indian theorizing about the requirements of deterrence, drawing heavily from American strategic literature, rests almost entirely on an uncritical acceptance of this edifice. It is time to take a closer look. The foundational concept of assured second strike capability and its derivatives emerged from a series of seminal writings that emanated from the American strategic establishment in the 1950s and 1960s, notably from the RAND Corporation (Basrur 2014) which better represents the intellectual bedrock of American nuclear doctrine and strategy of Albert Wohlstetter. His 1958 paper on the "Delicate Balance of Terror"—more widely disseminated in a *Foreign Affairs* article in 1959—presents the core precepts of deterrence as he saw them (Wohlstetter 1958, 1959). A set of ideas drawn from the writings of Patrick Blackett (Blackett 1961, 1962) which offers a powerful critique of the notion that secure second strike capability is vital to the working of nuclear deterrence and provide a sound intellectual basis for a truly minimalist approach toward nuclear deterrence. He was critical of Wohlstetter and provided an alternative basis for thinking about the requirements of nuclear deterrence which in effect rejected the notion that second strike capability is the *sine qua non* of successful nuclear deterrence. His debate with Wohlstetter is instructive because it draws attention to the roots of the question "how much is enough?" As will become evident, Blackett's analysis was more insightful than Wohlstetter's. Indian strategists would do well to consider Blackett's analysis with care (Basrur 2014).

Ironically, policy circles were familiar with Blackett's views on nuclear weapons. Nehru appointed him defence advisor, in which capacity he produced a report on the organization of India's defense apparatus (Blackett 1948). The report, which led to the establishment of the Defence Science Organisation, later the Defence Research and Development Organisation (DRDO), was warmly received by Nehru (Letter 1948). Blackett was also close to Homi Bhabha, often called the father of the Indian nuclear programme and a strong advocate of nuclear weapons for India, though Blackett himself had reservations about the value of nuclear weapons (Speech 1974). Blackett's position on nuclear weapons finds an echo in contemporary India in numerous ways. He was a staunch campaigner for nuclear disarmament and an early advocate of No First Use (Howard 1985).

Blackett offered a systematic refutation of the conception of deterrence that was predominant in American universities and in think tanks like the RAND Corporation (Basrur 2014). He was particularly severe on Wohlstetter, whose views on the requirements of deterrence crystallized into official doctrine and produced the central tenet of "secure second strike capability" that quickly became deeply embedded in most strategic thinking about nuclear weapons in the United States and later elsewhere (Blackett 1961, 1962; Wohlstetter 1958, 1959). The chief points made by Blackett were as follows: (Basrur 2014): First, one need not threaten to obliterate the opponent's society in order to deter. Second, a nuclear surprise attack that destroys much of one's arsenal is extremely unlikely to happen. Wohlstetter's reasoning was based on the American experience of Pearl Harbour, i.e. the possibility of catastrophic damage inflicted by a similar surprise attack. Third, Wohlstetter held that an attacker who struck first would have the advantage, which meant that the defender, in order to deter effectively, would have to (a) absorb the strike and have enough forces to retaliate; and (b) ensure that surviving retaliatory forces would be sufficiently strong to cause the desired damage by means of a successful second strike. The clear inference was that relative quantities and quality matter a great deal: the nuclear balance is important in ensuring that one has sufficient survivable weapons. The overarching argument put forward by Blackett was that the choices before an aggressor state are stark: only if it is fully confident that there will be no retaliation can it takes the risk of striking first—and no one can be that certain. Thus, deterrence rests ultimately not on the defender's certainty of hitting back after absorbing a first strike, but on the aggressor's *uncertainty of being able to avoid retaliation*. Even if the two sides are numerically unequal in the size and capabilities of their nuclear arsenals, a "stronger" power cannot risk the possibility of retaliation by a "weaker" one because it cannot know in advance the level of retaliation that it may have to face. In short, most arguments about assured second strike capability are not in tune with the reality faced by policy-makers.

The Limitations of Nuclear Deterrence

There are valid grounds to revisit India's nuclear doctrine, but on the conceptual front, the limitations of nuclear deterrence have become apparent. In important ways, India's acquisition of nuclear weapons has not increased its security. While nuclear weapons have obvious relevance for the external dimensions of national security, they cannot ameliorate threats to India's territorial integrity that arise from domestic discontent or from cross border militancy and terrorism emanating from Pakistan. In other words, nuclear weapons cannot provide any defense against the sub-conventional threats to India's national security from extremist elements within its own territory or, especially, against those who receive moral and material assistance from across the border. As Singh repeatedly warned, the internal threats to India's national security are critical to its overall national security challenges. Nuclear weapons provide no defense against these dangers. The evidence in this regard is overwhelming and discernible from continuing unrest in the state of Jammu and Kashmir and in northeast India and from Maoist violence in central and east India. In a larger sense, no doubt, nuclear deterrence permits peaceful conditions to be established, a situation that is conducive to economic progress and the stimulation of regional trade and commerce. However, an entire spectrum of security threats also arises, ranging from border incursions to sub-conventional warfare and cross border terrorism and militancy. Nuclear weapons provide no security against this range of existential security threats.

Pakistan Ups the Ante

The establishment of nuclear deterrence vis-à-vis Pakistan had only limited value for India's overall national security. It did not deter Pakistan's cross-border incursions in winter 1998 and spring 1999 into the Kargil sector of Jammu and Kashmir, which led to a short but intense conflict ending in the ouster of Pakistan's regular and irregular forces. Yet despite India's overwhelming superiority in conventional arms, the effects of nuclear deterrence inhibited it from attacking Pakistan's lines of communications across the border or from enlarging the theater of conflict along the border to relieve pressure on the beleaguered Kargil sector. Significantly, these operations revealed that a nuclearized Pakistan had constrained New Delhi from launching a counteroffensive elsewhere along the Line of Control or into Pakistan to relieve pressure on Indian forces in Kargil. New Delhi decided that it would exhibit restraint and not expand the theater of conflict. Political considerations were said to be at play, as India wished to establish that it was a responsible nuclear power by not escalating the conflict. There was also a subliminal desire among Indian leaders to paint Pakistan into a corner by highlighting its irresponsible conduct in attacking across recognized borders without any provocation. There is little doubt, however, that this restraint was also informed by New Delhi's awareness that an escalation of this border conflict could become uncontrollable and leads inexorably toward the nuclear threshold.

Pakistan's decision to deploy tactical nuclear weapons in a battlefield mode along the India-Pakistan border can be surmised from a report by Hans M. Kristensen and Robert Norris of the Federation of American Scientists that identified Pakistan and China as either having or developing non-strategic nuclear weapons. Pakistan had made clear, Kristensen told the *Times of India*, that it was developing its nuclear-capable Nasr (or Hatf IX) missile for use against invading Indian troop formations that Pakistan doesn't have the conventional capabilities to defeat. These weapons, according to Indian experts, are meant to be used along the border in case of any skirmish with the Indian Army. The Nasr is described as a 60-kilometer (37-mile) ballistic missile launched from a mobile twin-canister launcher. According to Pakistan's Inter Services Public Relations, the Nasr also has "shoot and scoot attributes" to serve as a quick response system to add deterrence value to Pakistan's strategic weapons development programme at shorter ranges...to deter evolving threats.

These developments have highlighted the insufficiency of India's no-first-use policy to deter Pakistan's destabilizing strategy. For one thing, this policy articulation frees Pakistan of the uncertainty and angst that India might contemplate the pre-emptive use of nuclear weapons to deal with terrorist attacks or limited conventional strikes by Pakistan. Pakistan could also go to the extent of deploying its short-range Nasr missile without being concerned that India would target it with its own nuclear missiles. For another, the determinism inherent in India's nuclear doctrine that any level of nuclear attack will invite massive retaliation is too extreme to gain much credibility. It defies logic to threaten an adversary with nuclear annihilation to deter or defend against a tactical nuclear strike on an advancing military formation. Pakistan, for its part, has not countenanced a no-first-use policy on the grounds that the weaker conventionally armed power has to rely on nuclear weapons to ensure its security. However, conventional wisdom warns that deployment of nuclear weapons along the border makes these arms vulnerable to attack, which, in turn, could generate a "use or lose" mentality on the part of their possessor. Pakistan argues that locating tactical nuclear weapons along the India-Pakistan border in a state of battle-readiness enables it to counter India's Cold Start strategy, which envisages positioning offensive, battle-ready forces along the India-Pakistan border to deter any cross-border attack.

Pakistan claims that deploying its tactical nuclear weapons would provide it with 'full spectrum deterrence' against India. It is arguable that India's commitment to a no-first-use posture has encouraged Pakistan to adopt its present adventurist strategy, secure in the belief that it could undertake provocative actions without the angst that India might contemplate a nuclear riposte. Its provocative actions would include promoting cross border militancy and terrorism into India and even brazen actions like the attack on the Indian Parliament in 2001 or the Mumbai attacks in 2008. Arguably, the adoption of a deliberately vague policy in regard to nuclear retaliation by India, instead of the certitude of a no-first-use declaration, might have better served India's overall strategic ends. Apart from that, the no-first-use policy, which has been incorporated into India's nuclear doctrine, has several other infirmities.

An Inadequate Doctrine

The decision by the Cabinet Committee on Security to endorse India's nuclear doctrine (1999) makes clear that India will use nuclear weapons only to retaliate against a nuclear attack on its territories or on Indian forces anywhere; that nuclear weapons will not be used against non-nuclear states; but that, in the event of a major attack by biological or chemical weapons, India retains the option of retaliating with nuclear weapons. This enumeration of India's qualified no-first-use policy doctrine is flawed on several counts. First, it does not address the possibility of an attack by non-state actors, which is the present and imminent danger. And how would India address an attack by an international organization like al-Qaeda that is situated in several countries in the proximity of India? Second, how would a "major attack" with biological or chemical weapons be identified? What is "major" and what is "minor" is debatable. This issue is significant since biological and chemical weapons are not truly weapons of mass *destruction*, but they are certainly weapons of mass *disruption*. Non-state actors might favour these weapons due to the comparative ease of their manufacture, concealment, and transportation. Third, serious difficulties arise in any attempt to identify the perpetrator of a biological or chemical weapons attack that could be undertaken by state or non-state actors or, not inconceivably, by a non-state actor assisted by a state actor. This issue is ultimately a question of reliable forensics, which is at a rudimentary stage of development. The difficulty in identifying those guilty of chemical weapon attacks in Syria is instructive here.

India's no-first-use declaration cannot be separated from the country's overall nuclear doctrine as it has been articulated since 1999. Inadequate as it is, this doctrine deserves to be reviewed in the light of changes over the past fifteen years. The current nuclear doctrine dictates that nuclear retaliation against a first strike would be "massive" and designed to inflict "unacceptable damage" upon the attacker. This is an unrealistic certitude because, ethically, punishing large numbers of non-combatants contravenes the laws of war. Besides, threatening massive retaliation against any level of nuclear attack, which would inevitably trigger assured nuclear annihilation in a binary adversarial situation, is hardly a credible option. No doubt, it raises a ticklish question: Would India then favour a counterforce strategy? India's stated adherence to an assured and massive second strike suggests the latter. The present doctrine fetishizes acquisition of a "credible minimum deterrent". But India is seeking a force structure that is no different from that established by the United States or the former Soviet Union. India seeks a strategic triad comprising land-based, airborne, and underwater nuclear weapon systems that will require increasing resources.

It is arguable whether India's strategic circumstances require a naval component for its deterrent or whether the country requires only a submarine-based deterrent, on the assumption that the nuclear deterrent posture ultimately rests on the survivability of the nuclear arsenal. Land and air-based systems are more vulnerable to counterattack and destruction than submarine-based missiles are. That leads to the argument that taking the deterrent out to sea would ensure the acquisition of an invulnerable second strike capability. This question has not been seriously discussed in India, resulting in vociferous demands from the three services that the government concede some component of the nuclear deterrent to each of them.

Criticism is widespread that there is little transparency about the size and structure of India's nuclear forces and what its credible minimum deterrent comprises in terms of weapons systems. Instead of debating this issue, official spokesmen have argued that it is impossible to define what a credible minimum deterrent requires since there can be no "fixity" in this regard, which suggests that the contours of the credible minimum deterrence are a moving target. Incidentally, India's armed forces have been kept out of the nuclear decision-making process; hence, there is a touch of unreality about these declarations on nuclear force structures.

Conclusion and Suggestions

The entire calculus that underlies the central principle of deterrence orthodoxy—that "secure second strike capability" is vital for effective deterrence—lacks empirical grounding. All deterrence is, in this sense, minimum deterrence. Even a small risk of retaliation posed to a potential aggressor suffices to deter because it poses the risk of very high-level damage within a very short time frame—a calculus that challenges any potential political gain arising from war. Furthermore, one cannot have confidence in relying on controlled or "tactical" uses of nuclear weapons. The risk of escalation in the fog of war means that any crossing of the nuclear threshold can very quickly result in indiscriminate mass destruction. Logically, there is no need for deterrence to rest on assured retaliation or to worry about the "vulnerability" of one's forces. Indian policy-makers and strategists need to rethink the intellectual foundations of nuclear deterrence. A number of critical points need to be contemplated with care.

Serious consideration needs to be given to a more realistic doctrine that rests on the principles outlined by Blackett and confirmed by historical experience across the board. A study Group comprising civilian and military experts should be appointed to articulate a truly minimalist doctrine of deterrence. The construction of an optimal minimum deterrence doctrine should be based on extensive debate over the ideas of minimalists like Blackett and General K. Sundarji as well as a careful scrutiny of strategic history.

The contradiction between 'Minimum Deterrence' and 'Maximum Credible' should be overcome and what is that 'minimum' should be defined in terms of quantity and quality.

The concept of "assured/secure second strike capability" may be discarded as it is empty of meaningful content. There is no evidence whatsoever that this principle actually works. Its primary function is to encourage the open-ended expansion of nuclear arsenals, which may benefit the sectional interests of specific organizations, but not national security interests. Even the powerful country like U.S.A. has no such principle like 'second strike' and it has the principle for first strike. Does India have sufficient retaliations capacity to absorb the first strike and go for an assured second strike?

The term "credible" should be dropped from the nomenclature of Indian deterrence doctrine. If states with less than 1% of the forces possessed by their rivals can exercise deterrence, then "credibility" is a doubtful strategy. One has only to look at one's own perception of adversaries: do Indian decision-makers worry very much about the credibility of their adversaries' weapons? This approach logically encourages minimalist perceptions of deterrence requirements.

Careful consideration needs to be given to the numbers and types of weapons systems desirable for effective deterrence. Excessive augmentation of capabilities waste resources that would be better utilized for other needs.

Above all, it is time for civilian officials to obtain a better understanding of the requirements of nuclear deterrence. Political responsibility requires that civilian policy makers come to grips with the complexities of the "nuclear revolution".

References

Basrur, Rajesh (2014, July). Deterrence, Second Strike and Credibility: Revisiting India's Nuclear Doctrine. *IPCS, Issue Brief*, 255.

Carranza, Mario E. (2007, December). From Nonproliferation to Post-Proliferation: Explaining the U.S.-India Nuclear Deal. *Contemporary Security Policy*, 28(3): 464-93.

Chellaney, Brahma (1994, Summer). Non-proliferation: An Indian Critique of US Export Controls. *Orbis*, 38(3).

CNN News, 'Clinton Says India is on "Wrong Side of History" with Nuclear Tests' 16 May 1998.

http://www.state.gov/r/pa/prs/ps/2007/aug/90050.htm.

Kapur, Ashok (2007). Canada-India Nuclear Negotiations: Context and Process. In Karthika Sasikumar and Wade L. Huntley (Eds.), *Canadian Policy on Nuclear Cooperation with India: Confronting New Dilemmas*. Vancouver: Simons Centre for Disarmament and Non-Proliferation Research.

Karnad, Bharat (2008, February 22). Nuclear Test is a Must. *The Asian Age*.

Kux, Dennis (1992). *India and the United States: Estranged Democracies 1941-1991*. Washington, DC: National Defence University Press.

The Indo-U.S. Joint Statement, 18 July 2005, Washington, DC, at http://www.indianembassy.org/press_release/2005/July/21.htm

Paul, T.V. (2007, Autumn). The US-India Nuclear Accord: Implications for the Non-Proliferation Regime. *International Journal*, 62(4) and Paul, T.V. and Shankar, Mahesh (2007). Why the US-India Nuclear Accord is a Good Deal. *Survival*, 49(4): 111-22.

Perkovich George. "Global Implications of the U.S.-India Deal", *Daedalus*, 139(1), Winter 2010; Ashley J. Tellis, 'What Should We Expect from India as a Strategic Partner', in Henry Sokolski (ed.), *Gauging U.S.-Indian Strategic Cooperation*, Strategic Studies Institute, Carlisle, PA, 2007: 231-58; Mario E. Carranza, 'From Nonproliferation to Post-Proliferation: Explaining the U.S.-India Nuclear Deal', *Contemporary Security Policy*, 28(3), December 2007: 464-93; Lisa Curtis, "The Costs of a Failed U.S.-India Civil Nuclear Deal", Web Memo no. 1688, The Heritage Foundation, Washington, DC, 2 November 2007.

Perkovich, George (2010, Winter). Global Implications of the U.S.-India Deal. *Daedalus*, 139(1).

Shourie, Arun (2006, August 24). "'Parity', Did You Say?" *The Indian Express*.

Shourie, Arun (2006, August 23). "This is About Energy, Did You Say?" *The Indian Express*.

Rajaraman, R. "The India-US Nuclear Deal", No. 9.

Rajaraman, R. (2006, February 14). "Who's Afraid of the Nuke Deal". *The Indian Express*.

5

The Problem of Food Security in "Emerging" India: Some Reflections

Ambarish Mukhopadhyay

The image of India as an emerging power in world politics and a contender to global power status has become a very common one in recent times, thanks to print and electronic media. "Shining India", "Incredible India" has become the buzzwords. Such imagery has been boosted by India's economic growth, demographic trends and increasing military capabilities and interests. These factors have been instrumental for India's options to play an increasingly important role in Asia and beyond. India's vision in the contemporary world order is linked with its aspirations to play an even greater role in global politics, economy and security issues. However, India's role as an 'emerging' power needs to be examined with reference to both internal determinants—such as domestic politics, economic reforms, conventional and non-conventional security threats—and the global factors. Hailed as the world's largest democracy, more than sixty years of democratic governance in India has failed to be 'inclusive' in nature. It had to tackle a number of daunting challenges within the framework of a democratic order. Despite her mounting ambitions, India is still very much a developing nation on many indicators of human development (Mikian and Kolas 2014: 1). Some persistent problems that our country faces include poverty, rampant corruption and crime, caste war and communal violence, terrorist insurgency, resource depletion and environmental degradation, conventional and non-conventional security threats and so on. India's great power ambition coexists with extreme inequality and social vulnerability in the domestic front. Of the myriad problems faced by our country, challenges to human security are a major one. Food security is one of the essential components of human security. Problems of human security are major impediments to India's development and serious threats to the welfare and very survival of millions of Indian people.

Non-conventional security discourse started emerging since the mid-1980s. The traditional realist conceptualization of security came under sustained attack from a number of directions (Sheehan, 2006: 2). Critics pointed out that it was ignoring important aspects of an emerging world order. The debates during the 1980s and 1990s made the concept of security wider, exploring its meaning and application to a broader range of areas. The term "Human Security" was first coined in a report of the United Nations Development Programme (UNDP) in 1994. Human security was defined as: "safety from such chronic threats as hunger, disease and repression, and protection from sudden and hurtful disruption in the patterns of daily life". This very definition clearly indicates that the issue of food security is intrinsically linked with human security. The UN Commission of Human Security in its report (2003) stated that, "the vital core of human security is what constitutes a minimum level of survival. Human security is thus a very basic requirement that must be made before development requirements become relevant." Today human security has become one of the major agenda of national security discourse. And national security is a major component of national interest. A country aspiring to be a major global power must then prioritize promoting and protecting its national security—both in conventional and non-conventional senses of the term. It is in this context that we, in the present paper, make a modest attempt to look into the problem of food security in India.

II

The concept of 'food security' gained prominence on the international agenda since the 1970s. The term was first used at the FAO World Food Conference in 1974. A definition of food security emerged that focused mainly on increasing food supply, putting emphasis on the necessary maintenance of adequate food grain supplies and on national self-sufficiency by financing agricultural development (Thivet 2014: 17). Throughout the later decades, the food security concept has undergone a paradigm shift from food supply to food access and from the global/national level to the household/individual. It increasingly emphasized on ensuring both physical and economic access to the basic food that they need for all people at all times. Awareness regarding the importance of food problem gradually increased among the policy-makers, both at the domestic and international levels. The dangers of famine, food shortage, increasing food price, hunger and malnutrition of the world's poor were being seen not as isolated social problems, but as "a problem of international and national responsibility" (FAO 2003: 26). However, not much has been achieved in reality in this respect due to the reluctance of the major Western powers to set up multilateral and global arrangements for world food security. The responsibility has continued to rest on the individual state. Food security has become a major problem across the globe, particularly in the developing nations. It is a complex phenomenon which comprises a range of factors from access to utilization of the food products (Mountain Forum: Internet Source).

India, an emerging world power—with its unprecedented economic growth in recent times—faces serious challenges to feed its rapidly growing population. India is home to almost 17 per cent of the world's population (1.2 billion people). It has been estimated that by 2050, the country's population will rise to 1.6 billion people. Despite per capita income more than tripling in the last two decades, lifting it to the rank of the third largest economy, India is home to almost one-quarter of the world's undernourished people. According to the latest Food and Agriculture Organisation (FAO) data, India is presently home to more than 230 million hungry people, and holds the record for the absolute number of persons living in chronic hunger (FAO: Internet Source). Such disparities have contributed to India ranking 136th out of 186 countries in the

2013 UNDP Human Development Index and 94th out of 119 countries in the Global Hunger Index (Lehane 2014: 2). India has the second highest percentage of total arable land in the world, and has the world's largest areas under wheat, rice and cotton cultivation. The country is also the largest producer of milk, pulses and spices. India, with its current level of food production, can satisfy the needs of its population, export food and agricultural products, and has also accumulated near about 60 million tons of food grain as buffer stocks. But still millions of Indians suffer from malnutrition and hunger. Thus, the situation appears to be quite paradoxical. Scholars have called it the 'paradox of plenty'—which illustrates the fallacy of addressing hunger exclusively as a supply-side problem, and to an extent reasserts Amartya Sen's argument in his seminal work *Poverty and Famines* (1981) on the crucial importance of the ability of the individual and households to access food or to have entitlement to it (Thivet 2014: 16). Thus, the focus only on increasing food production cannot be the only way out to solve the food problem and achieve food security at the individual and household level. However, that has exactly been the major component of India's food policy since independence.

III

Within years of gaining independence, system of public food delivery was introduced in India in 1950 in the face of serious fluctuations of food prices. It had its origin in the 'rationing system' introduced during the British rule to tackle the problem of shortage of food grains. Independent India continued with food shortage. The development goals of the newly independent nations were centred on achieving self-sufficiency and self-reliance on food. The Five-year Plan documents clearly reveal this. The First Five-year Plan (1951-56) emphasized on increased food production as a matter of priority. Prime Minister Nehru stated that, "it is only when we obtain self-sufficiency in food that we can progress and develop ourselves". During the Second Plan period (1956-61), the Public Distribution System (PDS) further expanded. It was mainly due to the imports of food grains (especially wheat) at a large scale at low prices from

USA under PL 480 (US Public Law under the US Food for Peace Programme) and food aid. During the mid-sixties, the country faced a series of political and socio-economic crisis. The death of Pandit Nehru in 1964 created a big hiatus of leadership at the top echelon of the Congress party and the government. Subsequent border wars with the neighbours and their impacts shattered the economy. Series of draught largely affected the volume of domestic agricultural production leading to the food crisis of 1965-66. To fight out this crisis, the national government launched the New Agricultural Strategy—popularly known as the 'Green Revolution'—in 1966, with the sole aim of increasing food grain production. The policy-makers believed that was the only solution to the problems of food scarcity and hunger, and socio-economic inequality in the rural sector. The Green Revolution of the late 1960s saw an influx of new agricultural technologies—high-yielding varieties of seeds, chemical fertilizers and pesticides, on-farm equipment, subsidies for water and electricity to facilitate irrigation—with the hope of increasing agricultural production. As a result, India's agricultural production did explode, securing the nation's food self-sufficiency by the late 1970s. But this development failed to be sustainable. Since the end of the seventies, agricultural productivity has been consistently in decline. The New Agricultural Strategy led to an explosion in injudicious use of chemical fertilizers and pesticides, and wasteful water habits, causing decline in soil health, water logging and salinization of both water and land, and overall land degradation. All this led to the gradual decline of the amount of food production in India. The Green Revolution also failed to solve the problem of economic and social inequality, as was claimed by the framers of this policy. It rather resulted in further inequality. The most serious social impact of the Green Revolution was the increasing gap between a newly emerged class of 'modern' farmers, and the mass of 'backward' small peasants and agricultural labourers.

A shift in the country's policy occurred in the 1980s. Though late, there was a realization of the social, economic and regional inequalities created by the Green Revolution and the consequent dangers thereof. As L.I. Rudolph and

S.H. Rudolph have pointed out in one of their seminal works, a new food policy and agricultural strategy evolved, paying more attention to income distribution and basic needs (Rudolph and Rudolph 1987: 325). There was a national consensus regarding the need and importance of investment in agriculture so as to provide the growth with employment and equity that the strategies of the earlier five-year plans did not emphasize (Thivet 2014: 20). A series of programmes were launched—such as Food for Work, DPAP, Small Farmers Development Agency, Rural Labour Employment Guarantee Scheme, Antyodaya, Cash Rural Employment—for promotion of rural employment and enhanced investment in agriculture.

The 1990s unleashed a new era in the country's policy of economic development. With the implementation of the New Economic Policy (NEP) in 1991, the Indian Government started moving towards the path of economic reforms, influenced and directed by the world-wide process of liberalization, privatization and globalization. The model of free-market economy was warmly welcomed. The economic policy was given a significant neo-liberal orientation under the influence of the IMF and the World Bank. As regards the food policy, the Indian State gradually started to disengage itself from the strategy of self-sufficiency in food production. Market reforms and structural adjustment policies reduced the role of the state in the economy. This resulted in higher prices for food under the PDS. The State increasingly started favouring the rich farmers who have the capacity to commercialize their production. The interests of the majority of the consumers were not taken into account. Open market sales and massive exports were made from the PDS stock by the government. This shrunk the access to food for millions of Indians. Keeping in tune with the neo-liberal agenda, the scale of food subsidies was drastically reduced, as subsidy was viewed as a costly programme by the champions of free-market economy. Following the recommendation and direction of the World Bank, the policy of universal PDS was replaced by a targeted public distribution system (TDPS). The Bank wanted that the PDS be targeted to the 'very poor' and that a distinction be made between the 'very poor' and the 'moderately poor'.

The objective was to reduce the public food subsidies bill and, consequently, the fiscal deficit of the country. The TDPS became exclusionary in nature, keeping a large number of the weakest sections of the population outside its net. The government later decided to widen the social safety net by introducing the Antyodaya Anna Yojana (AAY) and Mahatma Gandhi National Rural Employment Guarantee Act (MGNREGA) in 2001 and 2005, respectively. While the first one targeted to provide 35 kilos of rice and wheat at ₹ 2 per kg to the 'poorest of the poor', the second one promised to guarantee a minimum of 100 days of wage employment a year to rural households. At the level of implementation, these schemes, however, have revealed their shortcomings and not been able to keep up the promises fully.

The policy of economic liberalization has seriously affected the livelihood of the vast numbers of small and marginal farmers whose food security has been largely undermined. With the opening up of the Indian economy to the world market and pursuing the strategy of export-led growth, there has been "displacement of local food staples by export crops production (cocoa, coffee, tea, sugarcane, oilseeds, rubber, cotton, floriculture, prawn fisheries, tropical fruits) in the name of the Ricardian theory of comparative advantage" (Thivet 2014: 22). Moreover, a huge number of food grain producers are living under the threat of increased competition from foreign countries due to the removal of trade barriers and quantitative restrictions to imports. The neo-liberal agricultural policy of the Indian state has exacerbated food insecurity among the most vulnerable population in India. Series of starvation deaths every year in the remote draught-affected areas, and the epidemic of farmers' suicides in recent times bear testimony to this situation of insecurity. In addition to this, there is the problem of the health and safety of food. The incidence of food poisoning due to negligent storage and contamination is quite high. Hundreds of such cases are reported every year. We often come to know about the deaths of school children due to food poisoning from mid-day meals contaminated with pesticides. Unhygienic food preparation, storage, and poor quality of food result to the threat of ill health across the country. India produces near about

150 million tonne of food grains every year. Of this 10 per cent is lost prior to distribution. According to the estimates of the FAO, on an average, about 6 per cent of the total 10 per cent loss takes place during storage. During the last decade the food grain surplus in India has been around 60 million tonne. But in spite of such huge surpluses, India is presently home to around 25 per cent of the world's hungry (Lehane 2014: 4). Such a gap between food surplus and the percentage of hungry is a clear reflection of serious mismanagement of the food problem and the issue of food security in our country. It also challenges the idea that the problem of hunger is purely a matter of supply requiring technological solutions.

IV

The concept of 'food security', developed and popularized by the International Agencies like FAO since the mid-1970s, carries with it an image of a kind of humanistic and philanthropist State. The argument runs like this—it is the State which comes forward to protect the poor throughout the world, particularly in the developing countries, from the world-wide food crisis and ever increasing prices of food grains. It is the State which performs the noble task of supplying food grains at minimum prices to millions of hungry poor, and thus ensuring food security. Food security needs more and more production of food grains and distribution of the same through market mechanisms. In fact, the total amount of food grain production lags behind the demand for food. Apparently, such arguments seem quite logical. But the reality speaks otherwise. Data published by various international agencies on global food situation reveal that during the last three decades the amount of global food production has increased at a much higher rate than that of the total world population. Presently, there is enough food stock to provide each individual an amount of 2700 calories per day. Thus, it is not at all true that, population increase has led to food crisis. The fact is that the millions of poor and the marginalized throughout the world have minimum, and often, zero access to food. This is the real face of food crisis and insecurity. The Global Hunger Index states that almost 98 per cent of these people facing the spectre of hunger live in the countries of the South.

On the other side, there is the Global Obesity Index which measures the amount of accumulation of fat in human body due to over-eating. The problem of obesity was identified in the USA as early as in 1980. The World Health Organisation (WHO) in one of its reports in 2001 coined the term 'globosity' to refer to the world-wide increasing phenomenon of obesity, particularly among the wealthy and the affluent living in the Western countries. The main reason for this is the regular over-consumption of the 'Western affluent diet' (Bhattacharya 2014: 11). Such consumption pattern is being encouraged by the world-wide big foods corporate which control the global market of food business. We presently live under this corporate food regime which control and shape our food habits and consumption patterns to increase the profits of the corporate giants. Earlier, the usual norm was "production according to needs". Nowadays, it is the 'need' which is being produced by the corporate. A world-wide corporate network of food regime has steadily expanded. It has gradually captured each and every aspect of food production—the types and amount of food to be produced, the technologies to be used, export and import of food grains and food habits. Four very large corporate—Cargill, Drefus, Bange and ADM (Archer Daniels Midland) today control more than 80 to 90 per cent of the global food grains business. In addition, there are others such as Kellog, Del Monte, Unilever, Nestle, Mc Donald, etc. who play a major role in the corporate food regime. As a result of the over-arching influence of the corporate food regime, we are losing our local agri-ecology and food diversity; particularly in developing countries. The corporate want to promote a kind of 'homogeneity' in matters related with food and tries to pour everyone into a single cast—the Western lifestyle. The neo-liberal market economy, doing away with state restrictions and regulations, has proved the path for the triumph of the corporate food regime.

We have to understand the issue of 'food security' in this perspective of food regime, and do away with the narrow view of food problem as an issue of food supply and food distribution. The business of the global food corporate has resulted in food insecurity and seriously jeopardized the Right to Food of the common people in different parts of the world. To fight back this situation, there have been protests and search for alternatives since the early 1990s. A joint organisation named 'La Via Campesina' (Campesina meaning 'small farmers') in the city of Mons at Belgium in 1993 under the initiatives of the farmers and members of activist movements. At present 164 local and national organisations spread over 75 countries of the world are members of La Via Campesina. At the World Food Conference held in 1996, they protested against the globalization and corporatization of agriculture and raised the slogan of "Food Sovereignty", arguing for more localized and direct control by the people over their food supply, notably by ensuring that small and marginal farmers have access and control over productive resources such as land, water and seeds (Thivet 2014: 25). The main objective of La Via is the promotion and protection of food sovereignty. In February 2007, near about 500 hundred representatives from more than 80 countries participated in the 'Forum for Food Sovereignty' and adopted the Declaration of Nyeline. The Declaration states that, "Food Sovereignty is the right of people to healthy and culturally appropriate food produced through ecologically sound and sustainable methods, and their right to define their own food and agricultural systems. It puts those who produce, distribute and consume food at the heart of food systems and policies rather than the demands of markets and corporations" (Mitra 2014: 39). In 2008, the concept of 'food sovereignty' got constitutional recognition by a nation-state. Equador became the first country to incorporate 'food sovereignty' into their constitution. In the later phase, Venezuela, Mali, Bolivia, Nepal and Senegal followed suit.

If we have to tackle the problem of food insecurity and provide security of food to all, we need to look at the issue in a broader perspective of food sovereignty. Adequate and/or surplus stock of food grains is no guarantee to food security in the true sense of the term. Our experience shows that such security, which is dependent upon the global food-market, is very fragile indeed. We have to look at 'food security' and 'food sovereignty' as complementary to each other. Food security sets up a goal; food sovereignty shows the path and guides to reach that destination.

V

The policy-makers in our country seem to be least bothered to promote and protect food sovereignty, and to guarantee the Right to Food to the people. The benefits of globalization and economic liberalization have not touched the majority of the people in India. The entitlement to food of the most vulnerable has been eroded as a consequence of the reforms in the PDS and the agricultural sector. The New Economic Policy has worsened the problem of chronic hunger and malnutrition of millions of Indians. "Inequalities and inefficiencies in distribution of food and the uneven access to resources for food production" have become the hallmark of the present 'food security' scenario of our nation. The National Food Security Act 2013, which promised subsidized food grains to 75 per cent of the rural and 50 per cent of the urban population of our country, does not draw much attention any more as both the central and state governments are silently postponing its implementation citing political differences (Mathew 2015: 20). The Union Budget 2015-16 made drastic reductions in budget allocation for major national social programmes in the country. Allocation on schemes like Mid-day Meal, ICDS, Sarba Siksha Abhiyan, etc. have been considerably downsized. Some other schemes such as the Backward Regions Grant Fund have been completely done away with. The Central Government is presently refusing to fund the recurring revenue expenditure on many of the schemes, and the same has been left to the states.

The story of India's growth is being lauded since the implementation of the NEP in 1990s. Prime Minister Narendra Modi, "riding the wave of the GDP figures marked his first anniversary in power with further promises of dazzling economic growth" (Shah and Lerche 2015: 33). His government continues a paradigm of "inclusive growth" (!) applauded by the World Bank and IMF. It puts economic growth and strong, deregulated markets at the centre of poverty reduction, and argues that this model will lead to a trickle down effect that will reach the poor. The reality, however, speaks otherwise. The neo-liberal reforms have met fierce opposition from scholars and activists. Amartya Sen and Jean Dreeze in their work *An Uncertain Glory* (2013) have argued that growth, though important, was not enough to improve the living conditions of the poor. In fact, the '*mantra*' that economic growth by itself will reduce inequality and eliminate poverty, has been dispelled by other scholars also. The search for an 'alternative' to secure food security in our country thus seems imminent. A number of local initiatives towards alternative methods of agricultural production are being taken at different parts of the country. The 'Risi Kheti' in the village of Rasulia in Madhya Pradesh, 'Zero Budget Natural Farming' of Subhas Palekar in Maharashtra, 'Zero Farming' of Kailash Murti in Karnataka are some of such initiatives and experiments towards an alternative model of development. These are certainly rays of hope amidst the clouds of despair. However, these movements face a very strong opposition from the global corporate food regime. But still, the struggle for the alternative must go on. Unfortunately, the sun rays of the 'Shining India' have not entered into the mud huts and '*jhopris*' of the millions of downtrodden in the country. We need a more comprehensive view of food security. A paradigm shift is urgently required which will view food security in the larger perspective of food sovereignty. For, without the promotion and protection of food sovereignty, India cannot solve her problems of food security. Food sovereignty is the essential component of our national sovereignty. India's foremost task should be to guard that. Otherwise, her so-called 'emerging global power' position may soon turn to be very unstable and fragile—her 'glory' to be uncertain.

References

Bhattacharya, Sutanu (2014, September). Khaddyo Shasantantra (in Bengali). In *Ekok Matra*, September, Kolkata.

FAO (2003). *Trade Reforms and Food Security: Conceptualizing the Linkages*. From ftp.fao.org/dorcep/fao/005/y4671e00.pdf

FAO (2011). *The State of Food Security in the World 2011*. From www.fao.org/dorcep/014/i2330e.pdf

Lehane, Sinead (2014, June 3). India's Food and Water Security. *Strategic Analysis Paper*. Future Directions International, Australia.

Mathew, C.K. (2015, October 24). Food Security Act in Sleep Mode. In *EPW*, Vol. 50, No. 43.

Mikian, Jason and Kolas, Ashild (Eds.) (2014). *India's Human Security: Lost debates, forgotten people, intractable challenges*. London and New York: Routledge.

Mitra, Sabyasachi (2014, September). Sarbovoumatyoi Nirapotta (in Bengali). In *Ekok Matra*, Kolkata.

Mountain Forum (n.d.). Water Security and Climate Change: Challenges and Strategies. From http:/www.mtnforum.org/content/water-security-and-climate-change-challenges-and-strategies. (Accessed on August 13, 2014).

Rudolph, L.I. and Rudolph, S.H. (1987). *In Pursuit of Lakshmi: The Political Economy of the Indian* State. Hyderabad: Orient Longman.

Sen, Amartya (1981). *Poverty and Famines, An Essay on Entitlement and Deprivation*. Oxford: Clarendon Press.

Shah, Alpa and Lerche, Jens (2015, October 10). India's Democracy: Illusion of Inclusion. In *EPW*, Vol. 50, No. 41.

Sheehan, Michael (2006). *Internal Security: An Analytical Survey*. New Delhi: Viva Books Pvt. Ltd.

Thivet, Delphine (2014). A nation without hunger Threats to food security in contemporary India. In Jason Mikian and Ashild Kolas (Eds.), *India's Human Security: Lost debates, forgotten people, intractable challenges*. London and New York: Routledge.

6

Energy Security: The Strategic Outlook of UPA Government

Ankhi Sen Sanyal

The end of Cold War has opened up a plethora of debates over the security issues. The Realist School emphasized the primacy of state in the security discourse or the *raison d'etre* of the nation-state to survive and enhance its power in a conflict ridden international system. The Cold War marked the ascendency of military-industrial complex and military-bureaucratic structures in the national polity that dominated the national policy-making and resource allocation process (Chari and Gupta 2003: 1). However, following the collapse of the bipolar world and in the quest for a new international system the end of Cold War has led to a paradigmatic shift in the problems of insecurity in the world. This invigorated a debate on alternative approach to security by bringing an alternative to the realist version of security. National security no more remained the only dimension of territorial integrity, though it remained the enduring promise of national security. The lack of an agreed definition and the varied theoretical approaches of examining security extended the opportunity to redefine security. Therefore, since the end of the cold war security has been at the center stage of almost any discussion revolving around politics and development. The problems of non-military threats to national security like the struggle for resources embedded in the pursuit of energy security, food security and environmental security demanded a more comprehensive understanding of security which would be less restricted to the military aspects. This made national security a comprehensive idea. Brandt Report came to an agreement that the scope of national security must be broadened to incorporate ideas beyond military security and stretching to the political, social, economic, environment and energy concerns.

Martha Harris has identified that relationship between energy and security which evolved during the twentieth century as the global strategic context change from great-power competition to multilateral cooperation on specific issues like energy (Harris 2003: 157). These developments justifies how acquiring adequate energy resources has assumed a security dimension over the years. Energy security in the twentieth century was a quest for oil, money and national power with focus on expanding national control of energy resources in order to ensure national security and securing autonomous national control. Although this continues to be a major theme of national policies in many countries today but along with this certain realities in energy politics have cropped up that revives the relationship between energy and security which can be identified as follows:

(i) Energy security calls for fuel substitution, lower price energy and improved energy efficiencies.

(ii) Energy security is closely associated geopolitics in determining energy futures and about what policy approaches are most useful for ensuring energy security in the century ahead. This issue becomes more pertinent as the nations link their fates to one another through pipelines, grids, and cross investment.

(iii) Energy security involves energy market interdependence but the governments are still striving to expand interdependence by building special relationships with supplier countries through market-oriented approaches to develop new ways of fostering multilateral co-operation in order to promote energy and security interests in the coming days.

(iv) Energy security has increasingly become a matter of international co-operation for achieving stability in the oil-producing states.

(v) Energy security involves global integration of energy markets as a result of which Western nations have moved towards more constrained roles for the government in the regulation of energy industries. Recent experience with "deregulated" energy markets has exposed risks of price hikes and problems with reliability and market power that require continued government oversight and regulations.

(vi) Energy security also absorbs the new challenges stemming from piracy, ethnic unrest and terrorism which jeopardize energy security through potential disruptions in supply and damage to infrastructures and stable global energy markets, open transportation channels and security of infrastructure has become associated with national interest.

(vii) Energy security involves environmental-protection goals and the need for transition to a different and more environment-friendly energy mix. Since the environmental dimension of energy policy has many facets like pollution control, fuel mix, promotion of alternative fuels and energy conservation as well as global warming and the contested role of nuclear power, it is difficult to formulate a successful strategy of energy security for achieving reliable energy supply, economic efficiency and environmental protection in the long run.

(viii) Energy security also involves security of energy infrastructure. Energy pipelines, LNG terminals, transmission grids, and power plants are critical components of national infrastructure that are vulnerable to terrorists, hackers, disaffected local groups, human error and natural disasters like earthquakes.

The relationship between energy and security evolved during the twentieth century was a global strategic context change from great-power competition to a multilateral co-operation on specific issues. Energy security in the twentieth century was a quest for oil, money and national power with focus on expanding national control of energy resources in order to ensure national security. Although autonomous national control continues to be a major theme of national policies in developed as well as developing countries, the process of decision-making becomes more complex as the lobbies, government and the private sector actors make key decisions that affect national security. By the end of the century, environmental protection added a new dimension to the energy security issue surrounding which the developing and developed nations contends over how to assess the costs of environmental damage and who should bear them.

The ground realities, discussed above, against the changed international political scenario would be helpful to understand the strategic stand adopted by India over issues concerning energy security and how India proposes to define her stand on energy security. India co-relates energy security with issues of economic development. One of the objectives of the energy policy in India is to meet the basic needs of the poor. The target was to reduce fuel wood consumption and promoting the use of alternative efficient commercial energy for cooking. However certain factors like subsidies, promotional efforts and social acceptability, willingness to pay and cost to the society play vital roles in realizing the energy policies to the fullest. Pricing of energy products in India are entirely under government control and are used as effective policy tools to satisfy various national objectives. Although the product prices are generally affected by the external prices of oil and petroleum products, the differential pricing mechanism is so worked out as to either stagger the cost effects in gradual manner or cross-subsidize various products in a manner consistent with the objectives of economic growth, demand management and equity (Sarkar and Kadekodi 1988: 23). The Indian economy is at a critical stage of development where energy requirement is increasing at a phenomenal pace. India is the fourth largest energy consumer in the world after USA, China and Russia. The domestic availability of oil and gas constitutes 40% of the energy basket and India imports over 75% of its domestic requirement and is subjected to the vagaries of the volatile international price scenario. In order to achieve 8% projected GDP growth during Twelfth Plan period

(2012-17), oil and gas sector needs to grow in tandem with economy at a faster pace. The challenge is to provide supply of oil and gas on a sustainable basis and at affordable prices in order to protect the interests of both the consumers and producers.

According to the Twelfth Five-Year Plan even though domestic production of energy resources will increase, import dependence will continue at a high level where nearly 80% of the demand will have to be met through imports by the end of the Twelfth Plan period. Given the forecast of increases oil dependence moving towards self-sufficiency goal has been identified as a significant step in the "history of nation". Accordingly, New Vision has been rolled out that aims at reducing oil imports by 50% by 2020, 75% by 2025 and eventually achieve self-sufficiency and Energy Independence for India by 2030. The earlier Oil Minister M. Veerappa Moily promised quick decisions and creating an environment conducive for investments to flow in. The priority should be to intensify domestic oil and gas exploration to reduce import dependence. Emphasis will be on quick decision-making and innovation and not on cutting subsidies (Jayaswal 2013) Veerappa Moily further claimed that India's energy exploration activities suffered due to "bureaucratic obstructions" and ministers are "threatened" by the oil and gas import lobbies which wants India to remain dependent on energy imports and obstructing the government's move to raise domestic gas prices. India is the fifth biggest importer of liquefied natural gas after Japan, South Korea, U.K. and Spain and by 2016-17 the gas import facilities are expected to be over 50 million tons per annum supplying about 198 million standard cubic meters of gas per day. "Import lobby" wants to discourage domestic oil and gas producers draining out all the earnings in importing oil and gas. While domestic gas produced in India is priced at 4.20 per unit, the imported gas costs in the range of $16-18 per unit in the international spot markets by the domestic gas producers such as ONGC, Reliance Industries and its partner Bharat Petroleum (Jayaswal 2013).

Moily even claims that India must strive to complete energy independence by 2030. He is working for a detailed roadmap having well defined action plan to achieve the above target in a way that the import dependence is reduced by 50% by 2020, 75% by 2025 and 100% by 2030. India cannot afford to fulfill its 80% requirement through import and carry a burden of subsidy to the tune per annum and he goes on saying "This is the tall task I have set for myself and I am hopeful to achieve with wholehearted support and co-operation from all the stakeholders." He said challenges before the country were to increase domestic production of oil and gas, diversify into unconventional sources such as coal bed methane and shale gas, accelerate acquisition of hydrocarbon asset abroad, rationalize subsidies on petroleum products specially motor fuels, undertake a sustained campaign for conservation of petroleum products especially motor fuels, undertake a sustained campaign for conservation of petroleum products. As Moily observes, "Since energy is a critical driver of growth and development, our goal should be to make energy available, in the right mix and at the lowest possible economic and environmental costs." In addition to importing greater quantities of crude oil, the government has increased its focus on enhancing reserves and production through increased domestic exploration activity as well as securing equity oil overseas. Moily said that natural gas will continue to see the maximum action in the years ahead as India try and increase its current share of around 9% in the primary energy basket towards the current global average of 23% and this will require collective action from the government, industry and consumers. In order to achieve the 12th Plan target of 19.5% CAGR in the natural gas sector, India will increasingly look to import LNG through pipelines. To cater to a rise in the import of LNG, India has initiated investment plans for increasing its current RLNG handling capacity of 12.5 MMTPA to 45 MMTPA by 2017. By the year 2016-17 the government envisages a natural gas grid measuring 31,757 km of pipeline across the country. It is also working on the 1680 km long TAPI pipeline project through which 38 MMSCMD of natural gas is envisaged to flow from Turkmenistan by 2018. A Gas Sale Purchase Agreement (GSPA) for 30-year supply has already been signed by GAIL in May, 2012 with Turkmengaz. According to the International Energy Agency, India will need investment worth nearly $600 billion over the next 20 years across various segments of its hydrocarbon value chain to increase its energy supply and augment the enabling infrastructure. This provides ample investment and business opportunities for companies engaged in the oil and gas value chain (Strong Economic Partnership...).

Under the New Exploration Licensing Policy (NELP), the government has provided an investment climate in which all the required ingredients for attracting capital are present, such as level-playing, fields for all players, stable legislative and fiscal frameworks, a robust regulatory mechanism, enforceability of contracts and attractive fiscal incentives. The activities under the NELP regime have brought a sea change to the exploration scenario of the country. Around 70% of the sedimentary area has been brought under the active exploration which was less than 20% prior to NELP. The numbers of producing sedimentary basins have increased to 7. The Ministry of Petroleum and Natural Gas has been continuously improving the NELP regime by bringing in more transparency and enabling policies and enabling policies for facilitating E and P operations such as New Extension Policy, Rig Holiday Policy, etc. Policies have also been made for exploitation of unconventional resources such as CBM, Shale Gas and oil and encouraging the studies for Gas Hydrate in the country. Efforts are made to remove any bottlenecks towards augmenting investment in this ground. Shale gas can emerge as an important new source of energy for the future. India has several shale formations which seem to hold shale gas spread over several sedimentary basins like Cauvery, Krishna, Godavary, Cambay and Gondowana. The Directorate General of Hydrocarbons has initiated steps to identify prospective areas for shale gas exploration through formation of multi-organisational team comprising of national oil companies. In this direction Memorandum of Understanding has been signed between State Department, USA and Ministry of Energy for assessment of resources, skill development, investment promotion and assistance in regulatory frameworks.

Oil Minister Virappa Moily had constituted Vijay Kelkar Committee (Jayaswal 2013) to recommend ways to substantially reduce India's energy import dependency by 2030 and suggest steps for enhancing domestic oil and gas production from the unconventional energy sources. The committee will also propose institutional mechanism for appraisal of India's sedimentary basins and suggest effective utilization of Oil Industry Development Board for appraising the unexplored and partly explored acreages. The government wants the committee to suggest policy measure that would help in developing and promoting indigenous service industry in exploration and production of oil and gas. The Vijay Kelkar panel on energy security has been asked to suggest roadmap for freeing natural gas prices by March 2017 and prepare a roadmap for enhancing domestic production of oil and gas so as to substantially reduce the nation's import dependency by 2030. The panel has been asked to prepare a "Roadmap for Switching over to the market determined gas pricing" at the end of the 12th plan period. Currently most of the gas produced in the country is sold at sub-market price of USD 4.2 per million British thermal unit and the oil ministry has approached the cabinet for raising it by over 60% to USD 6775 as per a complex international hub and LNG price based formula suggested by Prime Minister appointed Rangarajan panel. While Rangarajan panel had suggested freeing of gas prices in 3-5 years, Moily wanted the Kelkar panel to clearly spell out a roadmap leading new price to roughly half of the market price (Strong Economic Partnership...).

ONGC has bought Videocon Industry's stake in Mozambique gas field and acquired 100% of shares in Videocon Mozambique Rovuma Ltd. for USD 2475 million as a significant step towards energy security of India. Rovuma field may hold 65 Trillion Cubic Feet of gas reserves, more than 10 times the reserves in Reliance Industries' eastern offshore KG-D6 fields. In March 2013 ONGC completed acquisition of Hess Corps' 2.7% stake in Azerbaijan and an associated pipeline for USD 1 billion. In November 2012, it announced the purchase of Conoco Philip's 8.4% stake in Kazakhstan's Kashagan project (PTI 2013).

Terming the South China Sea as a disputed region, China has warned India to refrain from undertaking oil exploration in the resource—rich Vietnamese blocks in order to ensure 'peace and stability' in the area and asked New Delhi not to explore it and get involved in the 'disputes'. The top Chinese foreign ministry official said that sovereignty of the islands in the region was a major issue and India should not carry out oil exploration till resolution of the vexed issue. Mr. Sun pointed that commercial nature of India's oil exploration in the region having huge oil and gas reserves were 'very complicated' and China was trying its best to find a peaceful solution to the problem. The issue of South China Sea region including Indian oil exploration has territorial disputes with some ASEAN countries including Vietnam and Philippines. Unfazed by Chinese objections India in October 2011 inked an agreement with Vietnam to expand and promote oil exploration in South China Sea which includes new investments and the exploration and supply of oil and gas to the two countries. The Chinese claim in the South China Sea has been rejected by both India and Vietnam. As per UN Records, the blocks belong to Vietnam. India said that the state-owned firms would continue to explore in South China Sea and made it clear that the entire Indian Ocean Region stretching from East African Coast to South China Sea remains crucial to its energy and national security (Beijing warns Delhi...).

India finds itself in a rather difficult situation following the West's sanction on Iran and the overt pressure being brought on it by the United States to curtail oil imports from the Gulf Nation. Iran is India's second largest supplies of crude oil after Saudi Arabia and given the growing energy requirements of the country, it is not a viable option to close the tap on Iran. The pressure has been since 2011 when the payments for Iranian oil imports through banks based in the West were choked but India found a way out by routing money through a Turkish bank. But with pressure mounting on Turkey to close the channel, India and Iran agreed to rupee payments with about half the value of imports to be paid thus. Now the pressure is to wind down imports from Iran totally and India appears to be succumbing to pressure. Mangalore Refinery and Petrochemicals Limited, the biggest consumers of Iranian crude is reported to reduce its imports for the financial year 2013-14. Iran accounts for 12 per cent of India's crude oil imports and it is not possible to find a viable replacement for that quantum in the prevailing market conditions for oil. India is said to be entering to barter deals with countries such as Russia by exchanging oil for wheat. India should offer similar bargains to Iran may be for refined petroleum products instead of food grains (Don't give up...).

More investors are backing wind energy projects as low valuations make the sector attractive. In 2013 over 1500 crores has been invested and deep-pocketed players such as Goldman Sachs are increasing their exposure in the sector. A number of leading risk capital firms, including Goldman and IDFC and development finance institutions like Asian Development Bank have entered as wind energy producers (Gooptu and Jai 2013).

- The Goldman Sachs invested $135 million in Re New Wind Power in June 2013
- ADB invested $30 million in NSL Renewable Power in May 2013
- An investor consortium including Proparco, DEG and South Korea PE firm Asia Clean Energy invested $60 million in NSL Renewable Power
- Leap Green Energy backed by JP Morgan Asset brought DLF's wind power assets for $44 million
- Gujarat Venture Finance invested 40 crores in SPV of UK based SITAC Group in January 2013.

India started exporting 250 megawatt power to Bangladesh from July 2013 which is expected to strengthen the diplomatic ties between two South Asian neighbours. The transmission line has been jointly set up by Power Grid Corporation of India and the Bangladesh Power Development Board. The proposed 125 km line will connect Berhampur in India to Bheramara in Bangladesh.

The President of India said that the need of the time for New Delhi was to build strong economic partnerships with other oil producing countries and their oil and gas industries to the mutual benefit of each other. Elaborating on the critical challenge of the growing energy demand in the country, the Minister (ex) of Petroleum and Natural Gas Shri Jaipal Reddy said that India is now focused on incorporating the Tripple Bottomline philosophy of People, Planet and Profit into their business models. The Government of India is working towards finding holistic solutions to the growing concern about environment and energy security in the country and the need to take initiatives to maximize the longevity of our existing assets and the need to realize India's energy potential completely.

Eight ministers along with former Finance Minister Pranab Mukherjee formed a group to consider the proposal of withdrawing public control on the price of petrol and diesel in the country. Petroleum Minister Murli Manohar Deora expressed his willingness to deregularize the prices of petrol and diesel since the price of unrefined oil had shot up to $80 in the world market and hence he considered it to be the ripe time to deregularize the petrol and diesel to check further rise of the price of the same (Strong Economic Partnership...). Given the forecast of increased oil dependence, V. Moily observed that moving towards self-sufficiency goal will be very significant step in the history of India. Moily underlined the tremendous potential for enhancing the domestic production of oil and gas and so far out of 205 million barrels of hydrocarbon resources only 73 billion of oil and oil equivalent gas could be explored and the remaining is yet to be unlocked through exploration. Hence, New Vision has been rolled out that aims at reducing oil imports by 50% by 2020, 75% by 2025 and eventually achieve self-sufficiency and Energy Independence for India by 2030. Steps taken by the Government of India to enhance domestic hydrocarbon production are:

- Permission of exploration in the mining areas
- Follow Rangarajan Committee Recommendations to improved overall governance mechanism of the upstream oil and gas industry
- Co-existence of National and energy security operations
- NELP
- Shale gas policy

- Coal Bed Methane policy
- Crude oil and natural gas production in new areas
- Overseas E&P activities
- Hydrocarbon potential in the country
- Roadmap for enhancing domestic oil and gas production.

The Government of India through overseas E&P activities allowed the indigenous companies to engage in bilateral and multilateral cooperation with various countries for oil and gas opportunities overseas. OVL has produced about 7.26 MMT of oil and equivalent gas during the year 2012-13 from Sudan, Vietnam, Venezuela, Russia, Syria, Brazil, South Sudan and Colombia. Oil PSUs like OVC, IOC, OIL, BPCL, HPCL and GAIL have acquired E&P assets in more than 20 countries. In 2012-13, Government of India has authorized OVL to acquire Participating Interests (PI) in the upstream and midstream oil and gas assets in Azerbaijan with an investment of US $1001 million. OIL and IICL have jointly acquired stakes in October 2012 in Carrizo Oil and Gas Inc's liquid rich shale assets in the Denver-Julesburg Basin in Colorado, USA (Strong Economic Partnership...).

The Prime Minister Dr. Manmohan Singh said that there is a need to develop all energy resources like coal, gas, oil, hydro and nuclear along with renewable like wind and solar power. He observed that from a long-term perspective, nuclear energy and solar energy could play an important role in addressing energy security needs in India. As India is blessed with the abundance of solar energy, it could be a major energy source in the coming years and we must invest in research and development for commercial use of the same. Several non-conventional energy sources fall in the domain of high technology and hence commercially not viable. Hence, the immediate need is to develop these technologies to make such energy available to the masses in the shortest possible time. Manmohan Singh said that energy security would assure supply of good quality energy at affordable prices. When the nation aims at 10% growth rate it must recognized the critical importance of energy security and at this stage Indian energy needs which will grow with the pace of economic development cannot be met with oil and gas for long. A new paradigm of energy security is needed to address development needs which will focus on judicious use of domestic and global resources along with

- Less energy intensive path of development
- Increasing use of non-conventional and renewable energy sources
- Aimed at reducing carbon emissions
- Improving efficiency in production and consumption
- Exploring new technological options
- New financing means
- Identifying new sources and building new bridges with global partners.

National Common Millennium Programme has made a commitment to develop renewable energy potential. The government has thereby launched the Rajiv Gandhi Vidyutikaran Yojana to provide electricity to all household by 2009. Hence pursuing a sound energy security strategy has become a vital national interest (PM calls for...). Accordingly a Energy Security Division was proposed to be established in the Ministry of External Affairs whose main objectives would be:

- To serve as a nodal point in MEA for Energy Security
- To sensitize and assist missions abroad in identifying possible opportunities for Indian companies
- To maintain close co-ordination with the concerned Ministries and support their international engagement through appropriate diplomatic interventions
- To support efforts of corporate entities in acquiring energy assets overseas and building strategic partnership with foreign companies
- To promote the transfer of new and emerging energy technologies to India
- To interface with leading energy security think tanks and experts in India and abroad on energy-related issues

The possibility of bilateral co-operation in the areas of natural gas, petrochemicals, hydrocarbons, non-conventional energy and joint ventures are explored with countries like Iran, Kuwait, Saudi Arabia, Yemen, United Arab Emirates, Oman, Brazil, Colombia, Mexico, Venezuela, Ecuador and Myanmar. The issue of energy co-operation has been taken up with countries like China, Japan, Korea, Russia, Central Asian Countries, Libya, Tunisia, Algeria, Egypt, Sudan, Mauritius, Mozambique, etc. MEA facilitated the entry of Indian energy companies in the markets of Latin America for acquisition of oil-fields and sourcing the crude oil from Mexico, Venezuela and Ecuador. The NELP is exploring opportunities and co-operation with other countries in new areas of energy like International Thermonuclear Experimental Reactor project, Future Gen Clean Coal Initiative, Integrated Ocean Development Programme for gas hydrates, etc. (New Division of Energy...).

Minister of Petroleum and Natural Gas under UPA Government, Murli Manohar Deora stated that need for energy security transcends national boundaries and requires joint and co-ordinate efforts of all developed and developing countries, international financial institutions, international aid agencies, national and regional institutions, government and private corporations to face the challenge as to how to provide all their citizens access to modern forms of energy at affordable prices and in an environmentally sustainable manner and access to modern forms of energy is imperative for accelerating socio-economic development (Deora calls for strategies...).

Former President Pratibha Patil said that India's endeavor is to make New Delhi a leader in the New and Renewable Energy sector in the shortest possible time and marked this call to promote the use of renewable energy as a National Movement. The Minister of New and Renewable Energy, Vilas Muttem was focused on the National Policy on Bio-fuels and Hydro Energy Road Map that was supposed to enhance renewable power capacity of the country during the 11th plan (We must recognize...).

The Union Minister of Petroleum and Natural Gas (ex) S. Jaipal Reddy as a policy towards energy security emphasized on proactive actions on three fronts with an objective to ensure energy security in the country: developing domestic reserves, assessing global energy sources and ensuring energy efficiency. He said for India, energy security is a truly central issue as India would likely emerge as the 3rd or 4th importers in the world of all energy forms, viz. oil, coal, gas and uranium and definitely energy security is a challenge today than before (Need proactive Action…). Hence specific concerns for India's energy security are as follows:

- Energy demand from coal will double India's global coal consumption by 2050
- Increasing strong reliance on renewable, hydro and nuclear power but limits to the sources of development of these energy
- Constrained availability of domestic gas unless large reliable supplies of gas are secured from overseas.

Mohammad Hamid Ansari provided a multi-dimensional definition of energy security endowing the idea with three aspects: access to energy and security of supply, availability of energy to all segments of society and energy conservation and environmental sustainability. The Parikha Committee Report of the Planning Commission had estimated that India needs to increase primary energy supply by 3-4 times of the 2003-04 levels and electricity generation capacity and supply by 5 to 6 times of the 2003-04 levels to sustain a growth rate of 8% through 2030. According to Hamid, the visions behind governments energy policy are multi pronged like (i) meet the demands for energy of all sectors at competitive prices; (ii) cater to the basic energy requirements necessary for survival of all households, if necessary through targeted subsidies for the benefit of the poor and vulnerable; (iii) achieve safe, clean and convenient forms of energy at minimum cost in a technically efficient, economically viable and environmentally sustainable manner.

Taking into account the oil security concerns of India, the government had decided to set up a strategic crude oil storage of five million tons at Mangalore and Vizag and a special purpose vehicle called 'Indian Strategic Petroleum Reserves Limited' had been incorporated to implement the strategic oil reserve project. One of the major initiatives taken towards enhancing energy security in the country is the concerted efforts to acquire equity oil and gas abroad and produce a prospective property. OVL and other National Oil Companies are already involved in 14 countries and in the process of being established in a further 33 countries worldwide, OVL acquired exploration blocks in Australia, Egypt, Qatar, Ivory Coast and Libya. India is also concerned about the requirements to reduce the cost of energy imports by reducing the dependence on crude oil. But due to acute shortage of gas from domestic sources and to ensure the prospect for energy security India proposed to import natural gas in the form of LNG as well as through transnational pipelines from gas rich countries in West Asia including Iran, Central Asia and South East Asia. Indian government is pursuing gas import through Pakistan and from Myanmar through Bangladesh. Efforts are underway to revive the Dabhol LNG Terminal. GAIL and IOC have signed agreement with National Iranian Gas Export Corporation to import LNG and participate in the Yadavaran Iranian Oilfield and Jufeyr field in Iran through service contracts. In January, 2005 the Asian Ministerial Round Table was held in New Delhi for promoting stability, security and sustainability in the Asian oil economy through regional co-operation. To reinforce the diplomatic thrust for energy security, an Advisory Committee on Oil Diplomacy for Energy Security was constituted. Simultaneously the National Mission on Biodiesel has been launched to encourage the supply and use of bio-fuels like ethanol, bio-diesel and hydrogen to supplement efforts to reduce import dependence for hydrocarbons. The Mission envisages large scale Jatropha plantation under the Ministry of Rural Development. The government has ambitious programme underway to utilize renewable energy. The New and Renewable Energy Policy 2005 promotes utilization of renewable energy sources through indigenous design, development and manufacture. This includes use of wind and solar energy for power generation. However the problems with regard to renewable energy sources remain mainly with land acquisition as most of the renewable energy systems is land intensive. Particularly bio-diesel blending and solar thermal electricity generation requires vast tracts of land which may be difficult to acquire in India. There are also problems of transporting renewable energy from areas of production to areas of consumption.

The then Prime Minister Dr. Manmohan Singh had created a new institutional mechanism called the Energy Co-ordination Committee to guide government policy in the energy sector while addressing the energy security concerns. The committee will identify key areas requiring energy policy initiative to meet the overall objectives of economic development, energy security and energy efficiency.

In line with one of the key thrust areas identified in the National Common Minimum Programme of the UPA Government, emphasis is being laid on enhancing energy security of the country through the following initiatives (One year of UPA...):

- Enhancing domestic oil and gas production
- Acquire oil and gas blocks abroad
- Strengthen oil and gas PSUs to reinforce their competitiveness globally
- Promote use of alternative fuels
- Minimize the adverse impacts of unprecedented and volatile risk in international oil prices.

At the domestic front the government has adopted multi-pronged strategies to enhance energy security of the country. On the domestic front these steps include intensive exploration of oil and gas through the

- NELP
- Exploration by National Oil Companies namely ONGC and OIL in their nomination blocks
- Increasing recovery of oil and gas from existing major producing fields by enhanced oil recovery or improved oil recovery techniques

- Exploring for alternative sources of hydrocarbons such as Coal Bed Methane, gas hydrate and underground coal gasification
- Creating strategic petroleum reserves.

In the words of the then Prime Minister "The achievement of energy security necessitates diversification of our energy resources, and the sources of their supply, as well as measures for conservation of energy. We ask need to be cognizant of the scale of investment is required, and the scope for public and the need for private investment, as well as legal and institutional framework required for promoting such investment.... Atomic energy will have to play a much larger role in the future in the quest for energy security...we must fully gear up domestic efforts in order to achieve the necessary growth in commercial nuclear energy" (PM's opening remarks...).

Salman Khurshid former Union Minister for External Affairs, said that India need to go for better integration with international markets for strategizing energy security and enhancing relations with energy exporting countries. At the energy Security Conference 2012 he further stated that India have made progress in linking India's electricity grid, the second largest with Nepal, Sri Lanka and Bangladesh. Of late the TAPI gas pipeline project has started to materialize which would increase the LNG capacity of the country (India need to fortify...). The Minister of Petroleum and Natural Gas Jitin Prasada said that for a developing country like India the 'energy security task is gigantic' which involves an economic growth of 8-10%, eradicate poverty and meet human development needs. For India energy security means 'energy to fight poverty' and the issue looming before is how, wherefrom and at what cost India can fulfill energy needs in a sustainable manner. Hence, India proceeds to support global initiatives that strengthen mutual energy security and revamping the architecture of global energy by encouraging diversification of energy sources, stability of energy supplies, security of energy transportation and creation of new energy infrastructure and its protection (Shri Jitin Prasada...).

At the Delhi Ministerial Dialogue on green economy and inclusive growth, the Minister of Environment and Forest stated that the issue of energy security and universal energy access is intricately linked with economic development and growth. Energy poverty coexists with inefficient energy use and continued heavy dependence on fossil fuel has contributed to greenhouse gas emission. Hence the need of the hour is to change the energy mix and ensure energy security without compromising on the need for high economic growth and meet the aspirations of the people in the country. Energy security thereby focuses on poor people, to raise their living standards through improved and secured energy, i.e. clean cooking and heating fuel supply (Delhi Ministerial Dialogue…). Keeping this broad view in agenda several new programmes were floated like "gaon-gaon bijli, ghar-ghar prakash" and "Rajiv Gandhi Akshay Urja Diwas to focus attention on the deployment of renewable energy systems and devices in rural and urban areas" (Hundred days of the…). While delivering a talk on "India's Energy Security in the context of the Power Sector" Jyotiriditya M. Scindia former Minister of State, Ministry of Power also emphasized on the access to electricity and meeting the energy requirements of the people of the country. To materialize this objective the government put forward 3A strategy, i.e. availability, accessibility and affordability. This has been implemented though the flagship programme of Rajiv Gandhi Grameen Vidyutikaran Yojana (Ministry of Power).

The Eleventh Five-Year Plan (2007-12) initiated Accelerated Power Development and Reform Programme (APDRP) to provide electricity access to all households and actually connect all BPL households under this programme. Power sector reforms was enacted through 'Electricity Act 2003' whose objective was to consolidate the laws relating to generation, transmission, distribution, trading and use of electricity and taking measures conducive for protecting the interests of the consumers and supply of electricity to all areas. In India energy planning has to provide for the ever growing demands of an economy on the move, as well as the needs of every household. It extends from full use of non-conventional, non-commercial and renewal resources to the optimum use of the sources of energy in the country along with unavoidable imports, to establish an efficient supply of network of commercial energy all over the country. The focus should be on achieving self-reliance affecting changes in the energy demand and supply pattern and the energy source pattern. The core of the idea of energy security should also include the measures to curb wastage and promote energy efficiency and energy conservation, supply of energy at affordable price and last but not the least maximize the shift from fossil fuel to renewable energy sources. Over and above the matters related to coal production, distribution and pricing demands more sincere intervention on the part of the government. The momentum which was visible owing to policies over oil, natural gas and renewable energy, to a large extent, was missing when it came to the issues pertaining to coal.

References

Beijing warns Delhi against oil hunt in South China Sea. (2012, March 26). *The Statesman.*

Chari, P.R. and Gupta, Sonika (Eds.) (2003). *Human Security in South Asia: Energy, Gender, Migration and Globalization.* New Delhi: Social Science Press.

Delhi Ministerial Dialogue on "Green Economy and Inclusive Growth". From http://pib.nic.in/newsite/erelease.aspx?relid=76257 (Accessed on December 27, 2011).

Deora calls for strategies for addressing energy security issues of developing countries. *Ministry of Petroleum and Natural Gas.* From http://pib.nic.in/newsite/erelease.aspx?Relid=59979 (Accessed on March 31, 2010).

Don't Give up Iran Oil (2012, March 12). *The Hindu.*

Emphasis will be on quick decisions, investments: Oil Minister Veerappa Moily (2012, October 29) *Economic Times.* From http://articles.economictimes.indiatimes.com/2012-10-29/news/34798399_1_import-dependence-oil-and-gas-decisions (Accessed on October 29, 2012).

Government has right to formulate gas usage policy: Parliament witness adjournments over gas issue (2009, August 4) *The Hindu.*

Gooptu, Biswarup and Jai, Shreya (2013, June 24). Low valuations lure investors to step up wind energy play: investors buy stakes in highly leveraged projects, replace ECBs with equity. *Economic Times.* From http://epaper.timesofindia.com/Default/Scripting/ArticleWin.asp?From=Search&Source=Find&Key=ETM/2013/06/24/6/Ar00600%2Exml&CollName=ET_MUMBAI_DAILY_2007&DOCID=636785&KEYWORD=%28%3Cmany%3E%3Cstem%3Energy%29&skin=ETNEW&AppName=1&PageLabel=6%20&View Mode=HTML

Harris, Martha (2003). Energy and Security. In Michael E. Brown (Ed.), *Grave New World: Security Challenges in the Twenty-First Century*. Washington, D.C.: Georgetown University Press.

Hundred days of the government—decisions and initiatives. From http://pib.nic.in/newsite/erelease.aspx?relid=3572 (Accessed on August 29, 2004).

India need to fortify relations with energy exporting countries. Shri Salman Khurshid. From http://www.pib.nic.in/newsite/erelease.aspx?relid=90608 (Accessed on December 13, 2012).

Jayaswal, Rajeev (2013, June 14). India's energy exploration suffering from bureaucratic obstructions: Veerappa Moily. *The Economic Times*. From http://articles.economictimes.indiatimes.com/2013-06-14/news/39976706_1_gas-import-dependence-domestic-gas-prices (Accessed on June 14, 2013).

———. (2013, April 1). "India can achieve complete energy independence by 2030", Oil Minister Veerappa Moily, *The Economic Times*. From http://articles.economictimes.indiatimes.com/2013-01-04/news/36148822_1_natural-gas-mmscmd-ring. (Accessed on April 1, 2013).

Ministry of Power. From http://pib.nic.in/newsite/erelease.aspx?relid=96987 (Accessed on July 3, 2013).

Need proactive Action on three fronts for ensuring energy security. Shri Jaipal Reddy. From http://pib.nic.in/newsite/erelease.aspx?Relid==88403 (Accessed on October 15, 2012).

New Division of Energy Security. From http://pib.nic.in/newsite/erelease.aspx? Relid=30972. (Accessed on September 6, 2007).

One year of UPA Government: Major Decisions and Initiatives. From http://pib.nic.in/newsite/erelease.aspx? Relid=9285 (Accessed on May 15, 2005).

PM calls for need to develop all energy resources. From http://www.pib.nic.newsite/erelease.aspx? Relid=30112 (Accessed on August 20, 2007).

PM Constitutes Energy Coordination Committee. Prime Minister's Office. From http://pib.nic.in/newsite/erelease.aspx?relid=10163 (Accessed on July 13, 2005).

PM's opening remarks at the first meeting of the Energy Coordination. From http://pmindia.nic.in/speech-details.php? Nodeid=158 (Accessed on August 6, 2005).

PTI (2013, June 10). ONGC jumps the gun, announces Videocon deal before it is due. *Economic Times*. From http://economictimes.indiatimes.com/news/news-by-industry/energy/oil-gas/ongc-jumps-the-gun--announces-videocon-deal-before-it-is-due/artcleshow/20526157.cms (Accessed on June 10, 2013).

Sarkar, Hiren and Kadekodi, Gopal K. (1988). Energy Pricing in India: Perspectives, Issues and Options. Switzerland: International Labour Organization.

Shri Jatin Prasada calls upon ASEM members to develop clean, renewable and new energy sources. Ministry of Petroleum and Natural Gas. From http://pib.nic.in/newsite/erelease.aspx?relid=49244 (Accessed on June 13, 2009).

Strong Economic Partnership Vital for Global Energy Security, Pranab Mukherjee, Ministry of Petroleum Natural Gas. From http://pib.nic.in/newsite/erelease.aspx? Relid=88402 (Accessed on October 20, 2012).

Suryamurthy, R. First Power feed to Bangladesh. *The Telegraph*. From http://www.telegraphindia.com/1130218/jsp/busibess/story_16573882.jsp#.UcLfTn1×5ct (Accessed on February 22, 2013).

Teler daam pher baranor ingit (Again an Indication of Hike in Oil Price). (2010, June 23). *Anandabazar Patrika* [Bengali Daily].

Veerappa Moily asks Kelkar panel to suggest roadmap for freeing gas prices. From http://economictimes.indiatimes.com/news/news-by-industry/energy/power/veerappa-moily-asks-kelkar-panel-to-suggest-roadmap-for-freeing gas prices/articleshow/201739 (Accessed on May 21, 2013).

"Vice President inaugurates 'India Energy Conference'", Vice President's Secretariat. From http://pib.nic.in/newsite/erelease .aspx?relid=43332 (Accessed on October 3, 2008).

We Must Recognize Critical Importance of Energy Security-President. From http://pib.nic.in/newsite/erelease.aspx?relid=33028 (Accessed on November 22, 2007).

Section Two

7

Connecting with Diaspora: BJP's Foreign Policy Mantra in the Twenty-first Century

Rashmi Bhure and *Smriti Singh*

> Now, these Indians abroad, what are they? Are they Indian citizens? Are they going to be citizens of India or not? If they are not, then our interest in them becomes cultural and humanitarian, not political. (Gopal 1987: 506)
>
> —Prime Minister Jawaharlal Nehru

> My conviction is that Indian diaspora is a great capital for us in the global context. The more we nurture it, the more stronger will be our presence globally (Pravasi Bharatiya...).
>
> —Prime Minister Narendra Modi

The above statements by two different Prime Minister in two different eras clearly reveal that there is a shift in India's attitude and its policy towards its Diaspora. "Diaspora" is a word traditionally used to represent the scattered Jewish population during 586 B.C. due to Babylonian Exile which was then followed by their desire to return to their homeland. In later years in the words of 'Robin Cohen' the term "Diaspora" started encompassing or representing various other groups having 'victim tradition' (Cohen 1996: 508), which gradually in the late 20th and early 21st century became a loose word to be used by the countries around the world to address their overseas kins having ancestrally, ethnically, traditionally, culturally, historically or politically linked to them or to a particular community or a group.

Indian Diaspora is no more different from this. They are the individuals or a group of individuals of Indian origin or there posterity and are now staying or are the citizens of the foreign country but they continue to share common history and preserve their distinct identity with regards to their culture, language and religious practices and many of them do maintain some or the other relation with their motherland India which is confined to politically recognized border in the post-independence era.

Indian diaspora have a long history of migration across the world but the group of population or their kin who are now recognized as a part of Indian Diaspora have mainly migrated during the colonial and the postcolonial period. During British rule many Indians migrated as temporary labourers under Indentured labour system and kangani/maistry system particularly, on sugar and rubber plantation to British colonies in Africa, Asia, and Caribbean. British could easily transport the Indians as labourers to other countries mainly due to two reasons—one, the growing poverty in India and secondly, the forcefully inbuilt existence of slave mentality among the Indians towards their British masters. Though in the initial years there were lot of restrictions that were imposed upon the migration of Indians starting with the passport act of 1917 by the British Government followed by the restriction based on racial discrimination imposed by various host country on the entry of Indians in their respective country, all this led to the decline of the Indians migrating to the other country. But those who migrated under the British rule formed an inseparable part of the Indian diaspora, which mainly consist of unskilled labourers.

In the postcolonial era the migration was primarily voluntary and comprised mostly the skilled labourers who went far off in search of better economic opportunities and the outcome of it was the so-called "Brain Drain". It is important to note here that the migration in both the cases was mainly the offshoot of economic compulsion like in pre-independence era it was by force but after independence it was by choice for 'greener

pastures' which led to the creation of diverse economic group of Indian Diaspora across 106 countries in the world. Indian diasporic population on the basis of citizenship consists of:

1. Non-Resident Indian (NRIs) who hold Indian Passport
2. Person of Indian Origin (PIO)
3. Overseas Citizen of India (OCI)[1]

As per the report of Ministry of Overseas Indian Affairs as on January 2015 NRIs are 11379746, PIOs are 15725280 and Overseas Indians are 27105026 (Population...), they are considered as the second largest diaspora in the world (The Ministry of...) only after China.

India Disentangling from Diaspora

It is ironical that during the colonial period various freedom fighters in India sought help from the Overseas Indians to fight against the Britishers, but in the postcolonial era the Indian leaders took a u-turn by disengaging themselves from the Indians abroad. This was made clear by the first Prime Minister of India Jawaharlal Nehru in 1957 during his Lok Sabha speech:

> We have left it to Indians abroad whether they continue to remain Indian nationals or to adopt the nationality of whichever country they live in. It is entirely for them to decide. If they remain Indian nationals, then all they can claim abroad is favoured alien treatment. They become aliens and they should get as good a treatment as any other aliens get. (Appadorai 1982: 42)

The main reason behind such a stand was the belief of Nehru and other Indian leaders in the policy of Panchsheel, NAM (Non-Aligned Movement) and the concept of Sovereignty. These policies enunciated that India believed in the principle of non-interference in the domestic and foreign policy matters of any country and expected the vice versa. Thus India developed an indifferent attitude towards many diaspora issues and left them for the host countries to resolve. On the other side, India had experienced the foreign rule and also experienced the tragedy of partition which created a problem for the Indian administrators to define the citizenship rules. Moreover, in

1950's India a newly born democratic country trying to stabilize its polity and economy was in no mood and position to take the added responsibility of the Indian diaspora. Hence, India's Foreign policy in the early decades after independence was mostly the culmination of its domestic necessity wherein the closed economic policy was adopted by the Indian Government thus both politically and economically delinking itself from the diasporic community.

This legacy of Nehru's foreign policy was further continued by Prime Minister Indira Gandhi when she came to power in 1967. She basically followed the footstep of Jawaharlal Nehru and thus continued to distant India from the Indians abroad. During this period the idea of "Brain Drain" emerged and the migrants were being criticized for their role in foreign countries development instead of their own. In all probabilities the other reason for the continuity of such policy was the rise of regionalism and regional political parties in India. The regional parties such as Akali Dal, Dravida Munnetra Kazhagam (DMK), and All-India Anna Dravida Munnetra Kazhagam (AIADMK) challenged her political hold; the regional sentiments which led to the emergence of separatist movement of Khalistan and Dravidasthan were being economically and politically supported by the Overseas Indians and have also strained the bilateral relation of India with the host country where this diasporic communities were located which created a negative image of the diasporic community in the eyes of Indian Government. The only interest that the government had in the diasporic community was the remittance received from the gulf countries as a result of migration of blue collar workers from India during Gulf oil boom of 1970's.

Rajiv Gandhi became Prime Minister of India in 1984, during his small tenure the country was facing the secessionist problem which resulted in rift between India and its overseas descent mainly in Sri Lanka. Despite this Rajiv Gandhi moved from his predecessor's policy of Non-Interference and brought certain shift in India's foreign policy. The shift in diaspora policy was visible with India's interference in 1987 during the Military coup in Fiji, which was directed against ethnic Indians or Indo-

Fijian Government. India was not only outwardly criticizing the Military Coup of Fiji at the local and International platform like United Nation but was also successful in expelling Fiji from Commonwealth Nations (Voigt-Graf 2008: 81-109). Though India could not help its diaspora substantially but the initiative on the part of Indian Government was the beginning of the long drawn policy towards the Indian Diaspora. During Rajiv Gandhi's tenure initiative was taken by the Indian Government for the creation of special diaspora investment cell in the Ministry of Finance (Mizanur and Yong 2015: 24).

Such small initiatives were taken by the Indian Governmen but were neither good enough to build the confidence amon the Indian diaspora towards India nor as strong as to tap th potential of the diaspora. Largely the process of "Disentanglin India from Diaspora" continued till 90's. The major shift i the Indian Government's Diaspora policy was seen only aft 90's when the country's economic policy was liberalized due t grave financial crisis.

'Brain Drain' or 'Economic Gain'

After Independence allegation was led against the skill workers of India that they instead of contributing towards t development of their motherland were migrating to develop countries and were serving them mainly due to the relaxation Immigrant norms of these countries. In 1960's and 70's ski and semi-skilled workers migrated to different countries. La number of semi-skilled workers migrated to the gulf coun with the discovery of oil and the emergence of OPEC count The Human Resources that was supposed to contribut the development of a newly independent country India instead migrating to other countries. The major point was associated with "Brain Drain" was that the migr was basically attached to the lack of economic opportu available within India. Human being can become a c within a country only if it's being utilized to its full ca this was not done in the post-independent India.

The Government of India started realizing the import Overseas Indians only after it received remittances from t

Countries that made significant contribution to the economy of India. These remittances kept increasing in the later years with further contribution from the skilled IT workers from the developed countries. In 1970's in order to increase the amount of remittances the Indian Government introduced the [NRE] Non-Resident (External) Rupee Amount (1970) and [FCNR (A)] Foreign Currency Non-Resident Account (1975) mainly to tap the resources of NRI. The ever increasing contribution of Remittance in the gross domestic product (GDP) of the developing country like India have been a boon in disguise with the increasing number of diasporic population and the liberalization of the Indian Economy. According to the World Bank report, India is setting new records and is maintaining its top position as remittance receiving country in the world in 2014, it received $70 billion as remittance (The World Bank...). This has brought the spotlight on the diasporic community and their important role in the Indian economy and politics.

The Reserve Bank of India (RBI) reports suggest that workers' remittances to India reached US $46.4 billion for fiscal year (FY) 2008-09 up from US $2.1 billion in FY 1990-91. (Afram 2012: 13). Remittances have constituted around 3 to 4 per cent of India's GDP thus providing considerable support to India's balance of payments it has also surpassed both foreign aid flows and FDI flows to India (Afram 2012: 13). The report of RBI establishes that the migration from India across the border is no more considered as 'Brain Drain' rather it has proved to be 'Economic Gain' for the country. It is not only adding to the Foreign Reserve of India, but is also acting as a 'Knowledge Diaspora' or 'Developmental Diaspora'. These facets of diaspora have been neglected for a long time by the Indian Government. In 1980's it mainly considered diaspora only as a source of income for the country. After realizing that the migratory population was not resulting in 'Brain Drain' but bringing about 'Economic Gain' there was a major breakthrough in India's policy towards the diaspora that led to 'recognizing them' as 'Indians' across the border.

The shift from 'They' to 'We' started with India adopting LPG policy, wherein the realization dawned that the Indian diaspora can be an economic resource for the country. With liberalization policy the Indian economy became open for foreign investment, wherein, the diaspora started participating actively. But yet they were lagging respect to the official assistance or recognition to their role which was to an extent demoralizing them. This status was only accorded to the Indian diaspora in the 21st century starting with the Report of High Level Committee on the Indian Diaspora (2002) followed by the Pravasi Bharatiya Divas celebration every year since 2003 and latter on with the establishment of The Ministry of Overseas Indian Affairs (MOIA) in 2004. These initiatives of Indian Government boosted the confidence of the Indian diaspora that though they are staying far away from India their motherland still remembers and recognizes the efforts of their sons and daughters across the globe.

Modi's New Initiative or Continuation of Vajpayee's Policy

The present upsurge in the Foreign Policy-making and more specifically the expansion of the diaspora policy under the Narendra Modi or BJP Government is a deliberate effort of the government to connect to its long lost children. The foundation of such activity was laid out by BJS (Bharatiya Jana Sangh) the parental organisation of BJP soon after independence. The parental organisation has always been critical of the failure of the Nehru Government to connect with the diaspora and to safeguard its interest.

It may not be wrong to say that, it was a deliberate attempt by the Atal Bihari Vajpayee's Government (1998-2004) to politically recognize the effort of the Indian diaspora and reciprocate in the similar manner unlike the previous government's who were using them just for 'economic gains'. Correspondingly the fact cannot be ignored that the political, economic and technological circumstances of the country were equally responsible for creating such atmosphere that was conducive for engaging with the Indian diaspora across the globe.

The footprints of A.B. Vajpayee's policy with respect to diaspora can be traced in his speech in 1957 as a parliamentarian criticizing the Nehru Government's disengagement towards Indian diaspora. He stated:

> I regret to say that we have not paid as much attention to them as we should have done. There are about 50 lakhs Indians living abroad.... All of them are the sons of Mother India and are the inheritors of the same Indian culture. We should try to bring them closer to us, but we have not been able to pay as much attention to them as we should have. These people are so far away from us and their difficulties are so great that today we hardly have the power to overcome those difficulties and solve their problems. (Ghatate 1998: 3)

This concern of Vajpayee towards diaspora was not just expressed as being the member of the opposition in the government but was also reiterated when he became the Foreign Minister during the Janata Party Government in 1977:

> On this occasion, when I speak on foreign policy for the first time from Government benches, I would like to send a message of greetings to the millions of sons and daughters of India who are working or residing in different parts of the world—be they under governmental cooperation or as private citizens. Each one of them in his way is a messenger of India and a symbol of our ancient civilization and culture. Though they may have chosen to go to work or reside abroad we shall never disown them or fail to appreciate and reciprocate their loyalty to the culture and heritage of their motherland.... We hope that even when they work for their own benefit, they will seek to identify themselves with the enlightened interest of the country of their domicile.... (Ghatate 1998: 103-04)

Vajpayee's well stated ideas over the years regarding the Indian diaspora, later became part of the BJP's foreign policy agenda.

The initial policies that were made by the Indian Government in early 1990's with the motive of attracting finance from the diaspora were mainly confined to the Non-Resident Indians

(NRI) and the larger communities of Persons of Indian descent were neglected. This group of people got recognition by the Indian Government only in the 21st century wherein they came to be recognized as Person of Indian Origin (PIO) and Overseas Citizens of India (OCI) as per their citizenship rules.

The major breakthrough with respect to the Indian diaspora policy came during Vajpayee's Government in order to reciprocate the active Indian diaspora who helped out India not just economically after the Pokharan II (1998) nuclear test, but also politically against the sanctions imposed by the US Government. The various Indian lobbies' had pressurized the US Government in favour of India. This was recognized by Prime Minister A.B. Vajpayee in his first Pravasi Bharatiya Diwas address in 2003:

> Friends, India has been deeply appreciative of the support of the Pravasi Bharatiya community at times of need. Whenever India has faced a challenge to its security or to its territorial integrity, you have tirelessly championed its cause and then when there was an effort to isolate India after our nuclear tests of 1998, you came forward to stand by India. Your enthusiastic response to our Resurgent India Bonds in 1998 helped us raise over 4 billion dollars when we needed it the most. (The Inaugural address...)

These efforts of the diaspora could not be ignored by the Vajpayee Government who has always taken keen interest in the Overseas Indians and thus the steps towards their formal recognition in India started with the setting up of the High Level Committee on Indian Diaspora in 2000. On the basis of their report and suggestion the first Pravasi Bharatiya Diwas was celebrated on 9 January 2003. It not only gave recognition to the NRI but also to the wider Indian diasporic community across the world. The idea of considering dual citizenship for PIO and getting associated with various Indian diaspora organisations like Asian American Hotel Owners Association (AAHOA), American Association of Physicians of Indian Origin (AAPI), etc. were initiated at this stage. The establishment of Ministry of Overseas Indian Affairs (MOIA) and the Internship

Programme for Diaspora Youth (IPDY) (later known as Know India Programme) in 2004 was another step towards engaging with diaspora. Thus there was an obvious shift from India's post-independence policy of "Disentangling from Diaspora" towards "Entangling with Diaspora".

The plant that was sown by the NDA Government under Vajpayee's leadership of officially engaging with the Indian diaspora and bringing about a drastic shift in India's diaspora policy altogether was further nurtured by the Manmohan Singh's UPA Government (2004-14). The UPA Government initiated various measures to engage with the diaspora, rather than merely concentrating on "take and take" the reciprocal relationship of "give and take" was further given a boost. It was during Manmohan Singh's tenure that the Indian diaspora proved its worth for India in a big way where they successfully lobbied for the Indo-US Nuclear deal and against the sanctions imposed by the US Government which was overtly accepted by the Manmohan Singh in 2007 Pravasi Bharatiya Diwas Celebration:

> U.S. law on civil nuclear energy an essential first step.... NRIs already making handsome contribution U.S. law on civil nuclear energy an important step forward. (Dhar 2007)

There were various policies and platforms that were created to forge a greater connection with the diaspora during Manmohan Singh's era like Overseas Citizenship of India Scheme (2006), Scholarship Programmes for Diaspora Children (2006-07), Overseas Indian Facilitation Centre (OIFC) (2007), India Development Foundation of Overseas Indians (IDF-OI) (2008), Tracing the Roots Scheme (2008), Indian Community Welfare Fund (ICWF) (2009), Study India Programme (2012), Mahatma Gandhi Pravasi Suraksha Yojana (MGPSY) (2012), Voting Rights for NRI (2011), etc. These initiatives created a sense of recognition among the Indian diaspora that their motherland still remembers them. Yet these actions were definitely not enough for the Indian diaspora to blindly trust Indian Government in times of need. The Indian Government's approach was considered to be biased towards the Indian diasporic community across the globe. The preferences were given to those countries where Indian diaspora was in large number or where the diaspora was economically vibrant. Indian Government was connecting with the diaspora culturally and financially but was not addressing to their immediate needs of safety and security in the foreign land.

This was clearly visible during the Arab spring (2010-11) wherein the Indian Government's response was delayed to the critical situation developing in Tunisia owing to India's larger economic and geopolitical interest in the region. India's cautious attitude when the uprising started in Tunisia was widely criticised. India officially responded and became active only after the conflict spread to Egypt and other parts of the Middle East and North Africa region. The change in India's official position can be explained that India's diasporic population in Tunisia was miniscule (199), whereas the population in Egypt (3600), Libya (15000) and other countries in the region was much larger this enforced India to become active in the region for the safety of its diaspora (India's Dilemma 2015: 4). The fact that India was distinguishing between the small populated diaspora in Tunisia and the large number of diaspora in the rest of the region was reconfirming its bias towards the diasporic community.

The major upsurge in diaspora policy was seen when BJP came back to power with full majority in 2014 election which was also the first election wherein the NRIs were casting their vote. The idea of officially connecting with the diaspora which was led by A.B. Vajpayee and groomed by Manmohan Singh was now being carried forward by Narendra Modi as the new Prime Minister of India. The BJP Government that came in power on the basis of the agenda of anti-corruption and development mainly focused on attracting more and more foreign investment and developing much stronger international relations by asserting India as the powerful and confident nation at the international platform. In order to achieve this agenda the new government aggressively started reaching to the Indian diaspora spread all over the world. It won't be wrong to say that the foreign policy of Modi Government is incomplete without his "Modiaspora Policy".

Unlike the previous government the visits of Prime Minister Narendra Modi to various countries across the world in last one year are not just focusing on building bilateral political relations but also aspire to build strong bonds with the Indian diaspora and invite them to invest in India. The Indian diaspora is now well considered as an asset by the Indian Government who can play a crucial role in India's development as one of the major power in the International politics. The history of world politics is all about demonstrating one's power in different ways in the international arena. Prime Minister Modi did the same by wooing the powerful Indian diaspora community during all his foreign visits. This fresh chemistry between India's Prime Minister and the diaspora was seen during not so common grand reception given to him at the Madison Square garden in the US in 2014. He addressed one of the most politically and economically significant diaspora community in the US, such gesture of directly connecting with diaspora was hardly done by any previous Prime Minister of India. This event had the snowball effect and was repeated by the diaspora community of the other host countries. At Allphone stadium, Sydney, Australia which was the first visit by any Indian Prime Minister in 28 years, followed by rebuilding the diaspora ties in Fiji, Canada, Ireland and UAE, etc. which was visited by the Prime Minister of India after 33 years, 42 years, 59 years and 34 years respectively. Significant number of Indian diasporic population stays in these countries.

These acts of showcasing India as a confident global player will help in building a trust relationship with its diaspora. Building the bridges with the diaspora continued and has become the core of Prime Minister Modi's foreign policy. This was observed during his second visit to the US in 2015 where he visited Silicon Valley and particularly met the Indian diaspora's powerful CEO's of Google, Facebook, Tesla Motors, Apple and other technological Professionals in order to bring more investment in India.

The "Modiaspora policy" addressed some important long raised issues of the diaspora community. Over the years the Indian Government was criticised for giving differential treatment to different categories of diaspora, the first step in this direction was taken to overcome the problem by merging the OCI and PIO card benefits. This was followed by the visa on arrival benefit for the diaspora of some countries. The creation of e-migrate portal to receive online application and complaint of Indian immigrants and the online platform called 'MADAD' is also created which is a grievances monitoring system. This will help to curb corrupt practices in migration procedure of India; this will be of great help for the blue collar workers in the gulf countries. On the other hand, the BJP Government through its various domestic financial policies like raising the limits on FDI in various sector and considering non-repatriable fund by the NRI/PIO/OCI as domestic investment rather than FDI (Press Information Bureau...) plan to increase the diaspora investment. It is also luring the diaspora to return to India through their "Make in India" and "Digital India" campaign.

The "Modiaspora policy" is stressing on adopting e-governance system widely in order to digitise the migration system and also to connect with the diaspora directly which is helping the diasporic community tremendously. Besides government's official website, social media like 'Twitter' and 'Facebook' is also used to connect with the diaspora. By using social media the Indian Government is at advantage while dealing with the problems of diaspora. This gives the Overseas Indians a sense of security, like the use of Twitter by the Government of India during the Yemen evacuation operation in 2015. The External Affairs Minister Sushma Swaraj directly responded with the Indian diaspora during this crisis. This crisis was a trust test for the Indian Government by its diaspora in which the BJP Government proved to be successful. India not only evacuated its own citizens but also helped people of more than 40 other countries (Evacuation from Yemen...). The use of social media by the BJP Government to directly contact and facilitate the diaspora to resolve their issues has definitely helped in reclaiming the lost faith of the middle class diaspora in the

Indian Government. They have now realized that it's not just about the finance of diaspora that matter's for the Government of India, but their security equally is the top priority. BJP is using technology not just at the governmental level but also at the party level to connect with the diaspora. The website "Overseas Friends of BJP" can be sighted here.

Apart from these initiatives the Supreme Court of India has already passed an order to the government and election commission to allow and facilitate NRIs to cast vote from their host country (NRIs can vote...) this will make sure that the NRI's become part of Indian politics and be a decisive factor in Indian politics.

The diaspora policy of BJP started by A.B. Vajpayee is not just being continued by "Modiaspora policy" but is also achieving new heights of engagement between India and its diaspora. It is certain that at present the diaspora has acquired a centre stage in India's foreign policy and there are hardly any chances that the government can retrieve back the old disengagement policy.

Note

1. The Indian Government has currently made provision of merging the PIO and OCI card, with this decision of the Government of India the grey line of distinction between PIO and OCI have vanished as PIO cardholder can now enjoy all the OCI cardholders benefit. There is also the least recognized fourth category of Indian diaspora they are the Stateless Person of Indian Origin (SPIO). They do not hold any proof to support their claim of being an Indian Citizen when they migrated to the host country. Neither do they have the citizenship of the host country, which refuses to recognize them. The size of this group of diaspora as recognized by the Overseas Indian Community Census (December 2001) 'Report of the High Level Committee' on the Indian Diaspora is very small.

References

Afram, Gabi G. (2012). *The Remittance Market in India: Opportunities, Challenges, and Policy Options*. Washington DC: The World Bank.

Appadorai, A. (1982). "The Prime Minister's Statement on India's Policy in regards to People of Indian Origin Abroad, 2 September 1957 and 17 December 1957". *Select Documents on India's Foreign*

Policy and Relations 1947-1972, Vol. I, September 1946-April 1961, Delhi: Oxford University Press.

Cohen, Robin (1996, July). "Diasporas and the Nation-State: From Victims to Challengers". *International Affairs* (Royal Institute of International Affairs 1944), Vol. 72, Iss. 3.

Dhar, Aarti (2007, January 8). Manmohan Singh tells diaspora to help build new India. *The Hindu*. From http://www.thehindu.com/todays-paper/manmohan-singh-tells-diaspora-to-help-build-new-india/article1779733.ece (Accessed on 14 October 2015).

'Evacuation from Yemen' (2015, April 09). Press Releases of Ministry of External Affairs. From http://www.mea.gov.in/press-releases.htm?dtl/25049/Evacuation from Yemen (Accessed on 17 October 2015).

Ghatate, N.M. (Ed.) (1998). *Atal Bihari Vajpayee: Four Decades in Parliament*. Foreign Affairs, Vol. III: Delhi: Shipra Publication.

Gopal, S. (1987). *Selected Work of Jawaharlal Nehru*, Second Series, Vol. 5. New Delhi: Jawaharlal Nehru Memorial Fund.

India's Dilemma in the Arab Spring (2015, January). To see the figures of Overseas Indian population in West Asia, *POMEAS Policy Paper*, No. 4.

Mizanur, Md Rahman and Yong, Tan Tai (Eds.) (2015). *International Migration and Development in South Asia*. New York: Routledge.

'NRIs can vote from abroad: govt. tells SC'. (2015, January 13). *The Hindu*. From http://www.thehindu.com/news/national/nris-can-vote-through-postal-ballots/article6780906.ece; "Decide NRI voting rights in 8 weeks: SC" *The Hindu*, 14 April 2015. http://www.thehindu.com/news/national/decide-nri-voting-rightsin-8-weeks-sc/article7099686.ece (Accessed on 18 October 2015).

'Population (Estimated/Assumed) of Overseas Indians Country-wise' (n.d). From http://moia.gov.in/writereaddata/pdf/Population Overseas Indian.pdf (Accessed on October 6, 2015).

"Pravasi Bharatiya Diwas: Indian diaspora a 'great capital', opportunities await you, says PM Modi". (2015, January 8). *The Economic Times*. From http://articles.economictimes.indiatimes.com/2015-01-08/news/57838270_1_indian-diaspora-clean-india-prime-minister-narendra-modi (Accessed on October 9, 2015).

Press Information Bureau, Government of India (2015, May 21). 'Review of Foreign Direct Investment (FDI) Policy on investments by Non-Resident Indians (NRIs), Persons of Indian Origin (PIOs) and Overseas Citizens of India (OCIs)'. From http://pib.nic.in/newsite/printrelease.aspx?relid=121914 (Accessed on 16 October 2015).

The Inaugural address by Atal Behari Vajpayee, Prime Minister of India at the Pravasi Bharatiya Diwas 2003. From http://indiandiaspora.nic.in/ch2.pdf (Accessed on 14 October 2015).

The Ministry of Overseas Indian Affairs. 'India and its Diaspora'. (n.d). From http://moia.gov.in/accessories.aspx?aid=10 (Accessed on October 6, 2015).

The World Bank (2015). Remittances growth to slow sharply in 2015, as Europe and Russia stay weak; pick up expected next year. From http://www.worldbank.org/en/news/press-release/2015/04/13/remittances-growth-to-slow-sharply-in-2015-as-europe-and-russia-stay-weak-pick-up-expected-next-year (Accessed on October 11, 2015).

Voigt-Graf, Carmen (2008). Transnationalism and the Indo-Fijian Diaspora: The Relationship of Indo-Fijians to India and its People. *Journal of Intercultural Studies*, 29(1): 81-109.

8

Indian Diaspora in the USA: Issues and Challenges

Badruddin

Historical Sketch

A diaspora is a large group of people dispersing or scattering with a similar heritage or homeland, who have since moved out to places all over the world. The word is now also used more generally to describe any large migration of refugees, language, or culture. Historically speaking, the US Census Bureau has commonly used Indians as indigenous people and the only diaspora to qualify for the American Indian, Native American and more commonly Asian American. However, the term was translated into Indian American in due course of time. India offers a unique example of diaspora community in the United States.

US, being economically strong, socially well connected and professionally well qualified, Indian diasporas have been instrumental in the development of infrastructure including IT, skill transfer, circular migration habits and transnational investment opportunities. Preservation of Indian culture through naturalization, inter-ethnic engagements and Indo-US Ties have been significantly valued by the Americans. US Census Bureau Current Population Survey, US Immigration Commission Dictionary of Races, Integrated Public Use Micro Data Series and Indian-American Community Survey have been helpful in giving qualitative and quantitative data about Indian diaspora. Rockefeller Foundation Aspen Institute—Migration Policy

Institute has been a rich source of information. Multifaceted information have been collected through U.S. Census Bureau, American Community Survey Data, Indigenous Peoples of the Americas, Asian Ancestry Group and Asian American.

Indian immigration to North America started as early as 1890s also known as the first wave of migration. Sikh and Gujarati community have existed in Abbotsford, British Columbia and Canada for over 100 years. Travelling via Hong Kong most of them reached to the West Coast of North America and finally settled down around British Columbia and California. In 1889, the first Hindu family arrived in America. Shri Swaminarayan Mandir Chicago build in 1851, became the first traditional Hindu Temple established by the Bochasanwasi Akshar Purushottam Swaminarayan (BAPS). Soon after there were many *Mandirs* placed around the country. First Gurdwara build in 1911 on South Fraser Way in Abbotsford, is the second oldest Sikh temple in North America. The Stockton Gurdwara, California retains its unique status of being the oldest existing Gurdwara in America was built in 1912. Very often, both Sikhs and Gujarati were called as 'Amerindians' who subsequently formed Asian Exclusion League—exclusively designed for the purpose of lobbying for expulsion of the Asian workforce—the Chinese, the Japanese, and the East Indians.

Broadly speaking, most immigrants were Sikhs from the Punjab region. They were referred to in the U.S. as Hindus (due to a common American misconception that everyone in India was a Hindu). Immigrants from the British India were called the East Indians to distinguish them from the Amerindians. It would be interesting to note that the U.S. Immigration Commission's Dictionary of Races defined the East Indians as any native of the East Indies. However, till 1923, Indian Americans were not eligible for citizenship. Gradually, however, situation changed when the Luce-Celler Act (1946) permitted to restore naturalization rights where Indian race of diverse communities were incorporated including those who migrated to America from England, Canada, Africa (South Africa, Kenya, Tanzania and Uganda), Asia Pacific (Malaysia, Singapore, Australia and Fiji), and Caribbean (Guyana, Trinidad & Tobago, Surinam and Jamaica). Thus, Indian diaspora covers widest spectrum of migration history, a rare example in the world history.

1960-70: Golden Periods of Emigration of Indian Professionals

As per available statistics to the US Census Bureau, largest influx of Indian moved to USA in sixties and seventies called as the 'Golden Intermediate Phase' despite racist immigration law. Sizeable sections of Sikh and Gujarati communities joined the American family under New Colour Blind Immigration Policy. During this golden phase large number of students from elite communities of India joined schools, colleges and aspirants of Engineering, Bio-technology, Nuclear Physics, Medicine, Dentistry besides opening of several cultural, social, religious and media services which were duly valued by the Americans time and again. During sixties and seventies India's Bollywood left unforgettable impress on Hollywood where large number of actors like Dilip Kumar, Raj Kapoor, Manoj Kumar, Waheeda Rehman, Rajesh Khanna, Dharmendra and many more were narrated, depicted, desired, confident, and crowned as globetrotting role models. 1960-70 periods also added greater sense of realization about the investment flow, skill, human technology, trade and business opportunities as important imperatives to judge the knowledge bank of Indian professionals in USA. In fact, 1970s was the major upsurge where Indians made substantial presence despite Restrictive Immigration Nationality Act earlier passed by the US Congress. Soon, Indians gained Lawful Permanent Residence: LPR (Naujoks 2013: 26).

Globalization and Economic Liberalization (1980-90)

Second generation of Indian Americans (1980-90) explored maximum talents in Silicon Valley, young minds below 30 years, mostly in software business including doctors, engineers, management consultants and academicians. Large numbers of companies like Amazon, Google, Microsoft, InfoTech, E-Bay, Android, etc. are the creations of Indian intelligentsia. Most of these entrepreneurs have great academic track records, and are well connected in valley often called as the world's biggest 'IT

Hub' where many Indians turned Angel of knowledge power. Many have turned Angel investors, advisors and mentors to other startups.

The third and contemporary wave of Indian in USA marked during the age of globalization and IT Revolution. Since 1990s, it is visible with the out migration of white collars professionals and the students to develop part of the capitalist west, particularly to US, UK and Canada. A joint project of Duke University and University of California Berkeley revealed that Indian immigrants have been better equipped in engineering and technology companies from 1995 to 2005 than immigrants from the UK, China, Taiwan and Japan combined. A recent study shows that 23% of Indian business school graduates take a job in United States. This gives rise to the much debated question of Brain Drain characteristically labor flow that includes: skills, technical qualifications, hard working and dedication towards works. Influxes of Indians continue to exhibit rising trends since 1980 as shown in the Table 1.

Table 1: Indians Diaspora in USA (NRI+PIO) Population ('000) and Community Distribution

<table>
<tr><th>Year</th><th>(Figure Rounded)</th><th>%age of Global Diaspora Share
(Rounded Average)</th><th>Community-wise Distribution
Data Based on: (2012)</th></tr>
<tr><td>1980</td><td>361</td><td>2%</td><td rowspan="9">51% Hinduism,
18% Christianity,
10% Islam,
5% Sikhism,
2% Jainism
14% Mixed Breed
Total: 100%
Languages: Hindi, English, Punjabi, Bengali & Other Languages</td></tr>
<tr><td>1985</td><td>425</td><td>2.5%</td></tr>
<tr><td>1990</td><td>451</td><td>3%</td></tr>
<tr><td>1995</td><td>347</td><td>5%</td></tr>
<tr><td>2000</td><td>1678</td><td>5%</td></tr>
<tr><td>2005*</td><td>1925</td><td>6%</td></tr>
<tr><td>2010*</td><td>2843</td><td>4.8%</td></tr>
<tr><td>2014*</td><td>3103</td><td>5.2%</td></tr>
<tr><td>2015</td><td>3105
(Projected Data)</td><td>5.5%</td></tr>
</table>

Source: George, Babu P. and Shyamsundar, Anuratha (2008). Counter Migration from US. *International Journal of South Asian Studies* (Pondicherry), Vol. 1(1) & www.migrationinformation.org

Table 1 clearly indicates both category of Non-Resident Indian (NRI) and Persons of Indian Origin (PIO) including large number of South Asian origin, except in 1995 where there are marginal decline due to recessions, impact of First Gulf War (1990s) and racial policies. As an average, the growths of Indian immigrants have been 3.5 per cent, correspondingly close to China, Mexico and Philippines. Table 1 also indicates that the annual flow of Indian Immigrants in US almost doubled as a percentage of total immigration rose from 2.50% in 1990 to 5% in 2000 and further went up to 6.90% by 2004. India remains in the list of top ten sending countries to the US with acquiring the second position after 2001. According to 2010 US Census, Indian population grew from 1687000 in 2000 to 284000 in 2010 and 310300 in 2014, as one of the fastest ethnic group in the US though it contributes even less than one per cent of total US population (*USA Today*: 2011).

It is duly noted that the US ethnic population rapidly grew during 1980 to 2005 where there had been the largest flow during the initial and peace period of IT Revolution between 25 to 35 years of age in exception of seniors. At the same time there has been a common understanding that any Indian in America irrespective of religion, caste and creed is from Hindu family though it is only the misunderstand of Americans some censorship on American media. India is not a Hindu *Rashtra* (nation) but it is *Rashtra* for all where secularism remains an integral to Indian democracy.

Geographical Distribution

Like Chinese, Pilipino and Mexican Diaspora, Indians too are widely spread all over America though some areas are well identified. But large sections live in metropolitan areas. New Jersey, New York, Illinois and California that continue to remain the most favourite destination often called as 'Little India'. New York, the Largest Business Centre, while California's Silicon Valley as IT Hub, remains the pet home of Indians. While states like Montana, Wyoming, South Dakota, Idaho, and Maine have least populated states of Asian Indians. As per US Census, 2014, State like Montana represents only 618 Indian, the lowest in all. In a nutshell, Indian migrants in US are highly decentralized. Out of all immigrants in USA, nearly 47% got Green Cards through

LPR (Lawful Permanent Resident) Status and are entitled for H-1B, L-1 and L-2 Visa.

Theory of Brain Drain to Brain Gain and Development Process

Brain Drain theory refers to export highly qualified knowledge of knowledge bankers like scientists, academicians, doctors, engineers, management consultants and similar profile rankers exported to alien culture, often called as White Collar Immigrants and human capital. It is also associated with prospective openings, rich resources, higher standard of living, and higher per capita income, well defined social and political system. It often results in contradictory ends where documented migrants often face racial segregation, portrayed by media as 'outsiders', 'low wage earners', 'low skilled workers', 'less paid' and 'less rewarded' despite substantial sacrifices. Various analytical index show that large number of agglomeration, mostly urban based come from Africa, South Asia, South East Asia including Korea and China who migrated to USA, UK, France, Germany and Australia being resource rich and brain drain generating power, thanks to their sound infrastructure and living conditions. At the same time, a notion of 'Model Indian Minority' and 'White Collar Americans' need a balancing approach, but cultural pluralism has certainly better say to maintain the rich heritage of America. In case of India, brain drain to brain gain theory is based on sustainable resources—human capital inflow in USA.

Large number of Indians who moved to America after completion of professional and academic degrees, managerial efficiency and entrepreneurship, found US a match maker, much better place in terms of remittances, opportunities, placement and work culture reward. Prospective openings in IT sectors, catering business, shopping malls, multiplexes, theatres, media and Bollywood—all matter and liked by the Americans. Consequently, Indians are highly paid, respected and dignified. In return, the Government of India receives dollars in billions from those alien Indians who send money to their nearest ones. No matter whether it is brain drain or brain gain, a free knowledge based economy is more important. Today, Indians are called as creators of 'Brain Gains' that will definitely power India into a glorious technology and studded future. It was confirmed by the visit of India's Prime Minister Narendra Modi at the Silicon Valley. But India needs to develop a well-planned strategy to transform brain drain into brain gain so as to benefit the home country. Out leaders should be matured enough to promote the spirit of true nationalism and will power to develop leadership.

Socio-Economic Profile of Indian Immigrants

Indian Americans are smart enough to express socio-cultural sentiment and are well connected, be it Indian epics, regional associations, dress, habits, culture, food, yoga, folk dance, festivals, fashion and Bollywood. All go well with alien culture where Indian American community has been recognized, law abiding and well adjustable with local conditions. Besides, the educational attainment of India, well conversant with American English, experience of Indian democracy, mind, action and ways of working—all have impressed the Americans. These have fetched financial rewards, name, fame and status. Moreover, Indians have been socially co-habited, duly qualified with the process of naturalization and offers the rare case of racial harmony. Another study indicates that India diaspora in USA are the top recipients of remittances with an average $70 Billion per annum (next to China) close to entire annual plan expenditure of India on education, thanks to IT boom that owes substantial reputation as the creator of Y2K. Large number of web pages through Google, and host of online services definitely offer lot more gain for the Americans. Thomas Friedman's work '*The World is Flat*' explains the trends in terms of brain drain whereby the brightest elements are Indians to earn better financial opportunities. India continues to rise in terms of remittances and inflow. For example during the year 1980, the remittance stood $2.6 billion which touched to $70 billion in 2014. In terms of workforce, Indian send largest percentage of Engineers-Architects (22%) followed by Management Consultants (19%), Medical Doctors-Dentists (16%), Teachers and Professors (4%), Waiter-Cook (4%), Scientists (3%), Transport Services (5%), Office Clerks (3%), Artists and Writers (2%), Social Services (1.5%), Legal Profession (1%), Unemployed (0.5%),

Miscellaneous (11%). In short, Indians are variedly divided in diverse professional fields in USA.

Cultural Profile

Love-Hate relationship which NRIs shared in eighties and nineties, are now progressively offering new opportunities and healthy two-way float of talent. Conversely, Indians in America during the age of globalization happily explore opportunities overseas without any guilt, fear and insecurity as they are well connected through socio-cultural means and economically happily livelihood better than anywhere in the world. Most importantly, Indian culture likes many others Asian counterparts, put emphasis on achievements and personal responsibility of individual as a reflection on the family and community. As a great assimilation, mixed European Asian background are becoming more prevalent and co-habitation of marriage between Red Indians (Asian Indians) and Whites (European Origin) has been in common practice. American women prefer Indian youngsters more than their own natives for variety of reasons, very much justified by US Census Bureau. The US Immigration Bureau has highlighted the realities of Indian talents and work next to that of Chinese diaspora.

One of the primary objectives of the Indian organisation has been to expose its culture to the next generation of Indian Americans to educate them about this new alien milieu. Indian cultural organizations have been doing well connected line job in promoting Indian festivals and parades in different parts of America. Indo-American Community has ever been recognized as one of the most influential law abiding and hard working communities. Indians migrated to US due to the freedom that the American society offers to every single individual to make their own way in life. Hard work brings financial reward, status, money and the material advantages. India offers a unique example of cultural diversity since ages even in the US due to close intimacy with American culture, religion and nationality. Virtually every regional and ethnic community that flourished in India has close links with regional social ethnic and cultural alignments of Hindus, Christians, Muslims and Sikhs who are well connected with various alignments. The prominent ones are: Geeta Ashram, Church of South India, Indian Muslim Americans and Sri Guru Singh Sabha. There are some regional associations like Tamil Cultural Association, Gujarati Marwari Society, American Sindhi Association, South Indian Association, etc.

It is only an indicative one as there are hundreds of more working through coordinated thought and action which show the strength of Indians in America. To take some names include: ISKCON, Swaminarayan Sampraday, BAPS Swaminarayan Sanstha, Hindu American Foundation, Paramahansa Yogananda, Bhakti Yoga, Plymouth Brethren, Pentecostal Mission, Saint Thomas Christian, Church of South India, Federation of Jain Associations in North America, Indian Jews, Indian Muslim Council—USA, etc. Most of these regional organizations also celebrate rituals and ceremonies like Holi, Deepawali, Dussehra, Gurupurab, Eid, Guru Nanak Jayanti, and follow food habits, dance, dress codes, etc., with great enthusiasm. Despite wide variation in concentration of Indians in US, they are well organized through religious and regional organizations on frequent intervals unlike the inhabitants of India where North Indians are different from South India. In India, Tamils have disliking about Biharis, Marathas hate outsiders and treat them as criminals, Kashmirs' have different view about India while North East have more inclination towards China, etc. The reverse is true about Indians in America where Indians irrespective of language, region, religion and caste are well connected and well managed, socially, professionally or otherwise. Members of Indian Diaspora have deep, positive and emotionally attached. The Government of India has created several programmes and initiatives that aim to encourage and amplify the contributions of Indian Americans through Ministry of Overseas Affairs.

Indian as Knowledge Banker and Education: IT and Miscellaneous Sectors

Indian being the fifth largest economy, next to that of USA, China, UK and Japan, has potential resource for IT lovers and professionals that benefit the stakeholders in number of ways. The Electronic Knowledge Management Culture (EKMC) offered new avenues and wider prospects for Indian IT professionals in

US. The signing of World Trade Organization on 1st January 1995 opened the floodgates for Indian IT professionals as when American faced a massive skills shortage in IT. In fact, the success and achievements of Indians in US have attracted the attention worldwide. Massachusetts, Harvard, Chicago, Washington, Los Angeles, Michigan, Arizona, Ohio, New York and California based its IT schools continue to attract highest IT professionals from India apart from hundreds of more IT related institutes in USA. Almost every University in US has earned reputation of having large of IT lovers from India (Subramanyam 2003: 18). After all, India's massive role in promoting higher education during the last decades resulted in large number of trained personnel who have been ever willing to seek jobs and professions in US. Attraction of higher income, welfare policies, low poverty, opportunities self-expression, and early permit to H1-B Visa and Green Cards, all are important for Indians (George and Shyamsundar 2008). Migration during the age of globalization and transnational sensitivities brought rich dividends for Indian IT lovers seeking wider opportunities in USA.

By continuing to provide economy services, utilizing the large pool of highly skilled IT professionals available, more and more organizations throughout the USA, UK and Europe are outsourcing work to Indian companies. IT development budgets allowed for crucial development work to be carried out in-house, or sent to bespoke service providers of California's Silicon Valley. It is now the hub of IT centre, the largest hi-tech city centre in the world, became the source of attraction in 1991 that appeared as a group of business opportunity for the Indian community in the US. Large number of Indian professionals relied heavily on the strength of huge pool of skilled computer expert and software professionals and thereby created several segments. According to a comparative study of higher education of 13 countries Taiwan remains on the top followed by India, Pakistan, Israel and so on. In case of Taiwan it is only the recent one where enrolment process started in 2000 while India's case is as old as 1980s and thereby India earns the richest dividends in terms of enrolment in US universities and colleges.

Table 2: Distinctive Professional Achievement of Indians: 1980 to 2015 (Only Top Most Profiles)

Sl. No.	Profile Personality	Year	Field of Specialization
1.	Suhas Patil	1981	Co-founded Cirrus Logic
2.	Vinod Khosla	1982	Sun Microsystems
3.	Subrahmanyam Chandrasekhar	1983	Nobel Prize for Physics
4.	Joy Cherian,	1987	First Indian Commissioner of the United States Equal Employment Opportunity Commission
5.	Sanjay Mehrotra	1988	Co-founded SanDisk
6.	Rohit Jagessar	1989	Founder of India's first Satellite radio station in USA
7.	Rajat Gupta	1994	First Indian-born CEO of MNC, McKinsey & Company
8.	Pradeep Sindhu	1996	Co-Founded Juniper Networks
9.	Kalpana Chawla	1997	First Indian American Astronaut
10.	Subrahmanyan Chandrasekhar	1999	Indian-born American astrophysicist and a Nobel laureate
11.	Calyampudi Radhakrishna Rao	2002	World-renowned statistician is awarded National Medal of Science by President George W. Bush
12.	Bobby Jindal	2007	Elected governor of Louisiana
13.	Raj Chetty	2008	Professor of Economics at Harvard University
14.	Aneesh Paul Chopra	2009	American Federal Chief Technology Officer
15.	Subra Suresh	2010	Dean of Engineering at MIT as Director of National Science Foundation
16.	Rohit Gupta	2011	Winner of over 100 international awards and accolades for his films Life! Camera Action...
17.	Ami Bera	2012	Elected to the House of Representatives from California
18.	Sri Srinivasan	2013	Judge of the United States Court of Appeals for the District of Columbia
19.	Vivek Murthy	2014	Surgeon General of the United States
20	Sundar Pichai	2015	Chairman and CEO of Google

Source: https://en.wikipedia.org/wiki/Indian_Americans

Several IT Graduates left India and emerged as important entrepreneurs in Silicon Valley. As per official record, 15% of India's total labor goes to IT sectors, a miracle of over 300000 employed in various capacities. The estimated annual buying power of Indian Americans in the US is around $20 billion. Indians are running Fortune 500 companies. The list of Indians who have made outstanding contributions in IT and other sectors a shown in the Table 2.

The above list is only an indicative one and the list of Indian entrepreneurs is exhaustive. Presently, there are more than 100000 Indian-Americans of elite profile, professionally highly qualified and it is rather impossible highlight about each of them. Separate Indian-American Encyclopedia is required to highlight the achievements in depth.

Table 3 has given an interesting illustration about the Indian-Americans right from primary to PhD levels where Indians are overweight. In general, 34% Indians have earned degrees from miscellaneous institutes including public and private ones followed by 30% bachelor, 22% Masters, 8% professional and 5% doctorate much higher than local Americans and Blacks-Negros.

Table 3: Educational Attainment of Indian Americans, White and Black Population Above Age 25 in the United States: A Cumulative Data (2000-2012)

%age	Indian-Americans	Whites (European race)	Negros (Blacks)
Primary upto 12th Standard	23	46	58
Some College	34	23	15
Bachelor	30	17	9
Master	22	6	4
Professional	8	2	1
Doctorate (PhDs)	5	1	0
Total	100	100	100

Source: http://images.google.co.in/imgres?imgurl=http://www.india-seminar.com/

Several studies show that Indians in American universities and colleges widely decentralized all over America, be it Texas, New York, California, Illinois, Pennsylvania, Michigan, Massachusetts, Louisiana, Maryland, Missouri, Alabama and Columbia. However, Texas, New York and California remain the first choice. Indians are found in almost all major universities of Texas State that include: University of Houston System, University of North Texas System, University of Texas System, Texas A&M University System, Texas State University System and Texas Tech University System where large number of Indian students and professors are academically and professionally engaged. Similarly, some famous Universities in New York like, New York Institute of Technology, New York Law School, New York University of Architecture, New York University, Rockefeller University and Saint John's University, are the largest home for Indian-Americans. Besides, Ohio, Michigan, Virginia, Maryland, Alabama, Carolina, Columbia and Washington also attract large numeral of Indian talents.

Corporate World and Professional Involvement

Unlike China, India has not been able to come up due to several patenting and intellectual property right copy right conditions. Concentrates on patents, trademarks, copyrights, trade secrets, licensing, litigation and other related fields remains serious concern for India. Patent Trial and Appeal Board and Patent and Trademark Office (the PTO) under the direction of US Supreme Court and certain limitations are binding. Despite PTO, India continues to shine in corporate sectors. In US, large number of motel and hotels, and catering series are owned by Indians. In host of corporate sectors Indians are found much superior and suitably rewarded. American marketers are now waking up to the buying power of the US Indians. NRIs make 10 per cent of the US Wealth and 200,000 of them are millionaires. With estimated asset of $78 billion, American NRIs account for over third of Global NRI Wealth (Karmali 2003: 92). For verity of reasons, American Indian Males represent higher occupation in selected sectors like teaching, medical professions, and administrative assistants; women are better equipped but they have limited demographic representation in US. It is well-known fact that most of the females are White Americans who have either married with Indian Americans or socially mixed with them for variety of reasons. However, it remains significantly diverse in professional entrepreneurship and selection of jobs.

Indian Diaspora and Political Leverage on American Soil

Despite racial segregation in several scores, large numbers of Indians have made substantial sacrifices in framing American policies and decision-makings in various distinctive fields. These works through Congressional India Caucus Indian Business Council (IBC), Indian Abroad Centre for Political Awareness and Indian American Forum for Political Education and number of others have effectively put across issues of concern to the Indian community.

As on year 2014, there are 120 out of 435 legislatures from PIOs and NRIs. These people played decisive role through electoral gains, popular representation, media image, work culture and parity with American democracy. Some prominent examples are: Bobby Jindal (Governor of Luciana), Kumar Barve (Legislature of Maryland Assembly), Bala Srinivas (Mayor, Hollywood Park), Vishwas More (Senator, Bush Administration), Sunil Aghi (Democratic Campaigner), Richard Rahul Verma (US Ambassador in India) and many more. The influx of Indian software professionals, now integral to US decision-makings, has resulted into serious scholarly debate. The US Immigration Department continues to accept the value of Indian-Americans as major national resource and readymade asset. The 'hi tech visa' for Indians have brought technology revolution, thanks to American economy that largely grew with support of Indians.

The above list is only indicating one. There are also large number of prominent profile that include: Nimi McConigley (Senator of Minnesota), Bala K. Srinivas (Mayor, Hollywood Park, Texas), John Abraham (Mayor, New Jersey), Arjun Jhaveri (Mayor, Burien, Washington), Bob Dole (Senators in Clinton Administration), Dr Arati Prabhakar worked as the director of national institute of standards and technology: NISI (Walia 2003). Some more names like Islam A. Siddiqui (Chief Agricultural Negotiator in the Office in Obama Administration since 2009), Farah Pandith (Special Representative to Muslim Communities—United States Department of State since 2009), Nikki Haley (Governor of South Carolina since 2010), Kamala Harris (Active Political Commentator since 2010), Ami Bera (elected to the House of Representatives from California in 2012), Arun M. Kumar (Assistant Secretary and Director General of the US and Foreign Commercial Service since 2013), Dinesh D'Souza (Gossiper Political Film All Times since 2013) and Neel Kashkari (Governor, California gubernatorial election, 2014), etc. are also important. But the list is still incomplete.

Media and Entertainment

Host of Indian community occupy important positions in the mainstream British media, including organizations like the *CNN*, *Daily Telegraph*, *Times of India*, *Indian Express*, *Indian American News*, *Financial Times*, etc. Their presence in these organizations contributes to a better understanding of India and more balanced projection of issues of concern to India. The ethnic Indian media has a strong and powerful presence throughout the country. The list is exhaustive. However, some important media outlets are as follows (Alam 2007: 77).

Newspapers, Journals and Magazines: *India Abroad*, *News India Times*, *Awaz*, *Biz India*, *Desi Talk*, *Express India*, *Great Gujarati*, *Gujarati Mitra*, *Gujarat Times*, *Himalayan News*, *The Hindi Times*, *Hindi Jagat*, *Hindu Wishwa*, *The Indian Express*, *India Focus*, *Indo-US Business Journal*, *India Currents*, *Indian Life and Style*, *India Light*, *India Living Magazine*, *India Monitor*, *India Positive*, *India Post*, *India Reporter*, *Lokmat*, *Lokvani*, *Malayalee Sabdam*, *Mantram*, *Marathi Vishwas*, *NRI Times*, *NRI Today*, *Prasar Bharti*, *Punjab Times*, *Rajni*, *Ranauk Mela*, *Sandesh International*, *Sher-e-Punjab*, *Silicon India*, *Spirit India*, etc.

Radio, TV and Satellite Networks

These are available all over America as per geographical location and population. Hindi radio and stations are available in areas with high Indian populations. For example, Easy96.com in the New York City metropolitan area, KLOK 1170 AM IN San Francisco, RBC Radio; Radio Humsafar, Desi Junction in Chicago; Radio Salaam Namaste and Fun Asia Radio in Dallas; and Music Masala, Sangeet Radio, Radio Naya Andaz in Houston and Washington Bangla Radio on Internet from the Washington DC Metro Area have well known networking. There are also some radio stations broadcasting in Tamil and Telugu within these communities. Houston-based Kannada Kaaranji radio focuses on a multitude of programmes for children and adults (Houstonkannada.com). Diya TV South Asian TV network, is available in San Francisco KTSF, Chicago WRJK-LD, Los Angeles KSCI, Dallas KLEG-CD, Houston KVQT-LD free to air and can be watched with a TV antenna. Several cable and satellite television providers offer Indian channels: Sony TV, Zee TV, TV Asia, Star Plus, Sahara One, Colors, Big Magic, regional channels, and others have offered Indian content for subscription, such as the Cricket World Cup. Many metropolitan areas with large Indian-American populations now have movie theatres which specialize in showing Indian movies, especially from Bollywood. In July 2005, MTV premiered a spin-off network called MTV Desi which targets Indian Americans (Music Videos). It has been discontinued by MTV. In 2012, the film *Not a Feather, but a Dot* directed by Teju Prasad, was released which investigates the history, perceptions and changes in the Indian-American community over the last century.

NRI and Philanthropy

Diaspora Philanthropy from the US to India is a rich, complex, controversial and debated. Indians have traveled and emigrated beyond the Indian subcontinent for nearly two thousand years. However, the philanthropic activities began only in later 18th century. By World War II, the flow of Indians from Punjab, Bengal, Gujarat and Uttar Pradesh added philanthropic strength and helped to build support for Indian independence, and probably the first significant political action by the Indians. During sixties, the Liberal Immigration Act 1965, the average annual entry of Indians in USA reached to 20,000. The US Bureau of Census recorded tenfold increases by 1990. By the end of 2015, the demographic profile touched to some 3.7 million. Obviously, large numbers of them have philanthropic engagements through providing sustainable social services in India and elsewhere.

Some Indian-Americans that the debut they owe to their homeland country, have helped greatly. Host of Indians with great value system continue to contribute sizeable amount at no cost. Indian community has been contributing towards the charitable causes in India, motivated to offer handsome sum in the form of love and affection as long as the emotional attachments continue in the form of "Pay Back time". While considering the fertile areas, the IT sectors stand at the top.

Donations have been made by Silicon Valley Indians towards the educational projects. IIT alumni Associations have been sincere and continue to support social welfare projects like child and women welfare, establishment of charitable institutions like schools, colleges, health centres and community services.

A number of charitable trusts in the US have shown strong desire to make solid contribution to India's economic development. For example, a US based IT Magnate and venture capitalist Kanwal Rekhi helped to establish *The Indus Entrepreneurs* or *Tie,* a non-profitable professionals' network which also helped Indo-American Joint Venture. Rekhi donated $2 million to IIT-Bombay, the famous IT InfoTech, Infosys, and Wipro have come up like anything though the sudden collapse of Satyam shares have raised doubts and uncertainties. K.B. Chandrashekhar, a former Wipro Software Engineer, now founder of Exodus Communications, donated heavy sum to Madras Institute of Technology. Fellow co-founder B.V. Jagdeesh donated $ one million towards schools in Bangalore. Vinod Gupta of *InfoUSA* founded Vinod Gupta School of Management in India and set up polytechnic in Rampur, his native place. A San Jose Pathologist Dr Nilima Sabharwal founded *Home of Hope* which raised $20,000 for Chennai orphanage. New York based Taxi Driver Om Dutta Sharma set up girls schools while a retired plastic surgeon from New York Sharad Dixit nominated for Noble Peace Prize for performing and supervising some 44,000 free surgeries to fight deformities in India. Pavan Nigam, a co-founder of *Health eon WebMD* launched free IT Training Institute in Kanpur while Prabhu Goel founded Gateway Design Automation contributed $10 million to set up the *Foundation of Excellence* to fund education of deserving underprivileged students in India. Examples are also available where Indians have been awarded for the outstanding contributions in IT related fields. Ms Bala Krishnamurthy has credit for developing robotic system in Chicago who was awarded internationally acclaimed 'Engel Berger Award' during the year 2007 (Indian American Woman). Give and take cases have also been noted to promote philanthropic activities. Tata Trust gifted some $50 million to his alma mater, Cornell University to establish and expand partnership with Indian scientists that build on its strength in applied agriculture research (Tata Gives $50 m). American Indian Film Director, Mira Nair played greater role in spreading awareness about AIDS in Bollywood to admire the Indian community. Yoga Guru Ambassador Baba Rama Deva launched 'Yoga for Health' at Long Island, New York on 30 June 2008 to spread the message of *Upnishads* and *Vedas*. New brand of Yogic Postures became a unique philanthropic example in the world (Ramdev's Yoga Brand). In short philanthropic activities have come through donations, peace messages, environmental awareness and academic purists where Indians have played remarkable role.

Conclusion

While in India the changing perception about the skilled migration has been driven by the role of NRIs in IT, Education, Health and Bio Technology. Growing awareness towards the investment flows, skill, knowledge, technology transfer, trade and business opportunities. Understandably, Indians in US represent direct measurable benefits and are able to leverage a network to raise funding opportunities, access distribution of wealth and spawn of better enterprises. India continues to earn rich dividends through knowledge gain, handwork and higher qualifications that definitely bridge the racial and nationalist gaps. Varieties of diplomatic and political channels do help significantly to end the hue and cry thanks to American counterparts.

Paradoxically however, 9/11 Episode has brought changes in the attitudes and policies, and there is a greater need to develop better convincing ability through proper diplomatic and social channels. Cases have also been found the clash between first and second generation Indian Americans who do not want to rise up the IT lovers and new professionals. While the American Born Confused Desi (ABCD) is another lame Indian diaspora culture that has to be clarified to older generation Indian-Americans to change their perception (Alam 2007: 78). American attitude about poverty and class promoted Indian immigrants group identity creates both pain and social marginalization unlike the

British and hence the Indians need a cautious watch on every political activity.

Mechanism need to be found within the Indian community for discussion of important issues in diaspora philanthropy. Opportunities and challenges for dialogue on the effectiveness of development aid to India between the diaspora and institutions with a longer history of such work in India need to be examined. *13th Pravasi Bhartiya Divas* (7-9 January 2015) held at Gandhinagar Gujarat provide much needed platform to the Overseas Indian Community for exchange of views on ways and means. The key objective was to fulfill the aspiration and expectations from the land of their ancestors. It also provided opportunities for exploring mutually beneficial trade and business relations and for networking the Indian American community. Finding of the Convention was to make interactive and useful relations between India and USA. Asian Indian community now has become integral part of US Community by exhibiting itself as a 'Model Minority'. The experience has also shown that neither complete assimilation nor separatism have place in the context of America who continues consider them as 'White Collars' despite the well-known fact. On balance, the cultural pluralism model certainly has the potential to communicate the society and cultural division by maintaining the rich heritage of America. But the real challenge is to work out a suitable intermediate base which can sustain the basic democratic infrastructure of the US Society. It is yet to be seen as how far the emotions, hard works and talents of American Indians are brought to the mainstream of society.

Findings

Diaspora has benefited India by transferring money and making investments there and sharing the skills, reasoning, technologies and transferring social networks. Despite such benefits, the over representation of the highly skilled in the pool of Indian emigrants to the US relatives to India's demography raises some serious concerns about the depletion of India's talent pool in large number of scores, especially science and technology. But the diaspora is an important source of investment to India, not only directly from diaspora entrepreneurs but also from diaspora members in their role as corporate executives in the mainstream of American business society.

Despite substantial sacrifices, sections of Indian diaspora suffer due to racial discrimination and are politically targeted at workplace. These are often correlated with Indophobia and outsourcing. Even rumors related to religious stereotype of American Hindus, Muslims and Sikhs have also been falsely documented, especially after terrorist attack on WTC, New York in September 2001. The question about mistaken targets, attitude about bustard Indians, extent of moral and material damages sometimes go beyond calculation.

Despite odds and challenges, the US has been a favorite place for Indians to emigrate. In terms of living condition, US is known for having a very sound infrastructure, opportunities to experience a better world, and positive relation between the brain drain phenomenon. Greater sense of realization and growing awareness about Indian diaspora communities towards the investment flows, skill, knowledge, technology transfer, trade and business opportunities are important imperatives to judge the talents of Indians working in US or in anywhere in the world. Attraction of higher income, welfare policies, opportunities self-expression, and Indian American InfoTech touch to get their act together with the US policy have resulted serious scholarly debate ever since.

References

Alam, Mohammed Badrul (2007). Situating Asian Indians Diaspora in the United States: An Exploratory Study. *Man in India*, Vol. 87 (1 & 2).

George, Babu P. and Shyamsundar, Anuratha (2008). The Factors that Affect Indian Migrants' Decision to Stay in or Counter Migration from the United States Counter Migration from United States. *International Journal of South Asian Studies (Pondicherry)*, Vol. 1(1), Information Downloaded from http://www.pondiuni.org

Houstonkannada.com. From www.houstonkannada.com (Accessed on July 2, 2013).

https://en.wikipedia.org/wiki/Indian_Americans

http://images.google.co.in/imgres?imgurl=http://www.india-seminar.com

http://www.ausgovindia.com/ndli/files/dest5.jpg

http://www.openforumusa.com/images/Stats-on-Indian-Americans.gif

http://www.tribuneindia.com/2006/20060924/spectrum/main2.html

Indian American Woman, Bala Gets US Tech Award (2007, June 16). *Navhind Times.*

Karmali, Nazneen (2003, May 12-25). Doing the *Desi* Thing. *Business India* (Mumbai).

Mira Nair Takes AIDS Message to Cinema Halls (2007, July 5). *Navhind Times.*

MIT World: The World is Flat (2014). From www. Mitworld.mit.edu. (Accessed on August 11, 2014).

Music Videos, Reality TV Shows, Celebrity News, Top Stories I MTV. From Mtvdesi.com. (Accessed on August 11, 2014).

Naujoks, Daniel (2013). *Migration Citizenship and Development.* New Delhi: Oxford University Press.

Ramdev's Yoga Brand launched. (2008, July 1). *Navhind Times.*

Subramanyam (2003, August 21). Indian IT Success Intrigues Foreign Students. *Economic Times.* New Delhi.

Tata Gives $50m to Cornell University. (2008, October 21). *Times of India* (Goa).

The Reality of Interracial Marriages. (2014). From www.multiracial.com. (Accessed on August 11, 2014).

USA Today (2011, May 17). Census shows growth among Asian Indians. USA Today. From http://usatoday30.usatoday.com/news/nation/census/2011-05-12-asian-indian-population-Census_n.htm, (Accessed on December 29, 2015).

Walia, Nona (2003, August 31). American *Desi*: Here Comes Generation Next. *Sunday Times of India* (New Delhi).

www.baps.org/Global-Network/North-America/Chicago.aspx

www.indiandiaspora.nic.in

www.migrationinformation.org

www.migrationpolicy.org/sites/default/files/.../RAD-IndiaII-FINAL.pdf

9

India's Central Asia Policy: Quest for Strategic Partnership

Sukanya Mukherjee

The Central Asian states in the post-Soviet phase confronted unaccounted number of challenges hitherto not familiar. Primarily the most important challenge was to overcome the Soviet legacy and replace it with a new system. It was indeed a daunting task before them because they faced two sets of critical challenges without even knowing how to overcome them. They dismantled the old socialist model based upon centrally planned command economic and political systems and in its place developed alternative system. The core objective was to prevent an economic collapse and ensure security in an increasingly volatile region. In fact, geo-politics pushed the Central Asian states into the vortex of international politics. The beginning of the war on terror and the military presence of Western forces led by the US further enhanced their geo-political significance. This apart, Central Asia is also endowed with huge amount of natural reserves such as crude oil, natural gas, etc. It was in this backdrop India had to reorient its Central Asia policy to maximize its national interests through promotion of some kind of strategic partnership. In this context the present paper makes a very humble attempt to focus on some of the key questions as follows:

(a) What is the geo-strategic importance of Central Asia in India's foreign policy framework?

(b) Why does India take keen interests in Central Asia?

(c) What are the major challenges before New Delhi in respect of strengthening its foothold in Central Asia?

Historical Background

The relations between India and Central Asia date back to antiquity. In past, the relations between these two regions were mainly limited in cultural field or some extent to commercial field. The interaction between India and Central Asia intensified further when the Islamized Central Asian Turks established their control over north India in the early thirteenth century. During the latter half of sixteenth and seventeenth century, the consolidation of Mughal Empire in India gave a boost to India's interaction with Central Asia. The political stability and economic prosperity under the Mughals led to the growth of India's trade with that region and an increase in the number of Indian traders and bankers there. The colonization of India by the British and the annexation of Central Asia to the Tsarist Empire led to the decline of trade between the two regions and consequent decrease in India's ties with that region. The interesting part is that after the partition in 1947 and the creation of Pakistan, India was cut off from its historical and natural neighbours: Iran, Afghanistan and Central Asia (Pandey 2012: 2).

The disintegration of former Soviet Union in 1991 created new possibilities and prospects for Indian foreign policy. During the Soviet period, there was a lack of direct political relation between India and the Soviet Central Asian Republics (Pandey 2012: 2). But the collapse of the USSR in 1991 paved the path for India to re-establish the age-old ties with the five newly independent countries of Central Asia namely Kazakhstan, Kyrgyzstan, Tajikistan, Turkmenistan and Uzbekistan (somewhere it also includes Azerbaijan). It is in this backdrop, the paper aims to assess India's policy towards Central Asia in the post-Soviet years.

Geo-strategic Importance of Central Asia

Central Asia occupies a very important place in India's geo-strategic thinking. Geo-politically Central Asia has been described as "one of the world's most strategic zones, between

Russia, China and a troubled Middle East—a region coveted both by its larger neighbours and major world powers" (Bal 2004: 38). The five Central Asian republics are abundantly endowed with natural resources. For example, in respect of geographical position, Kazakhstan, one of the most important Central Asian countries is as large as Western Europe, more than twice the size of the other four nations of Central Asia combined, and the ninth largest country in the world. Kazakhstan's enormous mineral deposits make it a world leader in reserves in coal, chromite, lead, zinc and its uranium deposits are estimated to be the second largest in the world. However, in Kazakhstan, petroleum and uranium has gained the most attention (Asian Development Bank 2010: 31). The Central Asian region, with its modest reservoir of hydrocarbons is important to India due to its geo-strategic and geopolitical reasons. These considerations along with energy security considerations in the short-term suggest that India would make a greater effort to access hydrocarbons from the Central Asian region and also develop its own natural gas resources in the North-East on a priority basis (Jatar 2004: 304).

Besides having natural resources, the Central Asian countries are also endowed with such commodities like cotton, gold, copper, aluminum, iron, etc. India has realized that if a strong relation is developed with Central Asian countries, it would be immensely benefited. Added with these, the countries of Central Asia represent investment markets where establishment of joint ventures in the core sector can prove to be extremely rewarding (Sarma 2010: 33). The industrial units in CARs are looking for foreign investments for the upgradation/modification of its units which is very good opportunity for India to step into the region strategically.

It has also become crucial for India, much more than before, to moderate the changing security relationship across its northwest frontiers. From India's point of view, the instability in Central Asia may have immense implications for its regional power balance (Attri 2010: 67). So, the geo-strategic importance of Central Asia to India is very significant from different perspectives.

Strategic Engagement with Central Asia

After the collapse of the Soviet Union in 1991, when the five Central Asian countries Kazakhstan, Kyrgyzstan, Tajikistan, Turkmenistan and Uzbekistan gained in dependence despite having complex legacy which includes central planning, distorted economic structures, boundary problem, they had made some economic reforms in the process of economic liberalization. India's bilateral trade relations with each Central Asian states is not equal, it's varying in respect of time, governmental process, international situation, etc. During the last few decades India has made substantial progress in the economic field—it is the fourth-largest economy with purchasing power, one of the largest foodstuff manufacturers that possesses diversified and extensive industrial base capable to compete. Indian companies are very active at the international level in spheres of marketing, production, purchasing research and development. India is also a leading country in the sphere of information technology (IT) and fourth-largest pharmaceutical industry in the world (Rakhimov 2013: 25). In this backdrop, if we focus on the growth rate of Indian trade with the five Central Asian countries in recent times, we can see that there is upward trend. During last couple of years the high growth rate of India's trade with Kazakhstan, Turkmenistan and Uzbekistan has created a new landmark to realize the objectives of India's 'Connect Central Asia' Policy. The growth of India-Central Asia trade from 2010 to 2015 is tabulated below:

Table 1: India-Central Asia Trade, 2010-11 to 2014-15

(US $ million)

Country	2010-11	2011-12	2012-13	2013-14	2014-15
Kazakhstan	310.59	436.25	426.22	917.84	952.35
Kyrgyzstan	26.98	31.44	37.07	35.18	38.53
Tajikistan	41.33	30.13	48.01	55.13	58.09
Turkmenistan	35.89	63.1	78.25	87.73	105.03
Uzbekistan	81.05	126.43	156.75	145.56	226.31

Source: Department of Commerce, Export Import Data Bank, Government of India, Accessed at http://commerce.nic.in/eidb/Default.asp

India is an emerging market economy in the process of industrialization, and Central Asia is rich in minerals and raw materials. At the same time, Central Asian countries are small economies, and they depend on foreign trade for meeting many of their needs. This situation leads to a huge potential in trade between India and Central Asia (Agrawal and Sangita 2013: 13). Apart from Kazakhstan and Uzbekistan, India's volume of trade with other Central Asian countries has been minimal. In this context, it is important to mention that India has a very close and cordial relation with Kazakhstan, and was one of the first countries that the Kazakh president visited after his country gained independence (Gidadhubli 2007: 34).

Table 2: India's Trade of Imports from Central Asia

(US $ million)

Country	2010-11	2011-12	2012-13	2013-14	2014-15	2015-2016 (Apr-Nov)
Kazakhstan	138.42	191.86	139.99	656.33	701.67	242.23
Kyrgyzstan	1.20	0.89	2.09	0.64	0.77	0.69
Tajikistan	23.02	8.86	12.86	0.86	4.39	8.68
Turkmenistan	9.73	19.46	8.33	14.10	13.05	43.64
Uzbekistan	20.63	37.04	31.85	31.50	55.86	26.03
Total	192.99	258.11	195.12	703.43	775.74	321.27

Source: Department of Commerce, Export Import Data Bank, Government of India, (Accessed at http://commerce.nic.in/eidb/Default.asp)

In recent years, New Delhi has stepped up its engagement with the Central Asian Republics with the aim of building a long-term partnership. The high level visits from both sides—Kazakh President Nursultan Nazarbayev's visit to Delhi and President Pratibha Patil's vist to Tajikistan in 2009, Prime Minister Manmohan Singh's visit to Kazakhstan in 2011—are all reflective of growing political ties between India and the Central Asian region (Kothari 2014: 242). If we focus on the subject of India's trade of imports from Central Asian countries, we can see the growth rate of importing trade has gradually increased. For example, in the year 2014-15, the Kazakhstan-India trade of imports reached at 701.67 US$ million where it was only 138.42 US$ million in the year 2010-11. Similarly, the Turkmenistan-India trade of imports has reached at 43.64 US$ million in the year 2015-16 (Apr-Nov) where it was very limited in 2010-11 (only 9.73 US$ million) (Department of Commerce 2016).

On the other side, the five Central Asian countries also import some valuable basic needs from India such as coffee, tea, mineral oils, pharmaceutical products, electrical machinery and equipment, vehicles, ceramic products, etc. in which Kazakhstan has ranked as the highest importing country from India (Agrawal and Sangita 2013: 13). In this context, it is also important to mention that presently, Central Asian countries has been one of the largest beneficiaries under the Indian Technical and Economic Cooperation (ITEC) programme, offering human resource development training to about 300 candidates annually from this region. India has set up small-scale projects in the region in diverse sectors, such as food processing, technical training and information technology and also courses in English (Rakhimov 2013: 25).

In June 2012, New Delhi launched a new 'Connect Central Asia' policy. This signaled that India would seek to build stronger political relations and strengthen strategic and security cooperation with Central Asian states. It proposed to step up India's engagement in the Shanghai Cooperation Organisation (SCO) and the establishment of a new Comprehensive Economic Cooperation Agreement to integrate its markets with those of Central Asia (Campbell 2013: 2). In practical terms it promised a cross-regional energy infrastructure, new flight connections with Central Asian states, and the development of IT, banking, and pharmaceutical industries in order to strengthen economic links.

In order to provide a major boost to promote cooperation and understanding, India has already initiated an annual India-Central Asia Dialogue, a Track II initiative. Two rounds of such dialogue have already taken place. The first India-Central Asia dialogue was held in 2012 in Kyrgyzstan and the second in 2013 in Kazakhstan. In 2012, India's policy approach towards Central Asia was explained by E. Ahmad, the then Minister of State for External Affairs, in June in Bishkek during the first India-Central Asia Dialogue, where he said, "India is now looking intently at the region through the framework of its

'Connect Central Asia' Policy, which is based on pro-active political, economic and people-to-people engagement with Central Asian countries, both individually and collectively." In the same year, India's Central Asia policy got a new push during External Affairs Minister, S.M. Krishna's two-day visit to Tajikistan on July 2-3, 2012. This visit could be explained in the context of India's growing interest in cultivating stronger ties with the Eurasian region through its 'Connect Central Asia' policy under the new mantra of the four Cs, namely 'Commerce, Connectivity, Consular and Community'. The main objective behind this Track II India-Central Asia Dialogue is to start a regular annual dialogue forum among academics, scholars, government officials and business representatives from India and the CARs with the aim of providing inputs to governments on both sides (Roy 2013: 304).

Importance of PM's Visit to the Region

Prime Minister, Narendra Modi's visit to five Central Asian countries from 6th to 13th July, 2015 has been a landmark development in the process of building strategic partnership between the two sides. Many important treaties have already been signed between India and Central Asia after the visit of Narendra Modi to CARs. Some of the path-breaking developments deserve attention. Firstly, Kazakhstan president Nursultan Nazarbayev's daring decision to sign a major contract for a renewed long-term supply of 5,000 Metric tons (MT) of uranium to India during the next five years is the most significant takeaway of the Prime Minister's visit. This is in fact proving more promising than achievements on the hydrocarbons side. Secondly, India's ONGC-Videsh Ltd. (OVL) has finally made its first breakthrough when Modi launched the drilling operations for oil exploration in the Satpayev block on 7th July 2015 (Stobdan 2015). Thirdly, the TAPI (Turkmenistan-Afghanistan-Pakistan-India) gas pipeline seems to be a reality in the near future, after its successful inauguration on December 13, 2015. On that day, the Vice President of India Hamid Ansari, Pakistan Prime Minister Nawaz Sharif and leaders from Turkmenistan and Afghanistan broke the ground for the ambitious USD 7.6 billion TAPI pipeline project which would provide natural gas to energy-hungry India to run its power plants. After signing this agreement Turkmenistan president Gurbanguly Berdimuhamedow hoped that the project would get operationalised by December 2019. The 1800-kilometre long TAPI gas pipeline will have a capacity to carry 90 million standard cubic metres a day (mmscmd) gas for a 30-year period. India and Pakistan would get 38 mmscmd each, while the remaining 14 mmscmd will be supplied to Afghanistan (TAPI gas pipeline...). In Ashgabat, these Prime Minister called the TAPI project a "key pillar" and pushed for its realization "quickly" (Stobdan 2015). If the India-Central Asia trade corridor once develops, it would facilitate the flow of goods from the region to India as well as Central Asia too. For instance, this trade corridor would help India to import precious minerals as lead, zinc, copper, titanium, bauxite, gold and silver and rare earth metals from Kazakhstan and Kyrgyzstan. From Uzbekistan there is a scope for importing cotton, gold, mineral fertilizers and ferrous and non-ferrous metals while Tajikistan would be able to provide aluminium, vegetable oil and textiles (Bhonsle 2013: 13).

Major Challenges: As far as India's Central Asia policy is concerned, New Delhi confronts the following important challenges:

Lack of Geographical Proximity: India does not have any direct geographical attachment with the Central Asian states. This geographical distance sometime creates obstacle in the process of building strategic relations with CARs. In the absence of any common boundary between the two sides, India and Central Asian countries are dependent on shortest trade route via Afghanistan and Pakistan. A new beginning has been made since TAPI (Turkmenistan-Afghanistan-Pakistan-India) gas pipeline seems to be a reality. This development implies that trade between India and Central Asia can easily take place through the shortest trade route via Afghanistan and Pakistan. However, the sustained China-Pakistan alignment and US-Pakistan ties have essentially served for India to erect a barrier-wall for a direct access to Eurasian region. If India overlooks the fast developing transport and pipeline network, intersecting with growing Sino-Russian, Sino-Pakistani and Pakistani-Russian partnership, they could adversely affect India's long-term interest. A creative diplomacy is therefore urgently needed to overcome the physical barrier with Central Asia (Stobdan 2015: 22).

Information Gap and Language Barrier: The wave of modernized information technology has changed the traditional process of information exchange between states. But there are a chance of information gap might be happen between these two regions. In this context, the language barrier between India and Central Asian countries is also an impediment for the development of the relations.

Role of External Players: Central Asia in the post-Soviet years has emerged as an arena of 'great game' among external players. Russia, China, US, Japan, Iran, Turkey, EU, India, Afghanistan, Pakistan, all have substantial economic and security interests in the region (Gupta 2013: 3). In the economic sphere, Russia is well positioned to remain the leading player in Central Asia for years to come. This is especially true for the energy sector. The major share of the oil and gas pipeline system from Kazakhstan, Turkmenistan and Uzbekistan is directed towards Russia (Boonstra 2008: 76). Another powerful state China entered Central Asia's energy market in 1997, when China National Petroleum Corporation (CNPC) acquired a 60.3% stake in Kazakhstan's Akotobe Munai Gas, gained access to three oilfields and an exploration block. On the other hand, India's first acquisition was only in 2011 and much smaller—a 25% stake in a single oil block (Kothari 2014: 240). Practically, it has become tough for New Delhi to compete with Beijing to grab the super facility from the region.

Conclusion

Today, the Central Asian region has emerged as a geopolitical space where numerous regional and external players are competing to enhance their influence and control over the energy resources of the Eurasian region. Therefore, given the multidimensional geopolitical interests and positioning of the various powers in the post-Soviet space, India's initiatives in the Central Asian region cannot be analyzed in isolation (Roy 2013: 301). The fundamentals of the Indian economy have clearly become strong and stable. Prevalent macroeconomic indicators are the best in the history of independent India with high growth, healthy foreign exchange reserves, increasing foreign investment, robust increase in exports and low inflation and interest rates. India is today one of the most dynamic and fastest growing economies of the world. It constitutes not only a vast and growing market, but also a competitive source of technologies and knowledge-based services. In all these achievements there is a significant share of Indian economic diplomacy. Countries across the globe are beginning to see India as an indispensable economic partner and seeking mutually rewarding economic and commercial links with its emerging economy (Mavlonov 2006: 444). However, despite fairly low per capita energy consumption, India is the world's fifth largest energy consumer and is likely to become the third largest by 2030 (Sachdeva 2011: 113).

India, as an emerging global player is trying to develop bilateral or multilateral partnership with the Central Asian countries with an aim of enhancing economic and political ties. At the same time, the Central Asian countries find themselves entangled with India and other regional actors, where they have been working towards striking the right balance to gain maximum economic and political gains. In such a situation, the CARs are building bilateral strategic partnerships and cooperative arrangements at regional and global levels to address the new security and economic challenges (Roy 2013: 302).

India's Central Asia policy is premised on a concrete foundation backed by pragmatic interests and needs of the both sides. India and Central Asia share common values and rich traditional legacy. Despite the fact that US, Russia and China are the three key external dominant players in the region, India has been working hard to make its presence felt though in a very small way. India's soft power approach towards Central Asia has been of immense help in cementing strategic ties between the two sides. In other words, Central Asia is considered to be a key area of developing strategic partnership under New Delhi's 'Connect Central Asia' policy. A meaningful and a cooperative relations between India and Central Asia can be established by adopting an innovative approach coupled with regular high level diplomatic exchanges (Joshi 2012: 60).

In short, as far as the promotion of strategic partnership between India and Central Asia are concerned, a good beginning has been made. Central Asian countries have responded favourably to India's new soft power approach towards the region. However, India cannot and should not rely merely on soft power approach; rather she will have to work hard to apply smart power approach in order to maximize its geo-strategic interests.

References

Agrawal, Pradeep and Sangita, Seema (2013). "India and Central Asia: Trade Routes and Trade Potential". *IEG Working paper No. 334.*

Asian Development Bank (2010). *Central Asia Atlas of Natural Resources.* Philippines: Asian Development Bank.

Attri, Ashok Kumar (2010). *India and Central Asian Republics.* New Delhi: Regal publications.

Bal, Suryakant Nijanand (2004). *Central Asia: A Strategy for India's Look-North Policy.* New Delhi: Lancer Publishers & Distributors.

Bhonsle, Rahul K. (2013). "India: Integrating Energy and Trade Relations with Central Asia". In Nasir Raza Khan (Ed.), *India, Central Asia and the World Powers* (111-16). Delhi: Primus Books.

Boonstra, Jos (2008). Rusia and Central Asia: From Disinterest to Eager Leadership. From http://fride.org/download/COM_Rusia_CentralAsia_ENG_oct08.pdf (Accessed on December 29, 2015).

Campbell, Ivan (2013, October). India's Role and Interests in Central Asia. *Saferworld.* From file:///C:/Users/RK/Downloads/indias-role-and-interests-in-central-asia%20(1).pdf (Accessed on January 12, 2016).

Department of Commerce, Export Import Data Bank, Government of India. From http://commerce.nic.in/eidb/Default.asp (Accessed on February 08, 2016).

Gidadhbli, R.G. (2007). India-Kazakhstan Economic Relations. In K. Santhanam, Kuralay Baizakova and Ramakant Dwivedi (Eds.), *India-Kazakhstan Perspectives: Regional and Interational Interactions I* (30-39). New Delhi: Anamaya Publishers.

Gupta, Arvind (2013). India and Central Asia: Need for a Pro-active Approach. *IDSA Policy Brief.* From www.idsa.in/system/files/PB_IndiaandCentralAsia.pdf (Accessed on December 28, 2015).

Jatar, S.C.N. (2004). "Indian energy strategies in Central Asia". In Indranil Banerjie (Ed.), *India and Central Asia* (302-28). Northold, Middlesex: Brunel Academic Publishers.

Joshi, Nirmala (2012). "India-Central Asia Energy Cooperation". In P.L. Dash (Ed.), *India and Central Asia: Two Decades of Transition* (50-61). New Delhi: Oxford University Press.

Kothari, Raj Kumar (2014). India's 'Connect Central Asia Policy': Emerging Economic and Security Dimensions. *Sociology and Anthropology*, Vol. 2(6).

Mavlonov, Ibrokhim R. (2006, April-June). Central Asia and South Asia: Potential of India's Multilateral Economic Diplomacy in Inter-Regional Cooperation. *Strategic Analysis: Quarterly Journal of the IDSA*, Vol. 30 (92): 424-48.

Pandey, Sanjay Kumar (2012). "India and the Importance of Central Asia". In P.L. Dash (Ed.), *India and Central Asia: Two Decades of Transition* (1-11). New Delhi: Oxford University Press.

Rakhimov, Mirzokhid (2013). "Regional Cooperation in Central Asia and Perspective of Central Asia-India Relations". In Nasir Raza Khan (Ed.), *India, Central Asia and the World Powers* (19-28). Delhi: Primus Books.

Roy, Meena Singh (2013, July-September). "India's 'Connect Central Asia' Policy: Building Cooperative Partnership". *Indian Foreign Affairs Journal*, 8(3), 301-16.

Sachdeva, Gulshan (2011). "Regional Economic Linkages". In Nirmala Joshi (Ed.), *Reconecting India and Central Asia: Emerging Security and Economic Dimensions* (105-62). New Delhi: Pentagon Press.

Sarma, Angira Sen (2010). *India and Central Asia: Redefining Energy and Trade Links*. New Delhi: Pentagon Press.

Stobdan, P. (2015, May). "Central Asia: India's Northern Exposure". *IDSA Monograph Series,* No. 44. New Delhi: Institute for Defence Studies and Analyses.

Stobdan, P. (2015, July 24). "The Modi Factor in Central Asia". *IDSA Isuue Brief*. From http://www.idsa.in/issuebrief/TheModifactorinCentralAsia_pstobdan_240714 (Accessed on February 10, 2016).

TAPI gas pipeline project: Turkmenistan starts work on gas link to Afghanistan, Pak, India. (2015, December 14). *The Indian Express*. From http://indianexpress.com/article/world/world-news/tapi-gas-pipeline-project-turkmenistan-starts-work-on-gas-link-to-afghanistan-pak-india/ (Accessed on December 28, 2015).

10

Political and Economic Review of Indian Ocean Region (IOR): Positioning India in The IOR

Peu Ghosh

Introduction

As the World is entering into a 'New-Geo-Energy' era, the importance of Indian Ocean Region (IOR) has jumped up to the list of priority areas in contemporary international politics. The IOR undoubtedly commands a significant position in geostrategic terms as well as economic and political activities in the current times. The major powers in this region and the presence of some extra-regional powers have catapulted this region to become a sensitive area of analysis.

The major players being India, China and Pakistan and among the extra-regional players the most prominent being the US, the world is witnessing a game of checks and balances or in other words a balance of power in IOR. This paper will attempt to assess this tricky game that is on in IOR by making a political and economic review and future prospect of IOR.

Political Review of IOR

A political review of IOR is essential to assess its importance in world politics and strategies of naval control and supremacy. The IOR comprises 36 States as littoral states. Hinterland States like Nepal and Afghanistan also view Indian Ocean as vital to their interests. Among the major powers India, China and Pakistan are said to be involved in strategic competition to bring in the IOR into their spheres of influence. The extra-regional Big-Power is the USA which already has a base at

Diego Garcia and now has devolved a design of 'Asia-Pivot' strategy in the IOR to counter regional forces in the IOR and establish a strong foothold. But before going into the pulls and pressures of international politics in IOR it will be a useful exercise to draw a political balance sheet of this region. From several reports of international agencies several dimensions of analysis have come to the fore.

The countries in the IOR can be categorized as belonging to the countries of the 'South', some being developing and yet some being low developed and some falling under the category of 'failed states'. The countries are a heterogeneous lot and the diversity is so vast that it becomes difficult to make a political assessment of the IOR. There is no simple way to characterize opportunity and risk. In some cases, civil conflict drives national behaviour and interaction with neighbouring states, in others it is the risk of local military conflicts, and in a few, the risk of broader regional conflicts.

Further, the IOR states can be categorized into five sub-regions that include the Middle East and Gulf, Red Sea and Horn, East Africa and Sub-Sahara, South Asia and Southeast Asia/Oceania.

The IOR is also one of the, most complex regions in the world if the demography of the region is considered. It includes a wide variety of different races, cultures and religions. The level of political stability, the quality of governance, demographic pressures, ethnic and sectarian tensions, and the pace of economic growth create an atmosphere where they can be either opportunity or risk for each state. This may trigger problems affecting mid and long-term development goals or questions of stability short of internal or civil conflict or full-fledged flaring up of civil strife.

If we go by the World Bank Worldwide Governance Indicators, which rank countries on six aspects of good governance: Voice and Accountability, Political Stability and Absence of Violence, Government Effectiveness, Rule of Law, Regulatory Quality, and Control of Corruption, we can evaluate the political scenario and risk factor of countries of this region. It is striking that there is a decline in many cases, and that the national rank varies sharply with given sub regions—for example from 16th best (Israel) to 160th worst (Yemen).

From the data prepared by the World Bank it becomes evident that IOR is not a region of stability and economic development to the fullest. The regional strategic environment is volatile and dangerous. The development in the sub regions particularly in Iraq, Afghanistan, Syria and Yemen pose challenges of violence, terrorism and instability in the IOR. It can be said that that the IOR is gradually becoming an "insecurity community". Matters have been made worst by *Great Game* among the littoral states as well as extra-regional powers.

Sub-region/ coutnry	HDI 2007	HDI 2011	HDI 2012	Rank 2013	Rank Change 2007-2012
GCC					
Bahrain	0.802	0.806	0.796	48	-4
Kuwait	0.787	0.760	0.790	54	-4
Oman		0.705	0.731	84	
Qatar	0.833	0.831	0.834	36	-3
Saudi Arabia	0.756	0.770	0.782	57	5
UAE	0.837	0.846	0.818	41	-3
Non GCC					
Iran	0.706	0.707	0.742	76	7
Iraq	0.567	0.573	0.590	131	1
Israel	0.892	0.888	0.900	16	-2
Jordan	0.695	0.698	0.700	100	-7
Lebanon	0.728	0.739	0.745	72	3
Syria	0.623	0.632	0.648	116	0
Yemen	0.444	0.462	0.458	160	-4
South Asia					
Bangladesh	0.488	0.500	0.515	146	1
India	0.525	0.547	0.554	136	-1
Pakistan	0.498	0.504	0.515	146	-1
Sri Lanka	0.693	0.691	0.715	92	5
ASEAN South East Asia					
Australia	0.931	0.929	0.938	2	0
Indonesia	0.595	0.617	0.629	121	1
Malasia	0.753	0.761	0.769	64	1
Myanmar	0.753	0.483	0.498	149	1
Singapore		0.866	0.895	18	7
Thailand	0.676	0.682	0.690	103	-1

World Bank Governance Ratings for All IOR States: 2013
UNDP Human Development Index for All IOR States 2007 to 2013

The IOR can be said to be the region which comprises the centre of gravity of international terrorism. Above this there is the threat of international piracy which is increasing in numbers in current times and thereby posing a tremendous challenge to the littoral states. India and some other littoral states though show a trend towards sustained economic progress yet most shows low level of economic development and high levels of poverty. Major natural disasters also occur in this area which also calls for action plans. Simultaneously, with a political assessment, an economic review of the region is also needed to assess the importance of this region and ensuing conflict and cooperation.

Economic Review of the Indian Ocean Region

IOR shows a multiplicity of features whether one considers demography or natural resources. Size-wise the Indian Ocean is a huge ocean almost covering 68.556 million square kilometers. Indian Ocean includes within its fold the Andaman Sea, Arabian Sea, Bay of Bengal, Flores Sea, Great Australian Bight, Gulf of Aden, Gulf of Oman, Java Sea, Mozambique Channel, Persian Gulf, Savu Sea, Straits of Malacca, Timor Sea and other big or small water bodies (Indian Ocean 2016).

Almost one-third of the population inhabits this region. The goods and services produced in this region is worth US$1 trillion. The IOR undoubtedly, therefore shows a potential for a huge market in the world economy. The natural resources of IOR are quite lucrative as IOR is rich in minerals, marine resources and there is a potential of tidal energy. It is a passage for world marine communication. It carries more than half of global container ships. Some IOR states showing sustained economic growth have significant technological capabilities. Human resources are also quite abundant in this region. Therefore, opportunities and risks of IOR are resulting in international competition for capturing market and therefore intensifying trading activities in IOR. On the other hand, certain states of IOR are becoming global competitors and trying to cut a niche for themselves in international trade.

One of the most noteworthy facts about the Indian Ocean is that it commands the world key lines communications not only within the region but also between the East and the West. Infact, the geo-strategic location of Indian Ocean makes it the heart of world maritime communication. It is also the critical global trade route including petroleum export and import. The important ports of IOR are Chennai, Kolkata and Mumbai (India), Colombo (Sri Lanka), Durban (South Africa), Jakarta (Indonesia), Melbourne (Australia) and Richards Bay (South Africa).

IOR is a region with countries that are developed, newly developed, oil-based and agriculture-based broadly. Apart from the above-mentioned disparities, the language, culture and political structure, is not similar in most of the countries. However, the IOR states have taken initiatives in working out a kind of regionalism based on economic cooperation among the IOR states.

Initiative for the formation of a *regional bloc* in the Indian Ocean was first mooted by the Foreign Minister of South Africa, Pik Botha, in 1993, and the thought was well received by a number of countries, including India, Mauritius and Australia. Later, other countries like Oman, Singapore and Kenya joined the forum in supporting the notion of forming regional economic cooperation in the Afro-Asia-Australia region. These seven countries including South Africa formed the "core" group which took the initiative in formalizing an economic cooperation in the Indian Ocean basin. What emerged out of a meeting among the "core" group states was a joint statement with a vision to practice Principles of Open Regionalism and Inclusivity of Membership, with the objectives of Trade Liberalization and Promoting Trade Co-operation. Activities would focus on Trade Facilitation, Investment Promotion and Economic Co-operation. The IOR-ARC was formally launched at the first Ministerial Meeting in Mauritius on 6-7 March 1997. Currently the name of this regional bloc has been changed to *Indian Ocean Rim Association (IORA).*

The countries of the IOR have increased their share in the global market at a very fast rate. The growth performance of the region and its sub-regions indicates that both exports and imports have increased at a faster rate with developing countries as compared to similar indices for the world as a whole.

The Indian Ocean Rim has substantial potential to become a zone of economic cooperation, and the advantages of making it a trade bloc would be manifold. A significant part of trade flow from the countries of the Indian Ocean is directed towards the region itself. It has been noticed that a large number of countries have shown a higher growth in the region itself than to the rest of the world. In fact, the intra-regional trade accounts for one-fourth of its total trade and the extent of intra-regional trade are increasing over the last few years.

The contribution of Singapore, Malaysia, Australia, Indonesia, India and South Africa is substantial in the total trade of the region. These six countries account for 97 per cent of the IORA countries' trade flows to the countries of the Indian Ocean. One of the pressing issues before the IOR has been the issue of identification of the most appropriate form of economic arrangement that the IOR will make in due course of time. Among the various forms of economic cooperation discussed, some arrangements like trade and investment facilitation process, preferential tariff arrangement (PTA), a simple form of regional arrangement with mutual investment and technology to reduce cost of tradable products within the region, etc. assume much importance for the formation of the IOR.

The IOR countries that showed the highest improvement in the Global Competitiveness Index Report are: Kenya and Mauritius by 10 points, followed by the UAE and Indonesia by six points. Out of the 10 IOR countries, four are from the GCC states: UAE, Qatar, Oman and Saudi Arabia. The non-GCC states showing improvement were: Indonesia, Kenya, Malaysia, Mauritius, Singapore, and South Africa.

The trends that emerge from the Country Risk Assessment of these two main Indices—using the change in Country Rank between 2010 and 2013—indicate that countries from the GCC Sub-region showed improvements in Rank in every Index. Singapore, Indonesia, Malaysia and Thailand in the South East

Asia Sub-region also showed consistent improvements in the Indices analyzed. This indicates that these two Sub-regions will be the main contributors to the IOR Economic and Financial development in the decades to come.

The geo-economic environment in the Indian Ocean witnessed the emergence of a new concept 'Blue Economy' led by Seychelles and Mauritius. The idea is becoming popular among a number of Indian Ocean littorals including Australia, Indonesia, Bangladesh, South Africa among others. The leaders are standing for their commitment to the sustainable development of living and non-living marine resources to enhance food and energy security.

The Government of Mauritius in collaboration with the Indian Ocean Rim Association hosted the First IORA Ministerial Blue Economy Conference, "Enhancing Blue Economy Cooperation for Sustainable Development in the IORA Region", at Le Meridien, Pointe aux Piments, Republic of Mauritius from 2-3 September 2015. An IORA Secretariat draft paper identified eight priority areas for cooperation in the Blue Economy:

1. Fisheries and Aquaculture
2. Renewable Ocean Energy
3. Seaports and Shipping
4. Seabed Exploration and Minerals
5. Marine Biotechnology, Research and Development
6. Tourism
7. Ocean Knowledge Clusters
8. SIDS and LDCs.

How best the IOR countries can use such windows of opportunities and gear up their economic cooperation and undertake plans of actions, will determine the direction of IOR region in world politics.

Positioning India in the Indian Ocean Region (IOR)

India's burgeoning position in the world politics with its economic growth in terms of GDP growth is expected to accelerate to 7.5 per cent in fiscal year 2015-16 necessarily places India as a power to reckon with in global affairs and also in its backyard, that is, the IOR. India needs a secure maritime environment to achieve sustained national development. In addition, many Indians see the Indian Ocean as India's backyard and perceive it as both natural and desirable for India to function as the leader and the predominant influence in this region. In the South Asian region, India has come to occupy a prime position but facing competition with Pakistan and problem of Chinese intrusions into her neighbourhood. India's political and naval leadership further down into the Indian Ocean is a matter of immense significance and has to be watched carefully over time. This arises from India's strategic and energy needs. To this end the India's security perimeter extends from the Strait of Malacca to the Strait of Hormuz and from the coast of Africa to the Western shores of Australia. India, according to strategic thinkers will have to play a very large role in the Indian Ocean if the prospects for peace and cooperation are to grow.

In the IOR, China is again the major rival of India both trying to occupy the same strategic space of IOR. China is the principal variable in the calculus of Indian Foreign and defense policy (Talbott 2004: 84). Undoubtedly, China's "rise will increasingly challenge Asian and global security. Just as India bore the brunt of the rise of international terrorism because of its geographical location, it will be frontally affected by the growing power of a next door...empire practicing classical balance-of-power politics" (Chellaney 2005).

Another observer has recently judged that there is no sign of China giving up its 'contain India' strategy in the form of (1) an unresolved territorial dispute; (2) arms sales to and military alliances with 'India-wary countries' (Pakistan, Bangladesh, Burma and now Nepal); (3) nuclear and missile proliferation in India's neighbourhood (Pakistan, Iran and Saudi Arabia); and (4) opposition to India's membership in global and regional organizations (Malik 2005). Narrowing its focus to the IOR, India cannot ignore growing capability of China's navy and of Beijing's growing maritime presence (McVadon 2004). In the Bay of Bengal and Arabian Sea, especially, New Delhi is sensitive to a variety of Chinese naval or maritime activities that observers have characterized collectively as a "string of pearls' strategy" (Gertz 2005) of containing India to South Asia and prevent its expansion into IOR. A key focus in this connection is Myanmar, where Chinese engineers and military personnel have long been engaged in airfield, road, railroad, pipeline, and port construction aimed at better connecting China with the Indian Ocean, both by sea and directly overland. Some of this activity, moreover, spills over onto Myanmar's offshore islands, including St. Matthews, near the mouth of the Malacca Strait, and the Coco Islands (Indian until their transfer to Burma in the 1950s), in the Bay of Bengal. On the latter, China is suspected of maintaining a communications monitoring facility that collects intelligence on Indian naval operations and missile testing. In addition to this "presence" in Myanmar, China is pursuing a variety of infrastructure links with Southeast Asia through the Greater Mekong Sub-region programme and is building container ports in Bangladesh at Chittagong, and in Sri Lanka at Hambantota linking the main east-west shipping route across the Indian Ocean. China has constructed a large naval base for Pakistan at Gwadar (Haider 2005). These are all aiming at containing the expansion of Indian beyond South Asia.

India also has to take into consideration the large U.S. military presence in the Indian Ocean to India's west—in the Arabian Sea and the Persian Gulf. India's *Maritime Doctrine* observes that "the unfolding events consequent to the war in Afghanistan has brought the threats emanating on our Western shores into sharper focus. The growing US and western presence and deployment of naval forces, the battle for oil dominance and its control in the littoral and hinterland...are factors that are likely to have a long-term impact on the overall security environment in the [Indian Ocean region]." In similar fashion, the *2004–2005 Annual Report* of India's Defense Ministry states, "The Indian Navy maintained its personnel and equipment in a high state of combat preparedness due to the continued presence of multinational maritime forces in the Indian Ocean Region resulting in a fast pace of activities in the area" (Ministry of Defence 2004-05: 46).

Keeping the strategic interest alive in the IOR, it may seem that the continuing development of ties with the United States will moderate Indian sensitivity to the U.S. presence in the Arabian Sea. In September and October 2005, for example, the two sides conducted their first naval maneuvers—MALABAR 05—employing U.S. and Indian aircraft carriers, and this occurred in the Arabian Sea. Washington's desire to nurture relations with India is in response to overlapping "China" and "terrorism" concerns in contemporary world politics. Therefore, the increased American role in the Indian Ocean region has increased India's "strategic space" and political military relevance in IOR. It's a peculiar balance-of-power for any decrease in American presence will increase Chinese pressure and thereby disturb the balance-of-power. Calculating China's IOR schemes of plans also is a factor in recent Indian efforts to increase Japan's profile in the IOR. This was manifested by the March 2005 Indo-Japanese agreement to develop jointly natural gas resources in the strategically sensitive Andaman Sea (Reuters 2005).

Besides strategic interest the other motivating factor behind India's interest in the IOR is energy. As the fourth-largest economy (in purchasing-power-parity terms) in the world, and one almost 70 per cent dependent on foreign oil (the figure is expected to rise to 85 per cent by 2020), India has an oil stake in the region that is significant and growing. Some Indian security analysts foresee energy security as India's primary strategic concern in the next twenty-five years and believe it must place itself on a virtual wartime footing to address it. India has to protect its offshore oil and gas fields, ongoing deep-sea oil drilling projects in its vast exclusive economic zone, and an extensive infrastructure of shore and offshore oil and gas wells, pumping stations and telemetry posts, ports and pipeline grids, and refineries. Additionally, Indian public and private-sector oil companies have invested several billion dollars in recent years in oil concessions in foreign countries, many of them in the region, including Sudan, Yemen, Iran, Iraq, and Burma. These investments are perceived to need military protection.

The relevant question that arises is whether India should concentrate on developing a Blue Water Navy to consolidate her position in IOR.

Developing a 'Blue Navy' for India: The Theory of Naval Supremacy

Alfred Thayer Mahan, the US Geo-Strategic thinker contended that with command of the sea, even if local and temporary, naval operations in support of land forces can be of decisive importance and that naval supremacy can be exercised by a transnational consortium acting in defense of a multinational system of free trade. Mahan wrote of sea power as a basis for a nation's fitness to play a great role in world affairs. He came up with compelling, navalist-oriented insights on matters of geography and territory, population and national character, and the soundness of a nation's governance. By placing the need for a powerful Navy at the centre of national interest, Mahan merged naval operations and political and economic destiny. Mahan foresaw that naval strategy during peace is primarily guided by the following principles. First, rather than allowing competitors to develop their own merchant shipping fleet to support their foreign trade, a great nation preempt them by the projection of sea power. These include a combination of defensive and offensive capabilities, deterrence, and the willingness to protect the flow of commerce.

Most likely Indian Ocean can become the hot-spot of rivalry and clash between India and China especially because of Chinese Maritime Silk Road (MSR) initiatives and its growing clout among a number of Indian Ocean states like Bangladesh, Maldives and Sri Lanka who also form the neighbourhood of India. During 2014, the Indian Ocean geostrategic environment, though peaceful, was a bit tenuous. The presence of Chinese submarines in the Indian Ocean created uneasiness in New Delhi. The Indian Navy seems to be beefing up capabilities to respond to the Chinese designs in the Indian Ocean. New Delhi believes that the MSR can potentially help China consolidate its naval/maritime strategy of access and basing in the Indian Ocean in support of PLA Navy's future operations.

The Indian Navy and the Coast Guard have been actively developing a sophisticated strategy that involves joint exercises, hot lines, exchange of intelligence and training with a number of navies. It will be useful to explore if the Indian Navy's National Command Control Communication Intelligence (NC3I) is suitably linked to the Singapore based Information Fusion Centre (IFC) established at Changi Command and Control Centre (CC2C), which has received much acclaim as an effective MDA hub in a pursuit to develop a 'blue navy' in the IOR, will yield valuable result. Mahan's dictum can be found to be reiterated by contemporary Indian naval strategist by modifying it to fit the context of IOR.

"Whoever controls the Indian Ocean dominates Asia. This ocean is the key to the seven seas in the twenty-first century, the destiny of the world will be decided in these waters."

> (US Rear Admiral Alfred Thayer Mahan quoted by Cdr. P.K. Ghosh in Maritime Security Challenges in South Asia and the Indian Ocean, 18 January 2004.)

As India juggles, the dual imperative to simultaneously compete and bypass an economically and militarily rising China, the outcome of its blue water quest will influence the balance of power in Asia for years to come.

The tremors of China's increasing claims in the South China Sea are already being felt across Asia, giving the Indian Navy more reason to beef up its fleet. While it might not be a primary player in the disputed waters, India would not want to be excluded from exploring assets in the resource-rich South China Sea or elsewhere as it scours far and wide for much-needed energy sources. A blue water navy would provide muscle for all these strategic imperatives, enhance regional power projection capabilities, more effectively protect India's expanding energy and trade routes, and enable stronger defense and trade ties with other nations.

However, the problem is that the India has an ageing naval fleet and replacement is often fraught with major delays. The Indian Navy is currently weak on submarine capabilities. Most of India's defense equipment is imported (mostly from Russia) and the country needs to develop its indigenous manufacturing capabilities. The navy's allocation in the defense budget would force it to make crucial trade-offs between developing one capability versus the other. Cost effective and timely modernization would be critical to fully realize India's blue water dreams. The outcomes of India's blue water quest will subtly but surely impact the region's long-term strategic calculus.

The Indian Navy's *Maritime Doctrine* released in 2004 also shows a major change in its outlook. Echoing the statement of Indian strategist, K.M. Panikkar, the document implies that the Indian Ocean is, in a singular way, Indian (Panikkar 1951: 84). Thus, Admiral Mehta, the Navy Chief of Staff remarked, "The Indian Ocean is named after us.... If required in this IOR, we will undertake humanitarian missions, stop piracy and gun running, and all those kinds of things in asymmetric warfare" (Suryanarayana 2007).

However, the Indian Navy does not see itself as primarily a defensive force. Specific undertakings of the Indian Navy include exercising sea control in designated areas of the Arabian Sea and the Bay of Bengal and at the entry/exit points of the IOR; in case of war to carry the conflict to the enemy's territory, to strangulate his trade/oil arteries, to destroy his war waging potential and naval assets and to ensure a decisive victory; to provide power projection force; and to work in conjunction with the two other services to preserve, protect and promote India's national interests (Sakhuja 2004).

The 2004 Maritime Doctrine takes into account China's naval-building and pays close attention to its submarine acquisition. The 2007 Maritime Military Strategy emphasizes three new issues: power projection including the development of expeditionary forces, securing Indian interests in a wide arc including the Indian Ocean, the Middle East/Persian Gulf and East Asia, and strike capabilities in littoral warfare to support land forces in war. It also lays emphasis on developing a sea-based nuclear deterrent. Figure 1 gives an indication of the Indian navy's growth.

1991			2012		
Batteries	Tonnage	Missile	Batteries	Tonnage	Missile
Aircraft Carriers X2	48,800	0	Aircrafts Carriers X1	29,000	0
Destroyers X5	25,000	30	Destroyers X8	43,470	134
Frigates X18	43,862	42	Frigates X14	43,862	130
Submarines X17	35,500	0	Submarines X16	35,500	52
Amphibious Craft X9	14,625	0	Amphibious Craft X11	14,625	0
Total tonnage	167,787		Total tonnage	217,426	

Figure 1: Indian Navy in 1991-2012

Source: http://futuredirections.org.au/publications/indian-ocean/1516-examining-the-sino-indian-maritime-competition-part-4-india-s-maritime-strategy.html

'Further India'

India has been cultivating closer relations with a number of states in the Bay of Bengal region and in Southeast Asia, often under the aegis of New Delhi's "Look East" policy. The Look-East policy as initiated in the early 1990s was against the backdrop of a struggling Indian economy and the sudden disappearance of the Cold War framework and has been to some extent a diplomatic success. As a consequence, India's ties with most of the states of the Bay of Bengal and Southeast Asia are central to Indian foreign policy.

The "Look East" policy also has produced positive gains with the Association of Southeast Asian Nations (ASEAN). India became a sectoral partner in 1991, a full dialogue partner in 1995, and a member of the ASEAN Regional Forum in 1996. In late 2004 India and ten ASEAN countries—meeting at the tenth summit in Vientiane—signed a historic pact for peace, progress, and shared prosperity. They also pledged to cooperate in fighting international terrorism and proliferation of weapons of mass destruction. The four-page accord and nine-page action plan envisaged cooperation in multilateral fora, particularly the World Trade Organisation; in addressing the challenges of economic, food, human, and energy security; and in boosting trade, investment, tourism, culture, sports, and people-to-people contacts. The pact commits India to creating a free trade area by 2011 with Brunei, Indonesia, Malaysia, Thailand, and Singapore, and by 2016 with the rest of ASEAN—the Philippines, Cambodia, Laos, Burma, and Vietnam.

India's perceived need to compete with China in Southeast Asia, particularly in its littoral nations, has helped produce a better relation with Singapore. It also underscores the importance India attaches to key *choke points*—that it may need to block a Chinese move toward or into the Indian Ocean (the principal mission behind developing of the Indian bases in the Andaman and Nicobar Islands).

Singapore is ideally situated to supplement the infrastructure in the Andamans with the facilities which in the same way may allow India to project power into the South China Sea and against China. With Singapore, India is gradually aiming at deepening her relationship. Trade has been growing rapidly, surging by nearly 50 per cent in 2004; a Comprehensive Economic Cooperation Agreement in June 2005 is supposed to boost trade further. In addition, a security pact in 2003 extended an existing programme of combined naval exercises to encompass air and ground maneuvers and initiated a high-level security dialogue and intelligence exchange. Singapore and India held their first air exercise late in 2004 and their first ground exercises from February to April 2005, in India. Notably, in February and March 2005 their annual naval maneuvers took place for the first time in the South China Sea (vice "Indian" waters). New Delhi also has stated willingness—in principle—to allow the Singapore Air Force to use Indian ranges on an extended basis. On the whole despite Chinese intentions to contain India, India has vision to 'further India' beyond South Asia.

Conclusion

Needless to say, that the IOR still remains a main hotspot major strategic issues and risks. In the light of these issues and the risks, it is likely that the Indian Ocean will become a region which will determine the future of international politics. The sub-regional stresses such as the civil war in Iraq or the intervention of the US or Iran-US relations and proliferation of nuclear arms and ensuing arms race may be a determining factor in the stability of IOR in the near future. The stability of Straits of Malacca is vital as it is a crucial route for the flow of petroleum to the East. India-Pakistan relation, that is, the ups and downs in it pertaining to issues of terrorism, Kashmir issues as well as arms race between the two may well extend to naval competition between the two. These may have higher implications and power rivalry may affect the stability of the IOR. China is another vital player between the two and the conflict and tensions between India and China and bonhomie in the Sino-Pak relations definitely will see repercussions in IOR as China is increasing its naval activity in IOR and presence in South China Sea. The presence of US in the IOR will invite Chinese competition for becoming a hegemon in the IOR. The US and China—as they indulge in co-operation and competition —must determine a road map of future course of actions to avoid the risks of some long-term clash or confrontation in the IOR. The US will continue to be the strategic anchor and security provider in the Indian Ocean and its role to 'correct security imbalances, challenge the hegemony of any dominant power and ensure regional stability' will make matters all the more complicated.

Future projections foretell that a naval conflict in the Gulf could also extend to the Gulf of Oman and Arabian Sea and might affect the traffic through the straits of Malacca. Piracy tops the list of risks in the IOR. The deployment of international task force has been actively engaged in controlling piracy near Somalia and in the Indian Ocean near the entry point to the Red Sea yet the risk of piracy still remains as the 'failed states' like Somalia continues to be caught in turmoil, instability and civil war. Somali-based pirates, using hijacked fishing trawlers as "mother ships" are extending their range and shifting their operations as far south as the Mozambique Channel, eastward to the vicinity of the Maldives, and northeastward to the Strait of Hormuz. Terrorism in the IOR is increasing and some states are incubators of terrorists. This region therefore, runs high risks of being the pivot of international terrorism. Besides the above mentioned risk factors, there still remain endemic transnational and maritime disputes and potential conflicts. There are many relatively low-level border, territorial, and maritime disputes between various IOR states. Even if they become violent, most will only affect limited numbers of local outside trading and investment activities. Followed by this is the offshore resource disputes in terms of petroleum or undersea mining contains the seed of future conflicts and cooperation.

For India, the proposition that China is building a 'string of pearls' along vital sealines of communication in the Indian Ocean has deep implications in terms of "Further India" or expanding beyond the South Asian region. Some analysts are contemplating about a premature policy of a 'necklace of diamonds' emerging in India's own plans for power projection. The idea of such a necklace is the reverberations of K.M. Panikkar's foresightedness as he emphasized the need for a ring of bases in the Indian Ocean to secure the nation. India has to chalk out a proper policy towards the IOR today and think clearly about the logic of power projection and the imperatives of forward presence in the IOR.

References

Chellaney, Brahma (2005, August). Should India Consider China a Friend or Rival? *Times of India.*

Gertz, Bill (2005, January 18). China Builds Up Strategic Sea Lanes. *Washington Times.* See also China Expands Its Southern Sphere of Influence. *Jane's Intelligence Review* (2005, May 23).

Haider, Ziad (2005, Winter/Spring). Baluchis, Beijing, and Pakistan's Gwadar Port. *Georgetown Journal of International Affairs*. Vol. 6(1): 95-103.

Indian Ocean (n.d). *CIA, World Factbook*. From https://www.cia.gov/library/publications/the-world-factbook/geos/xo.html, updated on 13 February 2016.

Talbott, Strobe (2004). *Engaging India: Diplomacy, Democracy and the Bomb*. Washington, D.C.: Brookings Institution Press.

Malik, Mohan (2005, April 14). China's Foreign Policy Is Still Dominated by the 'Contain India' Theory. *Force: The Complete Newsmagazine of National Security*. On the April 2005 visit of Premier Wen Jiabao and Chinese purchases of oil and natural gas, see Pramit Mitra, "Iran and India Extend Their Friendship," *South Asia Monitor,* 1 January 2005, available at www.csis.org. On China and Africa see Paul Mooney, "China's African Safari," *Yale Global Online*, 3 January 2005, and John Hill, "China Covets African Oil and Trade," *Jane's Intelligence Review,* 1 November 2004. The key work on Sino-Indian competition in the Indian Ocean is John W. Garver, "The IO in Sino-Indian Relations," in *Protracted Contest*, 275-312.

McVadon, Eric A. (2004, December 1-3). "The Asian Sea in Which Transformation Must Swim", paper presented at the conference on U.S. Defense Transformation: Implications for the Security of the Asia-Pacific Region, Asia-Pacific Center for Security Studies. See also James Brooke, "China's Navy Fans Out in the Pacific," *New York Times,* 30 December 2004, and Richard Halloran, "Chinese Sub Highlights Undersea Rivalries," *Japan Times,* 30 November 2004, available at www.japantimes.com. That the Chinese navy is currently operating, or planning to operate, submarines in or near the Bay of Bengal is suggested by "Three Submarines Damaged by Earthquake" (30 December 2004) and "2 Chinese Spy Ships Seized off Andamans" (30 November 2004), both *NEWSInsight,*newsinsight.net.

Ministry of Defence (2004-05, Annual Report). Government of India, New Delhi. From mod.nic.in/.

Panikkar, K.M. (1951). Panikkar's statement is "...to other countries the Indian Ocean is only one of the important oceanic areas, to India it is a vital sea. Her lifelines are concentrated in that area, her freedom is dependent on the freedom of that coastal surface. No industrial development, no commercial growth, no stable political structure is possible for her unless her shores are protected."—Panikkar, K.M., *India and the Indian Ocean*. London: Allen & Unwin.

Reuters (2005, March 26). Japan, India to Develop Natural Gas Resources. *Reuters*. From www.inlnews.yahoo.com.

Sakhuja, Vijay (2004, July 1). Indian Navy: Keeping Pace with Emerging Challenges. In Prabhakar, Lawrence W., Ho, Joshua H., and Bateman, Samuel, (Eds.), *The Evolving Maritime Balance of Power in the Asia-Pacific: Maritime Doctrines and Nuclear Weapons at Sea*, Institute of Defence and Strategic Studies, Singapore, 2006: 103-06; See also, "Maritime Doctrine Envisages Formidable Blue Water Capabilities", New Delhi Force, 2004, cited in Gilboy, George J., and Heginbotham, Eric, *Chinese and Indian Strategic Behaviour: Growing Power and Alarm*, Cambridge University Press, New York, 2012: 153.

Suryanarayana, P.S. (2007, May 21). No evil design behind proactive naval exercises: Admiral Mehta. *The Hindu*. From http://www.hindu.com/2007/05/21/stories/2007052104551300.htm—See more at: http://www.futuredirections.org.au/publications/indian-ocean/1516-examining-the-sino-indian-maritime-competition-part-4-india-s-maritime-strategy.html#sthash.Lg8PFO3R.dpuf

11

India's Water Sharing Disputes with Its Neighbours: A Challenge to Its Regional Ascendancy

Jayita Mukhopadhyay

> Water is life's matter and matrix, mother and medium. There is no life without water.
>
> —Albert Szent-Gyorgyi

Since time immemorial, availability of water has shaped the establishment and growth of human civilization. The blue gold is fast surpassing oil as the world's scarcest critical resource and World Bank has already prophesied that the 21st century will be an era of War over Water. Modern agriculture, industrialization, urbanization and spiraling growth of population have all contributed to exponential rise in the demand for water. And, as of now, water has no substitute. Water experts have sounded an alarm that within the next 25 years, half of the world's population could have trouble in finding enough freshwater for drinking and irrigation.

Water has emerged as a key strategic resource that could determine if Asia is headed toward cooperation or competition. The risk of water becoming a trigger for war or diplomatic strong-arming is especially high in Asia, which is home to three-fifths of the human population, yet has the lowest per-capita freshwater availability among all continents. Asia's per capita freshwater availability is less than half the global average. By 2025, two third of the global population is likely to be living in water scarce or water stressed conditions. And the majority of the world's people living in water related despair will be in Asia (Chellaney 2011: 8).

There is an undeniable shortage of water in Asia, particularly South Asia, precipitated by the changing climate and a tendency of water wastage in the region, and this shortage has the potential to create a major water crisis in the region. Unfortunately, India is caught up in the vortex of such water disputes with almost all its neighbouring states some of which dates back to the period of India's birth as a free nation. This paper begins with an attempt to highlight why the water disputes are major concerns for all the stakeholders, i.e. governments and people alike. This will be followed by a brief account of the water disputes between India and three of her prominent neighbours, Pakistan, China and Bangladesh. The paper ends with an attempt to suggest what can be done to grapple with these difficult issues so that they do not create obstacles to promotion of friendly relations between India and her neighbours, and to what extent India, as an emerging big power should actually walk the extra mile to eliminate chances of friction among neighbours on water sharing.

India with 16% of the world's population has only 4% of world's freshwater resources. Per capita availability of utilizable water in India has rapidly decreased due to unsustainable agricultural practices, unchecked industrial pollution and unplanned urbanization. The U.S. had the world's highest per capita water footprint, at 2,842 cubic meters per annum. As against this, in India, the individual footprint is only 1,089 cubic meters a year. As India struggles to cope with the water need of its burgeoning population and of rapidly modernising agricultural and industrial sectors, it finds itself locked in bitter tussle with all its prominent neighbours, Pakistan, Bangladesh, China over sharing of water of common rivers. The hydrological contours of India, both as an upper riparian and a lower riparian, is at the epicenter of new riparian politics and diplomacy over trans-boundary rivers. As India's relations with these countries have many outstanding issues, that complicates her riparian relations. The management of rivers does not take place in a vacuum but rather in a complex political and economic matrix. Riparian issues ultimately have a political connotation. Politics is about power, influence, resource allocation and policy implementation.

But politics is also about managing relationships between states and trade-offs. The implementation of river policies, even when purely design-related to the linking of rivers or constructions of dams and barrages, are undertaken within a political context. Riparian states differ in their views of what cooperation entails for them and not surprisingly, a power game ensues. Very often decision-makers, even if they are aware that a proposed treaty is sound from technical standpoint, raise objections when it comes to water sharing, as they don't want to be seen as 'giving in' to the legitimate demands of a hostile neighbour. Jingoistic sentiments are whipped up and real solutions become elusive in a politically charged milieu (IDSA Task Force Report...).

In the post liberalisation-globalisation era, successive Indian governments have aired their aspirations to gain the status of regional superpower for India, but the fact remains that India does not have the military clout to act as a regional policeman, neither there is any prevailing consensus in this country to gain a stature whereby India can have any impact on the course of actions of other countries of the region. Rather, India should try to be a broker of 'peace', a felicitator of regional cooperation. One stumbling block in the way of improving relation among India and her neighbours, as already noted, are the festering water disputes.

India-Pakistan Disputes

Following independence from Britain in 1947, India was subdivided into the separate nation states of India and Pakistan. During this partition, borders were drawn with little consideration to water resources. In particular, the borders near the Indus and its major tributaries—the Beas, Chenab, Jhelum, Ravi and Sutlej, all of which flow from India into Pakistan—were drawn without considering the conflict that such political boundaries might provoke. This division led to a number of disputes in which India, which is entirely upstream from Pakistan, allegedly attempted to restrict or alter flows, to the detriment of Pakistani quality of life. In 1960, India and Pakistan negotiated a settlement to the dispute under the auspices of the World Bank. The Indus Water Treaty divided the six major rivers of the Indus River system between the two nations. India was allocated complete ownership—or exclusive usage rights—to the three eastern rivers: the Sutlej, the Beas and the Ravi, while Pakistan was allocated nearly unfettered ownership to the three western rivers: the Indus, the Jhelum and the Chenab. As co-signer of the treaty, the World Bank continues to serve a procedural role in settling differences and disputes. Should either nation violate the terms of the treaty, through fault of interpretation or application, the matter is first brought to the Permanent Indus Commission, after which it is brought to a World Bank-appointed neutral arbitrator. Upon receiving the neutral arbitrator's ruling, the nations could seek reference to a court of arbitration or appeal to the International Court of Justice at The Hague, under Article IX (paragraphs 3 through 5) of the treaty (Salman 2008). While the Indus Water Treaty created a legal framework for governing water resources, it failed to mitigate several important areas of tension. Specifically three key points of the treaty have contributed to subsequent disputes. First, Pakistan is wholly dependent upon the Indus River system for its freshwater supply. While dwindling groundwater provides for some of Pakistan's needs, the Indus and its tributaries represent the only source of surface waters for the entire country, including its prominent agricultural sector. Second, the headwaters of all six rivers are within Indian territory, and, accordingly, the Indian Government can significantly limit the flow of water into Pakistan. Third, while India is not permitted to build projects on the Indus, Jhelum or Chenab rivers to divert or store water flowing to Pakistan, many of India's current or proposed dam projects do both. To compound matters, the Indus, Jhelum, and Chenab all flow through the volatile region of Jammu and Kashmir, where India and Pakistan have engaged in sporadic fighting during a decades-long territorial dispute. Together, these elements provide a basis for several major disputes as India and Pakistan seek to meet growing domestic water demand. The discrepancy between political borders and the natural course of rivers, coupled with the structure of the Indus Water Treaty, creates multiple areas of potential conflict between India and Pakistan. The greatest issue under dispute is India's construction of dams and other projects that divert water that would otherwise reach Pakistan. The most important current disputes involve the Baglihar Dam, the Tulbul Navigation/Wular Barrage, the Kishenganga Dam and Indian retention of water from the Beas, Ravi and Sutlej rivers. In most cases, Pakistan believes it has been the victim of Indian strong-arm tactics (Resource Dispute in South Asia...). Pakistani authorities very recently have raised the cavil that IWT is not in Pakistan's best interest and should be scrapped, and India has violated the Indus Waters Treaty many times by constructing 3200 dams and barrages on the river Jhelum, which deprives Pakistan of this major source ('Interview: The India-Pakistan...'). It is evident from these allegations that if not duly addressed, water disputes between India and her belligerent neighbour on the western front may flare up any moment.

India-China Disputes

India-China relations are complex and uneasy. In recent times, Chinese assertiveness against India has been more pronounced. It sees India as a rival and contender, which is not unusual in regional politics, and defines its 'pinprick policy' by raising the *ante*. While there is political assertiveness on the one hand, there is definite resource aggressiveness on the other, particularly relating to water resources (IDSA Task Force Report...). China is an extremely thirsty country and is one of the world's driest nations. With a population of 1.3 billion and much of its rivers polluted and silt-ridden, water undoubtedly becomes a prized strategic asset. China's hardening position on Arunachal Pradesh is not mere rhetoric. In laying claims to Arunachal it is claiming the almost 200 million cusecs of waters resources in the state. Some of the water data figures suggest that roughly 354 BCM of water flows from Tibet into India, of which 131 BCM is accounted in the Brahmaputra. Under China's 11th five-year plan (2006-10), a huge development thrust involving 180 projects worth more than 770 billion yuan has been earmarked for Tibet. It includes building roads, railways and airports and importantly the completion of two hydro-projects: Zhikong on Lhasa river (which is one of the five tributaries of the Yarlung-Tsangpo, which flows into India as the

Brahmaputra) and Shiquanhe which is the upper reach of the Indus in the Ngari Prefecture. China's increased infrastructural activities are a pointer to its long-term plan to build more dams and hydro-projects on the Indus, Sutlej and Yarlung-Tsangpo. Such an infrastructure boost can be linked to the proposed dam construction at the 'Great Bend' of Yarlung-Tsangpo.

As a lower riparian, India will be vulnerable to any major storage projects planned on the Yarlung-Tsangpo. Given the political situation between the two countries it is hard to imagine China playing the role of responsible upper riparian releasing re-regulated flows from powerhouses immediately back into river. China's consumption requirements and long distance transfer of waters will undoubtedly hurt the interests of India and more so Bangladesh (IDSA Task Force Report...).

India and China, in October 2013, signed a new agreement to strengthen cooperation on trans-border rivers that is aimed at allaying India's concerns over new dams on the Brahmaputra and facilitating the exchange of flood data. The agreement, signed after talks between Prime Minister Manmohan Singh and his Chinese counterpart Li Keqiang, said both countries agreed to strengthen their cooperation further on the trans-border rivers through the existing Expert Level Mechanism to provide flood-season data and emergency management. Under the new agreement, the Chinese side agreed to provide more flood data of Brahmaputra river from May to October instead of June to October that was in vogue under the previous agreements river water agreements in 2008 and 2010. India has expressed concerns over China's plans to construct more dams which New Delhi ears could restrict the flows of the Himalayan river flowing from Tibet. China for its parts assured India that its dams are run of the river projects not designed to hold water (China Allays fear...). However, a recent editorial in *The Statesman* has pointed out, "the website of the Yellow River Conservancy Commission of China's Ministry of Water Resources" has a 50-page report on the diversion of the Brahmaputra, and though Beijing denies any bad intention, the project remains on the 'official' website. The million dollar question is, can China be trusted? In November 2014, China's plans for the

Brahmaputra took a leap forward when the first unit of the $1.5 billion Zangmu Hydropower Station project, which is located in the middle reaches of the river, became operational. Once completed—five other generating units of this project are due for completion this year—the project is designed to generate 2.5 billion kilowatt hours of electricity annually. China's dams on the Brahmaputra may be run-of-the-river projects but they are "a matter of utmost concern to lower riparian countries," argues Ramaswamy Iyer, former secretary of Water Resources with the Government of India and currently an honorary research professor at the New Delhi-based Centre for Policy Research. A "break in the river between the point of diversion to the turbines and the point of return of the waters to the river... can be very long, upwards of 10 km in many cases, even 100 km in some cases; and there would be a series of such breaks in the river in the event of a cascade of projects," he points out. Besides, "far from being environmentally benign, as often claimed," a run-of-the-river hydroelectric project "spells death for the river". Turbines operate intermittently in these projects, "which means that the waters are held back in pondage and released when the turbines need to operate, resulting in huge diurnal variations—from 0 per cent to 400 per cent in a day—in downstream flows. No aquatic life or riparian population can cope with that order of diurnal variation" (Ramachandran 2015).

More worrying than China's construction of hydropower dams on the Brahmaputra is the proposed northward rerouting of its waters at the Great Bend. This diversion would result in a significant drop in the river's water level as it enters India. It will have a serious impact on agriculture and fishing in the downstream areas as the salinity of water will increase.

India Bangladesh Disputes

The distribution of Ganges water during Bangladesh's lean months has historically been a contentious issue between India and Bangladesh. The Farraka Barrage is the most important concern to Bangladesh. It diverts water through the Bhagirathi-Hoogli river system in an effort to flush sediment from India's port city of Kolkata. Bangladesh argues that the Farraka Barrage harms the agro-ecological and economic well-being of southern Bangladesh. Bilateral treaties provide a structure for resolving these points of discord. On December 12, 1996, Bangladesh and India signed the Ganges River Treaty, which regulates the seasonal allocation of waters reaching Farraka. Specifically, the treaty outlines the distribution of Ganges River waters during the lean period. It schedules division of water according to 10-day average availability of water at Farraka. The Joint Committee of Experts is staffed by the secretaries of water resources for each country and is charged by Article IX of the 1996 Ganges Treaty with negotiating agreements on common rivers between India and Bangladesh. Since its inception, the committee has met quite a few times, but has made little progress in resolving these disputes.

The Teesta River is another source of conflict between India and Bangladesh. In the late 1980s, India constructed the Gazoldoba Barrage 60 kilometers north of the Bangladesh border to divert water toward irrigation projects in northern West Bengal. In 1998, Bangladesh constructed the Teesta Barrage 20 kilometers south of the Indian border. Bangladesh has raised concerns about the distribution of the Teesta's waters. In particular, Bangladesh contends that India is increasingly diverting more water to Gazoldoba at the expense of Bangladeshis downstream (IDSA Task Force Report...).

The Teesta water sharing accord, proposed by earlier Manmohan Singh Government got derailed due to objections raised by West Bengal Chief Minister who purportedly acted as a crusader for the rights of people of north Bengal regarding their claims in Teesta water. River expert Kalyan Rudra has headed a commission to look into the Teesta water sharing issue. Though a report has been submitted, it has not been made public by West Bengal Government. According to some sources, the report has found the claim of Bangladesh for 25% share of the water permissible and not detrimental to India's interest and also in view of the fact that the health of the river on the Bangladesh side is at stake with an inadequate flow of water resulting in siltation (Mamata stalls Teesta...). Recent visit of

Prime Minister Narendra Modi to Bangladesh and the happy outcome of discussion between Prime Minister of Bangladesh Sheikh Hasina and Mr. Modi in the form of the finalisation of Land Border Agreement between the two countries generated intense euphoria, and yet, could not drown the frustration of the stakeholders, particularly on the side of Bangladesh, that there was lack of "definite progress on the contentious Teesta water sharing issue" (Bangladesh media hails...).

Water disputes are actually time bombs ticking away very fast and if not addressed properly, may upset regional integration as well as India's regional aspirations. Some noted analysts of South Asian politics have observed that regional cooperation and efforts at integration in South Asia is increasingly getting defined in economic terms, dictated by neoliberal market agenda. Consequently, there is a push to perceive water as an 'economic good,' a tradable commodity to be left to the market forces. In many parts of South Asia, ordinary people are forced to dole out good amount of money to purchase water, water tax is levied on water used in agriculture and industry. Bottled water industries are making huge profit (Mukhopadhyay 2012). An alternative and prudent approach will be to recognize water as a common pool resource, as a human right vital for survival, and as an environmental resource to be protected, and treated with the principles of sustainability. Social activists, academics, environmentalists and NGOs are of the opinion that this alternative approach will facilitate avoidance of friction over water sharing. Some noted hydrologists and environmentalists have observed that India, having the scientific and technical knowhow and better economic strength than her South Asian neighbours, should take the initiative, through multilateral foras like SAARC, to develop and implement framework for better water management. Efficient water governance that is fair, equitable, and environmentally sound, involving both governments and civil society actors are need of the hour (Singh 2008: 9-41). India experiences seasonal water abundance, and devastating floods which is counterbalanced by arid months. Rainwater harvesting, regular de-silting of rivers and water bodies to enhance storage capacity, healthy water use practices, avoiding wastage of water are some vital steps that can boost India's capacity of managing a valuable resource which will also take care of seasonal scarcity of water and ease the pressure on government when it negotiates treaties with water stressed neighbours. So far as trans-boundary rivers are concerned, entire river basin should be managed in totality so as to protect the river and its ecological milieu and India should be willing to yield water to its parched neighbours as much as possible if hydrologists do not find it detrimental for us, as it can generate huge amount of goodwill, improve regional cooperation and enhance India's stature as a benefactor, as recently concluded Land Border Agreement between India and Bangladesh has exhibited.

References

"Bangladesh media hails PM Narendra Modi on LBA but concerned over Teesta impasse", *The Indian Express*, http://indianexpress.com/article/india/india-others/bangladesh-media-hails-pm-modi-on-lba-but-concerned-over-teesta-impasse/

Chellaney, Brahma. *Water: Asia's New Battleground*. Washington, DC: Georgetown University Press, 2011: 8.

"China Allays fear over Brahmaputra Dam", *The Hindu*, October 23, 2013.

Gp Cap A.G. Bewoor, "The Way to Regional Power Status", *Indian Defence Review*, Vol. 25, January–March 2010, http://www.indiandefencereview.com/news/the-way-to-regional-power-status/

IDSA Task Force Report, "Water Security for India: The External Dynamics", http://www.indiawaterportal.org/articles/water-security-india-external-dynamics-idsa-task-force-report.

"Interview: The India-Pakistan Water Dispute" by Muhammad Akbar Notezai, The Diplomat, November 21, 2014, http://thediplomat.com/2014/11/interview-the-india-pakistan-water-dispute/

"Mamata stalls Teesta Water sharing agreement yet again," *The Times of India*, July 14, 2013.

Mukhopadhyay, Jayita. "Nor Any Drop to Drink", Special Article, *The Statesman*, Kolkata, 24 April, 2012.

Ramachandran, Sudha. "Water Wars: China, India and the Great Dam Rush", The Diplomat, April 03, 2015, http://thediplomat.com/2015/04/water-wars-china-india-and-the-great-dam-rush/

"Resource Dispute in South Asia: Water Scarcity and the Potential for Interstate Conflict", Prepared for the Office of South Asia Analysis,

U.S. Central Intelligence Agency, By Emma Condon, Patrick Hillmann, Justin King, Katharine Lang, Alison Patz. Workshop in International Public Affairs, June 1, 2009. Robert M. La Follette School of Public Affairs, University of Wisconsin–Madison www.researchgate.net/.../28627598_Resource_Disputes_in_South_Asia_Water_Scarcity_and_the_Potential_for_Interstate_Conflict

Singh, Richa. "Trans-boundary Water Politics and Conflicts in South Asia: Toward Water for Peace". New Delhi: Centre for Democracy and Social Action, 2008.

Section Three

12

The Tibetan Enigma and the Sino-Indian Boundary Dispute in the Twenty-first Century

Anindya Batabyal

Tibet remains an important factor as far as People's Republic of China's (P.R.C.) policy-making on the Sino-Indian boundary dispute is concerned. In fact, the issue of Tibet has been one of the most important and a core issue in India's bilateral relations with its northern neighbour. Many within the highest ranks of the Chinese political leadership still suspect that the Indian Government prefers an independent Tibet and covertly supports the separatist elements within and outside Tibet. The presence of over 1, 20,000 Tibetan refugees within India and the fact that the Tibetan spiritual leader Dalai Lama and the Tibetan Government in exile has its headquarter at Dharamshala located within the Indian state of Himachal Pradesh only adds further doubts in the minds of the Chinese political leadership regarding Indian Government's intention on Tibet. The presence of representatives from the Tibetan Government in exile during the swearing-in ceremony of India's Prime Minister Narendra Modi in May 2014 only accentuated this suspicion in the minds of the Chinese political leadership. The Sino-Indian boundary dispute is in fact intertwined with China's insecurities in Tibet, its anxieties about India's special cultural and historical ties with Tibet and the support provided to Tibetan spiritual leader Dalai Lama, who along with his followers runs his Tibetan Government in exile from India. This is in spite of the Sino-Indian Agreements of 1954 and 2003, through which the Indian Government recognized the Tibetan

Autonomous Region as part of the territory of the People's Republic of China. A dominant view that persists within the Chinese Communist Party is that unless Tibet is completely pacified and sinicized like Inner Mongolia, China would never give up the bargaining chip that an unsettled boundary vis-à-vis India provides it with (Malik 2009: 176). An unsettled frontier with India provides China the strategic leverage to keep India uncertain about its future intentions and nervous about its capabilities, while simultaneously exposing India's vulnerabilities as well as weaknesses. It also ensures Indian Government's good behaviour on matters, which are of vital concern of the Chinese political leadership. The main thrust of this paper is to highlight two important issues, which lie at the heart of India's bilateral ties with China. First, this article will argue that the issue of Tibet still remains as the core issue in India's relations with China. It is important to note in this connection that the 1962 border conflict between India and China was not primarily due to India's so-called 'forward policy' along the disputed Sino-Indian frontier as had been outlined by several scholars (Gupta 1974; Hoffman 1990; Maxwell 1970), but was a result of the then Chinese political leadership's misperceptions regarding Indian Government's intention on Tibet at that point of time. Second, this paper will also analyze the manner in which the issue of Sino-Indian boundary dispute is intimately linked with the issue of Tibet and it is impossible to discuss the former without making a reference to the latter.

I

Contemporary Chinese thinking on Tibet is part of what the Chinese nationalists refer to as China's national humiliation experienced at the hands of the imperialist powers in the past, particularly at a time when China was weak politically, militarily as well as economically. As constructed by modern Chinese nationalism, China was bullied, oppressed and also exploited between 1839 and 1949 by the foreign imperialist powers. An important element of this national humiliation was the seizure of Chinese territory by belligerent imperialist powers at a time when the Central Government in China was weak. These territories included areas populated by ethnic Han Chinese (for example Taiwan, Hong Kong, Macao) and also those occupied by non-Han people, which includes Tibet. It is important to note in this connection that Tibet had owned allegiance to the Chinese imperial government for centuries. China's political and military control over the non-Han ethnic populated areas including Tibet had been weak and most Chinese scholars have concluded that taking advantage of China's weakness at different periods in the past, these areas like Tibet had been seized by the imperialist powers from China. As nationalist thinking in China started to evolve since the early part of the twentieth century, Chinese political leaders across the political spectrum—imperial, nationalists and communists—struggled to enhance China's political and military presence in Tibet. However, the Tibetans were able to resist such attempts with the help of Great Britain till 1949.

In October 1949, the Chinese Communist Party under the leadership of Mao Zedong came to power with a firm determination to end the period of national humiliation of China on their own terms. In terms of Tibet, this meant asserting complete political and military control by the Chinese Communist Party led government. The concept of 'suzerainty' that implied certain kinds of limitations regarding Chinese presence in the Tibetan region was rejected as an instrument of imperialist aggression against China (Garver 2001: 33-35). The Chinese communist leadership since 1949 were of the firm view that the Chinese Government must exercise absolute and unlimited sovereign authority over Tibet. In the opinion of the then Chinese Communist Party leadership, exercise of absolute control over Tibet would help to make China powerful in two significant ways. First, it would provide China greater security against possible external military threats in the future. Second, the exploitation of Tibet's vast and extremely rich mineral as well as other natural resources was considered vital for China's economic development. In fact, development and exploitation of Tibet's rich natural resources remains crucial for China's overall economic development and its rise as a great power (Garver 2001: 35-36). Also, for the Chinese Communist Party, incorporation of Tibet has great prestige value inside China (Kalha 2012: 8). The occupation and incorporation of Tibet would firmly establish in the eyes of the Chinese People, the nationalist credentials of the then new communist regime. The new communist political leadership view the incorporation of Tibet as a strategic necessity without which the unity of the 'new' China could not be realized. Although the Han Chinese population constitutes almost ninety per cent of China's total population, they inhabit less than half of China's total landmass. The population of non-Han minorities inside China comprise only about one hundred million, but they crucially occupy almost half of China's total land area. In fact, it is significant to note that in the last two decades, there has been a demographic shift in the Tibetan region with Han Chinese people settling in the region from other parts of China and thereby almost reducing the ethnic Tibetans to a minority status within their own territory.

The essence of the Tibetan issue in bilateral ties between India and China is that this large, ethnically distinct and strategically located region, which was historically not subject to direct Chinese political control and military occupation, has since 1951 been brought under precisely such form of control by the Chinese Government. The governments of India and China viewed this fundamental transformation in the long-established status of Tibet very differently (Garver 2001: 32). Chinese political leadership viewed the Tibetan region as an integral part of China and was determined to bring it under its direct administrative and military control and perceived India's expression of concern regarding any developments inside Tibet as manifestations of India's interference in the internal affairs of China. On the contrary, the then Indian Government under Prime Minister Jawaharlal Nehru viewed the permanent stationing of Chinese troops along its northern frontiers in Tibet since 1951 as constituting a major adverse change in the national security situation for India. While India before 1951 had faced no danger of military attack from the north, since 1951, India had to confront a large battle hardened Chinese People's Liberation Army (P.L.A.). Further, sections within

Indian political leadership and the public at large also lamented at that point of time because of the manner in which the Chinese political leadership incrementally destroyed Tibet's unique and deeply Indian influenced culture. By 1959, preservation of Tibet's unique cultural heritage had become an important mainstream concern for India.

India had initially tried to resist but was gradually compelled to accommodate China's creation of a new political reality in Tibet, which brought the Tibetan region under direct political and military control of China. From the very beginning since 1951, it became apparent to the Chinese political leadership that the Indian Government would not militarily intervene in Tibet, primarily due its weakness on that front. It has also been said that the British Government at that point of time had advised the then Indian Prime Minister Jawaharlal Nehru of not to attack China (Kalha 2012: 11). Nehru had made this clear in his several statements on numerous occasions, even before the Chinese People's Liberation Army attacked Tibet. India by the end of the twentieth century had largely adjusted to the irrevocable loss of its long extant Tibetan buffer vis-à-vis China.

China on its part, while being able to impose its will in Tibet, experienced serious vulnerabilities there. A considerable section of the Tibetans are extremely hostile towards the rule of the Chinese Communist Party over Tibet. China rules over an overwhelmingly sullen Tibetan population who are deeply resentful towards Chinese military takeover of their ancestral homeland. Rebellion against Chinese rule in Tibet constitutes an ever present danger to the political leadership of the Chinese Communist Party. Such rebellion against Chinese Communist Party's rule in Tibet has occurred on several occasions since 1951, with the two recent occasions being in 1988 and 2008 (BBC News 2008; Yardley 2008). Also, sporadic protests against Chinese rule over Tibet have continued to take place since 2008. And on every occasion, Chinese Government has deployed military force to crush such Tibetan uprisings against Chinese rule in Tibet. It is important to note in this connection that when Tibet is relatively peaceful, it is possible for both India and China to keep their fundamental disagreements on the back burner and move forward with the process of normalization of bilateral ties (Norbu 1997: 1078-95). However, when there is political unrest in Tibet, as it was in 1959, 2008 and several times thereafter, it comes back on cast a big shadow on the bilateral ties between these two states.

Further, internationally, although no foreign government openly challenges China's claims over Tibet, public opinion in several states, including in many Western democracies and even in India, has been appalled by what has befallen the Tibetan people and their culture under Chinese rule. An important objective of the Chinese political leadership has been to prevent these factors from coming together in a manner that would undermine Chinese Government's control over Tibet, possibly leading to its loss from China. The very basis of China's policy towards India regarding Tibet has been to exert pressure in order to compel the Indian Government to refrain from adopting policies and pursuing actions that might endanger Chinese control over Tibet. The nature of pressure includes periodic diplomatic protests as well as full-scale war with India in 1962.

It is significant to point out in this context that Mao Zedong had told a visiting Nepali delegation to China in 1964 that the major cause of the problem in China's bilateral ties with India leading to the border conflict of 1962 was not the problem over the disputed McMahon Line, but the question over Tibet (Garver 2001: 59; Kalha 2012: 7). Contemporary Chinese Studies on the 1962 border conflict are in line with Mao Zedong's analysis because they also perceived an Indian effort to turn Tibet into a buffer zone between India and China as a major cause behind the 1962 conflict. The Tibetan issue was a critical and central factor that resulted in deterioration of bilateral ties between India and China that ultimately culminated in the 1962 border conflict. In the opinion of several Chinese scholars, Indian Government's support to the Tibetan separatists including the Dalai Lama was the decisive factor that led to the Sino-Indian border conflict of 1962. Some Chinese officials also believed that the Indian Government had provided encouragement to the Lhasa uprisings of 1959. Therefore, irrespective of whether India had adopted the forward policy along the disputed frontier with

China or not, the Tibetan issue became an important factor in the gradual deterioration of bilateral ties between India and China in the decade of the 1950's and Chinese political leaderships' misperception about Indian Government's intentions on Tibet had prepared the ground for the 1962 border conflict between these two Asian states.

II

From the Chinese perspective, the presence and putative political activities of the Dalai Lama and more than hundred thousand Tibetan activists in India since 1959 constitutes a major source of uneasiness and friction in bilateral relations with India. Although the Indian Government had recognized China's authority over Tibet through the 1954 Agreement and later by the Agreement of 2003 (signed during then Indian Premier Atal Behari Vajpayee's visit to China), Chinese Government views the granting of political asylum to Dalai Lama and the existence of the Tibetan Government in exile at Dharamshala in India even today with deep sense of suspicion and distrust. The Chinese political leadership has also been deeply concerned about the growth of India's military power, particularly its nuclear and ballistic missile capabilities in the aftermath of the 1998 nuclear tests conducted by India. The signing of the India-US civilian nuclear agreement in March 2006 and the India-United States Framework Agreement on Defence in June 2005 has further accentuated the Chinese leadership's concern about India because they viewed these developments as indicators of India's emergence as a major power (Malik 2009: 166-67). Also the India-US nuclear deal and the regular joint naval exercises between India and the United States has been viewed by the Chinese political leadership as an attempt to contain China's future rise (Frankel 2011: 1-17).

It is primarily against this backdrop that China has hardened its position in settling the long-standing boundary dispute with India in the last few years. Incursions by People's Liberation Army personnel into territories claimed by India all along the Line of Actual Control in both the eastern and western sectors have increased significantly in the last one decade. In spite of steady improvement in bilateral ties, particularly in the economic arena in the last two decades, the dispute over the frontier has remained as a constant source of irritant between these two Asian neighbours. Several rounds of negotiations at the level of joint working group on the boundary dispute between both sides have failed to achieve any breakthrough in settling the issue in the last two and a half decades. It seems that both India and China exhibit a peculiar case of 'constrained cooperation' in which the convergence of their economic interests tend to conceal their prevailing strategic and political differences. These strategic and political differences, of which the dispute over the frontier and the issue of Tibet are the foremost, have the potential to upstage the bilateral ties, even if temporarily, at any point of time. The incidents of border incursions at Depsang valley in April 2013, at Chumar area of Ladakh in September 2014 and at several places across the disputed frontier in the recent past needs to be viewed in this light (Joshi 2013; *The Indian Express* 2014). It is significant to note that in spite of several confidence building agreements in the last two decades between the governments of India and China in 1993, 1996, 2005 and 2012 and despite numerous meetings of the joint working group on the boundary dispute, incidents such as the one at the Depsang valley and at Chumar occurred when a platoon of Chinese PLA personnel intruded deep inside territory claimed by India.

Incidents involving incursions by the P.L.A. personnel are to a large extent due to the fact that the Line of Actual Control (LAC) has not been delineated on the ground till date and there exists large chunks of territory, which are claimed by both India and China. Given that both India and China have not mutually agreed upon the actual delineation of the LAC on the ground, sporadic incidents of transgressions across the frontier by both sides appears to be a useful ploy to exert their respective claims over territories across the LAC. The LAC is not physically demarcated on the ground and there seems to be reluctance on part of the Chinese Government to do so in order to keep India under constant political and strategic pressure. However, it also constitutes an astute strategy on part of the Chinese army and political leadership to buttress their claims all along the disputed frontier and keep the Indian political leadership under political and strategic pressure. In fact, the issue of Tibet has been very closely connected with the unsettled boundary dispute between India and China. Through an unsettled boundary, China wants to retain the strategic leverage by keeping India uncertain about its future intentions and preventing India from doing any mischief in Tibet, which could jeopardize Chinese interests. Tibet, in the psyche of the most of the Chinese political leaders still constitutes an arena where India could respond by following indirect strategies to any future augmentation of the security challenges that China poses to India through building close political, economic and military ties with states on India's periphery like Myanmar and Pakistan.

One of the core concerns of the Chinese Government is to stabilize Tibet and they have advocated, particularly in the last one decade that there are strong historical and cultural linkages between Tibet proper and the disputed areas, most notably Tawang. For the present Chinese political leadership, Tawang is not only a part of the Sino-Indian territorial dispute, but is also inseparably connected with the issue of stability of Tibet (Shukla 2015). In fact, the Chinese Government claims that Arunachal Pradesh, which it calls southern Tibet, is a major part of the territorial dispute with India and perhaps also associates the stability of Tibet with Tawang. According to one Chinese scholar, the Chinese people basically understand that the territorial dispute with India is concerned mainly in the eastern sector along the disputed McMahon Line, under which the area of Tawang falls. In the western sector, only the specialists are aware that India claims certain parts of the Aksai Chin region, which are under Chinese control at present.

There are important political and strategic reasons behind the recent thrust of the Chinese Government on laying claims over the area of Tawang. Quite significantly, some analysts believe that former Chinese President Hu Jintao's desire to control the choice of the next Dalai Lama had led to pressuring India to concede access to the Tawang monastery, which is crucial for exercising this choice (Malik 2007). It was from around 2006 onwards, during the tenure of Hu Jintao, that China had started to harden its position in settling the boundary dispute with India by reasserting its claims on the areas in the eastern sector, particularly Tawang. The deterioration of bilateral ties during the tenure of Hu Jintao, however, must not come as a surprise given his reputation as a hardliner over Tibet. After all, it is important to remember that late Deng Xiaoping had groomed him for the Chinese Communist Party leadership because of his prominent role in successful suppression of the Tibetan rebellion of 1988. Moreover, the rapid pace of development of road, rail and military infrastructure by China in Tibet close to its borders with India and Nepal is viewed as pre-empting the possibility of any prospective destabilization inside Tibet in the future.

Moreover, the assertiveness of the Chinese Government since 2006 on laying its claims on territories along the eastern sector can be seen from its objection to an Asian Development Bank (ADB) proposal in 2009 for developmental assistance to India for a watershed development project in Arunachal Pradesh to control floods. There was a major confrontation between India and China in the Asian Development Bank (ADB) in March 2009 as China was digging its heels in and was not giving consent to ADB's US$ 2.9 billion India development plan unless the mention of Arunachal Pradesh is removed from the plan document. Within this India development plan, a sum of US$ 60 million is marked for watershed development project, including flood management in Arunachal Pradesh (Samanta 2009). All the member states on the board of executive directors of ADB except China supported the funding plans for India (*India eNews* 2009). The ADB thereafter asked India to resolve the matter bilaterally provoking a very strong reaction from India. India had categorically told the ADB that it would rather withdraw from the entire plan than conceding on China's demands on Arunachal Pradesh by removing it from the stated ADB plan document for the sake of financial approval. India even stated its desire to look for alternative sources of funding if the matter was not resolved in India's favour (Samanta 2009). It is also significant to note in this connection that ADB does not have a policy for projects to be located in disputed areas. China considers the territory of Arunachal Pradesh as disputed and claims that the entire territory belongs to China. The Indian Foreign Minister Mr. S.M. Krishna stated in the Rajya Sabha that the Indian Government had categorically told the ADB member states that China's objection to ADB funding for India on political grounds is a clear violation of the ADB charter, which prohibits the bank from evaluating any proposal on grounds other than economic. He further stated that India has unequivocally told all the member states of the ADB including China in the strongest possible diplomatic language that the territory of Arunachal Pradesh is an integral part of India and its status is not negotiable. Ultimately, the ADB had accepted India's point of view on this particular issue.

In recent years, like in November 2011, the scheduled meeting of the India-China joint working group on the boundary dispute was suddenly postponed as India refused to budge on the issue of allowing Tibetan spiritual leader Dalai Lama to address the world congregation of Buddhists at New Delhi during the same time (*India Today* 2011). China was unhappy because the dates of the joint working group meeting and the world congregation of Buddhists at New Delhi had accidentally coincided. India maintained that being a functional democracy, it cannot possibly cancel an event that is cultural and religious and not political in its orientation. As India refused to cancel the event, the scheduled meeting of the India-China joint working group on the boundary dispute was postponed temporarily. All these instances show that the Tibetan issue and the activities of the Tibetan Spiritual leader Dalai Lama still constitutes a critical factor as far as India-China bilateral ties are concerned.

Conclusion

Therefore, there is no gainsaying the fact that the issue of settlement of the Sino-Indian boundary dispute is intimately connected with the issue of political stability in Tibet. Notwithstanding the real and positive economic changes inside Tibet since the launching of economic reforms in China under late Deng Xiaoping, the protests in Tibet since 1988 demonstrates that the region's integration into China still remains fragile. When Tibet remains relatively peaceful, there remains tranquillity in Sino-Indian bilateral ties. With the situation in Tibet becoming restive just prior to the Beijing Olympics in 2008, the Chinese Government went into overdrive around the world to limit its consequences, and no more directly than in India, the home of the Tibetan Government in exile. It can be seen that China has started to become more assertive in expressing its claims over the territory in Arunachal Pradesh almost around the same time. Also, the number of incursions by P.L.A. personnel across the disputed L.A.C. in both the eastern and western sectors increased several-fold from this time onwards. It was also around the same time in 2008 that the Chinese Government started the policy of issuing stapled visas (visas issued on a separate piece of paper stapled to passports) to Indian citizens domiciled in Jammu and Kashmir who wish to travel to China, thereby attempting to put a question mark over the territorial status of Jammu and Kashmir as part of India (Jacob 2011). There were several instances since 2008 when Indian citizens residing in Jammu and Kashmir were issued stapled visas by the Chinese Government. India-China bilateral ties have always been sensitive to the internal situation in Tibet (Raja Mohan 2013: 197). From the perspective of the Chinese Government, the issue of maintaining their control and stability in Tibet is more important than settling the boundary dispute with India (Shukla 2015). If political unrest in Tibet subsides and the region stabilizes in future, China might be more flexible in settling the boundary dispute with India. However, since 1988 and particularly after March 2008, there were several instances of political resistance by Tibetans against Chinese rule in Tibet resulting in armed clashes between the Chinese P.L.A. and the Tibetan protesters leading to the death of several Tibetans (BBC News 2011). There have been several incidents of self-immolation by Tibetan protesters in the last few years as a form of protest against the harsh Chinese Communist Party's rule inside Tibet. One of the latest incidents occurred in March 2012 when a Tibetan woman set herself on fire in China's South-Western Sichuan province to protest against Chinese rule in Tibet. According to one estimate, this was the twenty-third incident of self-immolation being carried out by the Tibetans between 2011 and 2012 (ABC News 2012).

Under the prevailing political situation in Tibet, a section of the Indian political elite display an increased willingness to play a hard-nosed game of political bargaining with China over Tibet. So far, the Indian Government has stayed away from adopting any such position that can be said to have constituted a major departure from the terms of the 1954 and the 2003 agreements with China. However, given the degree of current political unrest and discontentment inside Tibet against Chinese Communist Party's rule, the Chinese Government is apprehensive that if a future situation inside Tibet turns more explosive, it might provide ample political ammunition to the Indian Government to take political and strategic advantage out of such a situation. And this apprehension on part of the present Chinese political leadership is one of the most important reasons, which has led to a hardening of China's position in settling the disputed frontier with India in order to keep the latter under constant political and strategic pressure. It is interesting to note in this context that China has so far settled all its land-boundary related disputes with its other neighbouring states, with India being the sole exception. The issue of Tibet will remain as a critical factor in defining the future course of India's bilateral ties with China and will continue to cast its shadow on the unsettled boundary dispute between these two states.

References

ABC News (2012, March 05). Tibetan burns herself to death in China protest. From http://www.abc.net.au/news/2011-03-05/ (Accessed on February 14, 2015).

BBC News (2008, June 19). Q & A: China and Tibet. From http://news.bbc.co.uk/2/hi/7299221.stm (Accessed on February 10, 2015).

______. (2011, August 15). Q & A: China and the Tibetans. From http://www.bbc.co.uk/news/world14533879 (Accessed on February 08, 2015).

Frankel, Francine (2011). The Breakout of China-India Strategic Rivalry in Asia and the Indian Ocean. *Journal of International Affairs*, Spring/Summer, 64 (2): 1-17.

Garver, John (2001). *Protracted Contest: Sino-Indian Rivalry in the Twentieth Century*. New Delhi: Oxford University Press.

Gupta, Karunakar (1974). *The Hidden History of the Sino-Indian Frontier*. Calcutta: Minerva Associates.

Hoffman, Steven (1990). *India and the China Crisis*. Berkeley: University of California Press.

India eNews (2009, July 10). China objected to ADB loan to India for Arunachal Pradesh: Krishna. From http://www.indiaenews.com/india/20090710/207402.htm (Accessed on November 04, 2015).

India Today (2011, November 26). China demand on Dalai meet let to border talks cancellation. From http://indiatoday.intoday.in/story/ (Accessed on February 14, 2015).

Jacob, Jabin T. (2011, July 26). Focusing on Arunachal. *The New Indian Express*. From http://expressbuzz.com/edition/print.aspx?artid=298127 (Accessed on September 22, 2015).

Joshi, Manoj (2013, May 07). Making sense of the Depsang incursions. *The Hindu*. From http://www.thehindu.com/opinion/op-ed/making-sense-of-the-depsang-incursion/article4689838.ece (Accessed on January 31, 2016).

Kalha, R.J. (2012). Tibet as a Factor in Sino-Indian Relations: Past and Present. *Journal of Defence Studies*, 6(4): 7-26.

Malik, Mohan J. (2007, October 09). India-China Competition Revealed in Ongoing Border Disputes. *Power and Interest News Report* (PINR). From http://www.pinr.com/report.php?ac=view_printable&report_id=695&language (Accessed on 31 May 2015).

_______ (2009). India and China: As China Rises, India Stirs. In Harsh V. Pant (Ed.), *Indian Foreign Policy in a Uni polar World* (163-91). New Delhi: Routledge.

Maxwell, Neiville (1970). *India's China War*. New York: Pantheon Books.

Norbu, Dawa (1997). Tibet in Sino-Indian Relations: The Centrality of Marginality. *Asian Survey*, 37 (11): 1078-95.

Raja Mohan, C. (2013). *Samudra Manthan: Sino Indian Rivalry in the Indo-Pacific*. New Delhi: Oxford University Press.

Samanta, Pranab Dhal (2009, May 15). India-China face-off worsens over ADB loan for Arunachal. *The Indian Express*. From http://www.indianexpress.com/news/indiachina-faceoff-worsens-over-adb-loan-for-arunachal/459910/ (Accessed on October 30, 2015).

Shukla, Ajai (2015, May 14). Beijing Believes unrest in Tibet linked with Tawang: Zhang Li. *Business Standard*. From http://www.

business-standard.com/article/printer-friendly-version?article_id=115051301282_1 (Accessed on January 28, 2016).

The Indian Express (2014, September 20). Standoff worsens as Chinese troops enter Chumar region again. From http://indianexpress.com/article/india/india-others/another-chinese-intrusion-in-chumar/ (Accessed on January 31, 2016).

Yardley, Jim (2008, March 14). Monk Protest in Tibet Draw Chinese Security. *The New York Times*. From http://www.nytimes.com/2008/03/14/ (Accessed on February 10, 2015).

13

India and Japan: Strategic Partners in the New Era

Chandrima Chaudhuri

In 2006, the Indian Prime Minister Manmohan Singh stated at the Joint Session of the Diet that India and Japan needs to build a strong global and strategic partnership that will have a great significance for Asia and the world as a whole. With the new government coming to power in New Delhi, the shift from 'Look East Policy' to 'Act East Policy' was announced. The tenure of Prime Minister Modi also coincides with India's third decade of 'Look East Policy'. This was in reaction to the criticism that India in the past decades did not have a consistent policy towards this region. Thus in the last two decades there has been a shift from a low key relationship to strategic relationship between India and Japan. The relationship is on an all-time high with large number of diplomatic exchanges taking place. Since historical times, both these countries had showed no real sign of friction and thus they have carried forward their friendship till date. The relationship is based on mutual respect and shared values on democracy, rule of law and human rights. The bilateral ties are expected to get a boost from the personal camaraderie between Japan's Shinzo Abe and India's Narendra Modi.

Historical Background

India and Japan have a strong historical relationship could be seen from the fact that during the seventh century, Buddhism travelled to Japan from India through China and Korea. After that in the beginning of the twentieth century there have been cultural and intellectual exchanges between Rabindranath Tagore and Okakura Tenshin which had a huge impact on both the societies. The Japan-India Association was also set up in 1903. India admired the way in which the Japanese defeated the Russians in 1905. It served as an inspiration for them in their fight against the British. The Japanese occupation of the entire Southeast Asia between 1940-45 by driving out all the major powers like the British, Dutch, and American left a huge impression on the nationalist leaders. Japan also helped India in its struggle for independence by providing support to Netaji Subhash Chandra Bose and his INA (Indian National Army).

Post-War Period of Friendship and Goodwill

In the post-War period, Judge Radha Binod Rai's judgment during Tokyo Trials and Nehru's decision of renunciation war reparations helped in continuing the cordial relations with Japan. India refused to sign the San Francisco treaty as it considered it to be a Cold War arrangement. It established diplomatic relations with Japan in 1952 and in the same year signed a separate agreement as well to waiver off the reparation claims against Japan. India took proactive steps to engage with Japan at that time when most of the other countries had shunned it. This invited Japan to participate at the New Delhi Asian Games in 1951. It supported Japan's membership in the UN. India also strong supported Japanese participation in the Bandung Conference in 1955 even though Japan was a part of the US camp that time. All these have helped in creating a positive image of India in Japan. As a sign of friendly relations, the Japanese Prime Minister Nobusuke Kishi visited India which resulted in the flow of Japanese yen loans to India. In return Jawaharlal Nehru paid a visit to Japan later that year followed by the Indian President Rajendra Prasad's visit to Japan in 1958. Sinha and Nataraj (2013) mentions that "India was the first country to receive ODA from Japan in 1958 and still it is one of the largest receiver of Japanese ODA" (Sinha and Nataraj 2013). The visit by Japanese Prince Akihito and Princess Michiko to India in 1960 also helped in taking the relationship forward.

Cold War Era: Period of Temporary Setback

As a result of the Cold War politics, the world got divided into two camps. As a result, the ideological differences acted as obstacles in their path of developing friendly relations. Lack of mutual trust and conflicting interests between them affected the relationship negatively. The relationship hit an all-time low during the Cold War period with Japan concentrating on its own economic reconstruction while on the other hand India was struggling to maintain an independent foreign policy. India at that time wanted that the newly independent countries should not become victim to the bloc politics and thus started the non-alignment movement. Japan could not understand India's intentions and thought India to be a chaotic country. India on the other hand, thought Japan to be a part of the US camp and hence a part of the bloc politics something which India was completely opposed to. Japan also did not take any interest in India because of the isolationist economic policies of India during that period. Thus, these six decades of stagnation were the worst period in their bilateral relationship.

Post-Cold War Era: Improving Relationship

Indian Council for Research on International Economic Relations (2008) mentions that the relationship started improving and in the 1980s, these countries collaborated to produce small cars in India under the banner of Maruti-Suzuki (ICRIER 2008: 9). Initially, India's 'Look East Policy' launched by Prime Minister Narasimha Rao in 1990s did not generate much interest among the Japanese. It was only when Japan started facing economic problems and the success of the Look East Policy made it take notice of India. The visit of the Japanese Prime Minister Kaifu to India helped in warming up of relations. This was followed by the visit of Prime Minister Narasimha Rao to Japan in 1992 which also marked the 40th anniversary of post-war bilateral relations. This visit yielded positive results with both the heads of government deciding to add new dimensions to the relationship. But soon there was a break in the relationship with India conducting nuclear test in May 1998. During the period from 1998-2000 the relationship had hit rock bottom with Japan taking an aggressive stand against India's stand at different international forums. During that time Japan also had revised its ODA Charter which prevented from giving ODA to nuclear weapon states. Thus, it suspended its ODA and also called back its ambassador and suspended all channels of communication. This led India to believe that Japan did not did not understand India's position.

The visit by the Japanese Prime Minister Mori Yoshihiro in 2000 marked a new phase in the relationship with both the countries emphasizing on a "Global Partnership" in the 21st century. The US also started to improve its ties with India which gave a positive push to India-Japan relations as well. In the next year, Japan also removed the sanctions it had imposed on India because of the nuclear tests conducted by the latter. This has paved the way for high-level visits between these countries. The visit of Junichiro Koizumi in 2005 was also a turning point with the Manmohan Singh-Koizumi Statement being issued containing the 8-point initiative which finally helped in taking forward the bilateral relations. They decided to not only cooperate through bilateral channels, but also at multilateral level and global levels. Panda (2010) writes that in 2006, these governments decided to establish a "Strategic and Global Partnership between Japan and India" which was a "roadmap for building multi-layered bilateral relations" (Panda 2010: 4). Khan (2014) writes that they had also agreed to hold summit-level talks at an annual basis alternatively between Tokyo and Delhi which have been held without disruption since then (Khan 2014: 2). With Abe coming to power, this relationship got an upsurge. Chellaney (2007) writes that Abe has always been a supporter for strong India-Japan relations can be seen from the fact that, in his book *Towards a Beautiful Country: My Vision for Japan*, mentioned it might happen that "in another decade, Japan-India relations overtake Japan-US and Japan-China ties" (Chellaney 2007). During his visit to India, he was accompanied by a large group of businessmen, thus emphasizing on their interest to engage with India economically. This was followed by the Joint Declaration on Security Cooperation between India and Japan which emphasized apart from other things, the need to coordinate policies in maintaining peace and stability in the region. This was a significant declaration since Japan had signed such kind of declaration only with the US and Australia.

When Yukio Hatoyama from the Democratic Party of Japan (DPJ) came to power after Abe in Japan, India was skeptical whether he would continue the pace of this bilateral relation. But his visit to India in 2009 put to rest all doubts. Kesavan (2010) writes that "both the heads of the government decided to take forward the relationship by launching the action plan. This plan contained steps to be taken by these countries in nine areas, including strategic and defence cooperation mechanisms, maritime security, safety of transport, cooperation at the UN, disaster management, and cooperation on disarmament and non-proliferation. They also decided to hold annually a comprehensive 2+2 security dialogue at the cabinet/senior official level" (Kesavan 2010: 15).

The China Factor

In the recent times, the rise of China has brought about changes in the power structure in the Asia Pacific region. From the late 1990s, China started its military modernization which raised concerns among powers. Over the years, due to its aggressive claims in the South China Sea, the Southeast Asian powers started perceiving China as a threat. Japan's dispute with China over the Senkaku islands has resulted in boycott of Japanese products in China. On the other hand, India's border dispute with China has resulted in India and Japan cooperating to meet this China challenge. China has modernized its navy and has developed the blue water navy. Both these countries have recognized the fact that China is an integral part in the changing international scenario. Japan's India policy is largely shaped by the Chinese threat has been openly declared by the Japanese officials. Though India has till date not openly joined hands with Japan to balance China, but their security and defence cooperation are definite indicators of the fact that both these countries are in favour of freedom of navigation and safety of sea line of communications. China in the recent times has been asserting its claims aggressively in the South China which has affected adversely the interests of both India and Japan. Panda (2014) writes that India has economic stakes there since the ONGC Videsh had acquired oil blocks off Vietnam in 2011 (Panda 2014: 189). The strategic dimension of Abe's India policy was interpreted as a move to counterbalance the growing influence of China in Asia. But India is treading very cautiously in its move to balance China. China's rise, both militarily and economically, has been one of the significant factors that has shaped Japan's Asia policy in general and India in particular. China has become suspicious about the warming up of relations between India and Japan. The warm reception given to Modi during his visit to Japan in August 2014 by Abe created suspicions in the minds of the Chinese policy-makers by openly stating that the bilateral relations with India has "the greatest potential of any bilateral relationship anywhere in the world". Due to the hostile relations with China, Japan now has been trying to shift their investments to India. During Abe's first term, he had talked about a strategic quadrangle with Japan, India, Australia and the US. This created suspicions in the minds of the Chinese policy-makers who viewed this as an attempt to contain its presence in the region. But both these countries should keep in mind that China is their biggest trading partner and hence they cannot afford to provoke it.

The US Influence

Mr. Richard L. Armitage, former US deputy secretary of state, pointed out that US needs 'strong Japan' when he published the report "US-Japan Alliance" co-authored by him and Prof. Joseph S. Nye of the Harvard University. As a "Natural Ally" or a "Linchpin", US needs a strong India too. Japan and India are candidates to fill the power vacuum in Asia. Hence, "US would want to support the coalition of Japan and India" as reported by *The Times of India*, 2010 (India a natural ally...). The Indo-US nuclear deal signed in 2006 by which India received nuclear technology was a positive development for improvement in India-Japan relations as well. The US pushed Japan to improve its ties with India. Both the US and Japan are aware that a strong and stable India would benefit them in balancing China in region. Thus, currently there have been converges of economic and security interest between these three countries in the Asia Pacific region. The first trilateral exercises were conducted in 2007 between India, Japan and the US. Later that year, the Indo-US Malabar naval exercise was transformed into multilateral exercise involving the US, India, Japan, Australia and Singapore. Vardarajan (2007) argues that "China grew suspicious and started to protest against this initiative. India and Australia did not openly want to oppose China and thus, this initiative was stopped" (Varadarajan, 2007). In 2011, India and Japan and the US initiated a strategic partnership for discussion on maintaining the balance in Asia-Pacific and maritime security in the Indo-Pacific waters. These countries have been cooperating at the multilateral level like EAS and the ASEAN Defence Ministers' Meeting Plus to discuss political and security issues. At the same time, there is a need for these countries to cooperate at the economic level as well. Thus, the US wants to collaborate with both India and Japan to ensure that the rise of China is peaceful and it does not affect the regional stability.

Political Cooperation

Several mechanisms have been established by these countries for political cooperation which help in guaranteeing the relations remain cordial irrespective of whichever party remains in power. There have been a lot of meetings taking place between the Members of Parliament since 2004. Annual Summit between the Prime Ministers has been taking place since 2006. They have also organized the Annual Strategic Dialogue at the Foreign Minister level. Under the auspices of FICCI, the India-Japan forum was also established in 2005. In 2012, these countries celebrated the 60th-anniversary of establishing diplomatic relations. During the visit of Indian Prime Minister Manmohan Singh in 2013 a Joint Statement titled, "Strengthening the Strategic and Global Partnership between Japan and India beyond the 60th Anniversary of Diplomatic Relations" was signed. The Japanese Emperor Akihito and Empress Michiko visited India at the end of that year. Shinzo Abe was invited to be the Chief

Guest at India's Republic Day parade in 2014. These visits are an indication that India is also keen to engage with Japan.

Defence Cooperation

Japan thinks that India can maintain stability in the Indian Ocean as in the recent times, India has emerged as a strong naval power. Several mechanisms are available for security and defence purposes—the Foreign Ministers Strategic Dialogue and Defense Ministers Dialogue, a new dialogue between the respective national security advisors—launched following the establishment of Japan's National Security Secretariat, and a so-called 2+2 Dialogue amongst their foreign and defense secretary levels (i.e., not at full ministerial level). Apart from these mechanisms, there are dialogue mechanisms and joint exercises between these countries. India and Japan are both concerned about maintaining the peace and stability in the Indian Ocean and thus they have undertaken joint exercises to control piracy. India and Japan have common interests in maritime security. As a result, they started Japan-India Maritime Exercise (JIMEX) in 2012. They have been exchanging information and coordinating their policies on security issues in the Asia Pacific region. In 2013, the chief of army staff of India visited Japan followed by the Japanese chief of Self Defence Forces paying a visit to India. During Modi's visit to Japan, it was also agreed to remove some of the Indian defence enterprises from the "End Users list". After Abe came back to power in 2012, he removed the restrictions on the sale of defence related technology to India. They also have been negotiating on the sale of the Japanese amphibious aircraft US-2 to respond to China's 'string of pearls' in the Indian Ocean.

Civil Nuclear Cooperation

Unlike other areas, there has not been much progress in this field. Even though they have been holding talks since 2010 but there has been no substantive outcome so far. India and Japan hold opposing views on the Nuclear Non-Proliferation Treaty. While India considers this treaty to be discriminatory for the non-nuclear powers, Japan believes it to be necessary for a nuclear free world. Khan (2014) writes that "in 2011, the negotiations were started by the Japanese Foreign Minister Katsuya Okada during his visit to India and he considered it to be the toughest decision that he had to take" (Khan 2014: 2). While the business lobby in Japan puts pressure on the government to go forward with the deal as India provides a large number of contracts for the Japanese companies. But on the other hand, the anti-nuclear lobby and the media provide strong opposition to the deal. In 2011, the Fukushima nuclear accident in Japan halted the talks on the civil nuclear deal. Khan (2014) mentioned that "India needs some key components from Japan for installing nuclear power plants". Though many Japanese companies have signed agreements with India to help set up nuclear power plants, "but without the nuclear deal in force these companies cannot go ahead with the installation" (Khan 2014: 1). Japan not only wants to retain the right to suspend its cooperation in case India conducts nuclear test, but also does not want to give India the right to reprocess spent fuel. These countries still have to go a long way in overcoming the deadlock in the field of nuclear cooperation.

Economic Cooperation

The economic relationship till date has remained quite far below the potential. These countries have complementary economic structure where the service sector is the largest contributor to the economy. Pal Chaudhuri (2015) writes that the number of Japanese firms operating in India has risen from 301 in 2005 to 1072 in 2013 (Pal Chaudhuri 2015: 4). Currently, the Japanese FDI to India is very low, with India accounting for only 1.2 per cent. The Japanese investments can mainly be seen in sectors such as automobiles, service sector and drugs and pharmaceuticals. In 2006, India and Japan had teamed up for the construction of Delhi-Mumbai Industrial corridor where the Japanese had invested US$ 100 billion. After successfully completing the project, they have again collaborated for building Chennai-Bangalore industrial corridor. India has sought help from Japan to build infrastructure in its northeast states. China stopped exporting rare earth materials to Japan needed to manufacture high-tech products, India decided to provide them with it. Greater economic engagement with Japan would benefit

India by having access to the markets of the other countries in the region. Both the leading political parties of Japan have accepted the benefits of greater economic engagement with India. After much negotiation, the Comprehensive Economic Partnership Agreement was signed in 2011. Khan (2014) writes that "both the countries agreed to reduce tariffs on around 90,000 products and also provide equal treatment to each other's investors in order to improve the bilateral trade. Though the trade had increased in 2012 but it did not reach the expected target in 2013" (Khan 2014: 4). The investments have also not grown as expected. India being the second most populous country in the world has huge resources as well as market. Japan wants to tap that market for its manufactured goods. India can provide raw materials to the resource-hungry Japan. India can take advantage of Japan's technology to produce manufactured goods. The full potential of two-way trade has not been fully tapped. This is evident from the fact that the volume of bilateral trade between Japan and China is greater than its trade with India. Both the governments have been discussing how to improve the volume of trade. Modi during his visit to Japan reassured the investors about a change in the investment environment in India. As reported by the *Financial Times* (2014) "The visit of Modi to Japan resulted in Abe announcing to invest US$ 35 billion over a period of five years in Indian infrastructure" (The Latest Special Relationship...).

People to People Contacts

As early as 1870s, Indians started visiting Japan for commercial purposes. These Indians who were involved in the business of textiles and electronics had close linkages with India. They had also established the Indian Merchants Association in Yokohama (IMAY) in 1929. But in the past few decades a large number of Indian professionals working in both Indian and Japanese firms have settled in Japan. Over the years, the number of Indians staying in Japan has also increased. As a result, a locality in Tokyo-Nishikasai is called as 'mini-India'. This community apart from playing an important role in promoting Indian culture and values also mingle with their

Japanese neighbours as well. In course of time this community has become valuable members of the Japanese community.

In the recent times, a number of MOUs in the educational sector has been signed by these governments. The India Japan Science Council was established in 1993 which led to the holding of academic seminars, research projects and visits by scientists from both the countries. The University of Tokyo and the Tokyo Institute of Technology and the Indian Institute of Technology have collaborated for educational exchanges. Since 2007, under the Japan-East Asia Network of Exchange for Students and Youths (JENESYS) programme, a number of Indian students are selected to visit Japan. In 2010, the Japanese Ministry of Education and Science had established an Indian Centre. During Abe's visit to India in 2014, an implementation arrangement for the Science and Technology was signed.

Importance of Modi-Abe Meeting

The change in leadership in both the countries has brought about a new dynamism in the relationship. The visit of Narendra Modi to Japan within 100 days of his coming to power is a strong signal to the fact that India wants to build a substantial partnerships with it. The Japanese Prime Minister Shinzo Abe has also been very proactive in building a strategic partnership with India. India and Japan share the same democratic ideology which has helped in developing the relationship from a low-key to a strategic partnership over the years. The Modi Government has also emphasized the importance of Japan in transforming India's economy. He mentioned that he was very impressed by the efficiency of Japanese businessmen and wanted to replicate that in India. During the meeting, Abe pledged to invest US$ 35 million on development of infrastructure in India. One positive outcome of his visit was the elevation of this strategic relation to a "special strategic and global partnership". There was also a renewed push for greater economic engagement. They also agreed on cooperation in some new areas like construction of high speed railways and transport system, cleaning up of the Ganges and other rivers and development of cities in India. On these lines, they have also decided to cooperate on making

Varanasi a smart city similar to Kyoto in Japan. Japan has also agreed to provide the necessary skills to the Indians in starting a bullet train from Mumbai to Ahmedabad. They also signed a Memorandum of Cooperation and Exchanges in the field of Defence. They also stressed the importance of maritime cooperation. Modi and Abe issued the Tokyo Declaration in September, 2014 through which they committed themselves to increase their engagement for the successful implementation of the India-Japan Strategic and Global Partnership. The Modi Government had mentioned India's economic growth as one of its priorities in its election campaign. To achieve that economic growth, India requires Japanese investments.

Apart from the convergences of interest, there are hurdles in the path of smooth bilateral relations as well. The Japanese businessmen have to face a lot of problems in India like bureaucratic delays, complex taxation process, land acquisition and environmental clearances. As a result only a few of them make profits in India. But the Modi Government is interested in expanding India's manufacturing base. For that he has set up an initiative called 'Japan Plus' to attract Japanese investments. He has also promised to transform India from a hostile to an investment friendly country. Though both the countries have emphasized on the importance of a civilian nuclear deal but still not much progress has been achieved till date.

Conclusion

India and Japan are considered to be "natural allies" as there has been no major conflict of interest between these countries unlike their relations with China which is characterized by rivalries. Instead they share a common goal of maintaining peace and stability in the Asia Pacific region. Since 2000, India-Japan relations have been steadily moving forward. India considers Japan to be a critical partner in its "Look East Policy". The Modi Government has also changed its "Look East Policy" to "Act East Policy" to show its commitment to engage with this region. Given the assertive role of China in the East China Sea, Japan also wants India to play a significant role in the region. The US also has stakes in the Asia Pacific region and thus, it is also giving a push to India for actively engaging with Japan in order to maintain a balance in the region. The personal ties between Modi and Abe have heralded the dawn of a new era in the bilateral relationship. India and Japan would continue to remain important to each other for future development. The shared values and common geo-political interests will pave the way for a lasting relationship. The current Indian Government is continuing the position of the previous government regarding Japan. This can be seen from the fact that the Indian Prime Minister chose Japan as the first country to visit outside South Asia. During his visit, he had emphasized the importance of Japan in transformation of India. Thus, it can be seen that there has been enormous progress given the fact that the bilateral relationship between India and Japan has acquired momentum only in the last decade. The changing international scenario has provided them with common grounds to take forward this multifaceted relationship.

References

Chellaney, Brahma (2007, August 16). Japan, India: natural allies. *The Japan Times.*

ICRIER-Indian Council for Research on International Economic Relations (2008). *Changing Paradigm of Indo-Japan Relations: Opportunities and Challenges* (Working Paper No. 212).

India a natural ally of US: Pentagon (2010). *The Times of India.* From http://timesofindia.indiatimes.com/india/India-a-natural-ally-of-US-Pentagon/articleshow/6974025.cms (Accessed on August 21, 2015).

Kesavan, K.V. (2010). India and Japan Changing Dimensions of Partnership in the post-Cold War period. *ORF Occasional Paper* (14).

Khan, Shamshad A. (2014). The Elusive India-Japan Nuclear Deal: It is time to bridge the differences to clinch the deal. *Indian Council of World Affairs Policy Brief.*

Pal Chaudhuri, Pramit (2015). India and Japan: A Nascent Strategic Bonding. *S. Rajaratnam School of International Studies Policy Brief.*

Panda, Rajaram (2010). Changing Dynamics of India-Japan Relations: Future Trends. *Slavic Eurasian Research Centre. India-Japan Dialogue.*

Panda, Rajaram (2014). India-Japan Relations: Dawn of a New Relationship? *Indian Foreign Affairs Journal* 9(2).

Sinha, R. and Nataraj, G. (2013, June 18). Japanese ODA Stimulates Indian Infrastructure Development. *East Asia Forum*. From http://www.eastasiaforum.org/2013/06/18/japanese-oda-stimulates-indianinfrastructure-development/ (Accessed on August 20, 2015).

The Latest Special Relationship in Asia (2014). *The Financial Times*. (2014). From http://www.ft.com/intl/cms/s/0/d7558ebc-337d-11e4-85f1-00144feabdc0.html?siteedition=intl#axzz3CK4OHP4Y (Accessed on August 04, 2015).

Varadarajan, Siddharth (2007, June 20). Four power meeting drew Chinese demarche: US-Japan keen to rope in India in quadrilateral security cooperation. *Global Research*. From http:/www.globalresearch.ca/index/php?context=va&aid=6100 (Accessed on August 18, 2015).

14

Recent Trends in India-Pakistan Relations: Track II Diplomacy as an Alternative

Debasish Nandy

Introduction

Relations between India and Pakistan have been marked by hostility and bitterness since their birth. The descending curve of Indo-Pak relations reflected the bilateral antagonism. M.P. Singh and Veena Kukreja have rightly observed that during the last six decades, Indo-Pakistan relations have not gone beyond the framework of mutual suspicion and discord. This perception goes as an input into the decision-making apparatus and policy formulation, and further strengthens the same 'national psyche' (Singh and Kukreja 2005: 258). Both are concerned of each other's foreign and security policies. Islamabad and New Delhi have developed adversarial relationship with each other from the beginning. As Stephen P. Cohen opined that "the origins of Indo-Pakistan conflict have been traced to many sources: the cupidity of the British in their failed management of the partition; the deeply rooted antagonisms between the Subcontinent's major religious communities, Hindus and Muslims; the struggle for control over Kashmir and shortsightedness of leaders on both sides of the border" (Cohen 2005: 198). The strings of wars and crises that have erupted in the course of this enduring rivalry have left little room for optimism about its prospect (Paul 2005). In this paper, I will discuss on the complexities of Indo-Pak Relations and later on, shed light about the effectiveness of Track II diplomacy between the two.

Perceptional Differences between New Delhi and Islamabad

When a relationship starts with antagonism, then it might hardly transform into friendship. On the basis of 'two nation theory' India and Pakistan were created as two sovereign states with separate entity. India introduced a liberal democratic system with a secular point of view; on the other hand, Pakistan also adapted a democratic system with rigid Islamic rule. Just after independence persecutions on minorities were started by majority, where role of government was just like a silent spectator. Pakistan viewed India's secularism as a false consciousness. Both countries are federal with plural society. Pakistan is a worst example of pluralism, India, on the other hand, a classic example of pluralism. Regarding multiculturalism and communal tolerance, India's perception is different from Pakistan. Pakistan had started to built close ties with Islamic states. Its relationship with Islamic states has a dual purpose to seek an Islamic identity and obtain economic assistance (Chengappa 2004: 92). The founder of India's foreign policy, Jawaharlal Nehru's faith in *Panchsheel* laid the philosophical foundation of India's foreign policy. It was not an exclusive national objective but an inclusive, universal alternative to conflict, tension, violence and war. His policy of non-alignment was basically guided by internal political dynamics consisting of demand for social justice and liberal democratic system. Non-alignment (NAM) was an extension of the ideal (Nehru). India has pursued a consistent policy to keep at bay foreign powers from South Asian region. On the contrary, the leadership of Pakistan pursued an exaggerated and unrealistic policy of parity relationship with India. However, Indian democratic and liberal value system was not shown in Pakistan. For a long time, Pakistan was under military rule. There was a basic perceptional difference between militarily influenced Pakistan and democratized India in making of bilateralism. Pakistan's foreign policy perspectives were primarily framed by bureaucratic-military leadership. Due to this reason, New Delhi and Islamabad never attained the anticipated level of amity, cooperation and trust. Pakistan's imbalance of power vis-à-vis India is integral to its obsession with the Hindu dominated state policy (Chengappa 2004: 92).

Rajiv Gandhi was not interested in dealing with controversial issues. He showed specific concern for negotiations on non controversial issues in India's relations with Pakistan. During his tenure, as Prime Minister of India, both countries highlighted a mutual commitment not to attack each other. In diplomatic level, both countries talked several times to maintain status-quo and peace in border areas. But this was 'diplomacy of moment'. There was no consistency on behalf of Pakistan. Actually, Islamabad's policy towards New Delhi mostly is influenced by Washington. The US Government promised a huge military package of $4.02 billion for 1987-92 periods. To strengthen Pakistani air force Washington also supplied F-16 fighter planes to Pakistan. After receiving of this military hardware Pakistan had started to deployed more military to Indian border. Prime Minister I.K. Gujral adopted a friendly policy towards its neighbors. His policy is known as "Gujral Doctrine". The crux of this doctrine was to resolve the disputes with neighboring states with peaceful measures. Prime Minister Atal Behari Vajpayee also introduced "extended neighborhood policy".

The Impact of Pakistan's Internal Crises on Bilateral Relations

T.V. Paul, a South Asian Politics expert, has rightly pointed out that "the warrior state of Pakistan is, in part, built on a religious foundation. The dominant view in Pakistan is that as a Muslim state, Pakistan should exclusively protect Muslim interests. Successive Pakistani rulers, even when they were not devout Muslims, upheld vision. However, this Islamic identity is contested by the diverse ethnic affiliations of the Pakistanis even though almost all of them are Muslims" (Paul 2014: 127). Pakistan's quest for systematic national identity continues. The task of nation building in Pakistan involved a key problem, especially, the search for a national identity. In Pakistan, the stages of nation building have not been completed. A concept of nationalism has been imposed from the above. In spite of being an Islamic state, Pakistan has not been able to implement a policy of equilibrium for all of its Islamic ethnic groups. In a plural society, there is a general expectation that democratic state authority will adopt a policy of accommodation without any discrimination. Regarding ethnic deprivation, Pakistani Central Government is reluctant from the very beginnings, which lead to various civil wars in different parts of Pakistan. There are so many ethnic groups in Pakistan. Punjabi speaking migrants were settled in West Punjab. They were lucky, because most of the government jobs, political posts and higher military posts were occupied by Punjabi community. Punjabi domination was shown in every sector of Pakistan. From the very beginning, a deep dissatisfaction had been generated among the Muhajir, Sindh, Baluch and Pastuns community. Baluchistan remains an underdeveloped province in Pakistan. Due to bias and exclusion policy of federal government, Baluch had started a violent regional insurgent movement since 1970s. Today, Pakistan is known as a terrorist country, where fundamentalists and secessionists are playing key role. Through the equal distribution of revenues, proper development, and policy of inclusion, Pakistan's fragmented state system could be reconstructed. Pakistan, as a federal and plural society based country is totally failed to restore its democratic institutions by implementation of accommodative policy towards all. India's vibrant democratic system and relative national integration have become a matter of jealousy for Pakistan. In several occasions, Pakistan has taken anti-Indian standpoint. In practice, Pakistan has done a number of terrorist attacks in India with the help of ISIS and radical Islamic fundamentalist group. On the contrary, Pakistan has a common perception that, India is involved in various internal insurgencies in Pakistan like Muhajir Quami Movement, Baluchistan Movement, etc. Perceptional differences between India and Pakistan resulted permanent antagonism and rivalry.

The Changing Contours of Islamabad-New Delhi Relations: Some Issues and Incidents

According to D.C. Jha, "ever since India and Pakistan emerged as sovereign states in August 1947, they have been in a state of uneasy peace. The study of Indo-Pakistan relations thus has been mainly a study of conflict,...a number of political problems outstanding between the two countries" (Jha 1972). The physical division of India created numerous irritating problems between the both countries. India and Pakistan have fought three wars 1947-48, 1965, 1971, and the limited war of 1999. The border problem is one of the major irritating between India and Pakistan. Evacuee Property Problem also arose leading to serious differences between the two countries, particularly in the fifties. Dispute over waters of the western and eastern rivers of the subcontinent was an issue which made Indo-Pak hostility. Kashmir issue is a most important event between the two countries, which is unsolved till date. The Kashmir issue is not only a manifestation of the deeper problems, which characterizes Pakistan's policy towards India. A Pakistan expert, Bidanda M. Chengappa opined that Pakistan perceives a serious threat from India, which can be traced, to the pre-independence in British Indian history. Kashmir has a strategic importance. It shares common borders with four countries—Afghanistan, China, India and Pakistan. Pakistan is poised acquire nuclear symmetry with India. Whatever, capability Pakistan has achieved has reached a stage of irreversibility? It is an open secret, Pakistan has been augmenting its military capacity and in certain fields it has acquired an edge over India (Bhola 1991: 156). Major General Vinod Saighal has stated, "India has got the upper hand in the proxy war that Pakistan has been waging against India, is one form or another, for a number of years" (Singhal 2012: 53).

Till mid-1980s, Indo-Pak relationship conformed to the strong state/weak state pattern. In the structure of regional system, India was the strong state, the 'local superpower, Pakistan the weaker one (Riencourt 1982: 433). India had started to increase its military expenditure by mid 1980s. In 1985 India's total military expenditure was US$ 8,921 million against Pakistan's US$ 2,957 million (Military Balance: 1999). Arun Prakash, the Indian former Chief of Navy has opined that, very soon after going nuclear in 1998, India formally declared a policy of 'no-first-use of nuclear weapons'. Pakistan on the other hand, has based its strategy on a deliberately ambiguous threat of 'unilateral nuclear first-use'. The country has unfortunately declared some conventional "red lines", the crossing of which will supposedly trigger a nuclear response (Prakash 2011: 84).

In February 1999, the then Prime Minister of India, Mr. Atal Behari Vajpayee had paid a visit to Pakistan and started a bus service from India to Pakistan. Pervez Musharraf had come to power through a military coup on 10 October, 1999 by overthrowing the democratic civilian rule of Nawaz Sharif. This development reflects the dominance of the military and shifting civil-military relations in Pakistan. Bilateral relations touched rock bottom after (allegedly Pak-sponsored) terrorist attack on the Indian Parliament in December, 2001 which led to heavy mobilization of Indian troops on its western border fermenting the imminent danger of two nuclear neighbours going to war before tension were dissipated through 'back-channel' intervention by USA (Ghosh 2006: 236). Regarding 'Kashmir', Indian stand is very clear. India opted for 'composite dialogue' after the end of cross-border terrorism in Jammu and Kashmir. Pakistan on the other hand followed a different design; it identified "Kashmir as the core or key issue and categorically mentioned that 'trade' should come after 'Kashmir'" (Kronstadt 2007: 12-13).

The India-Pakistan peace initiative continues at a slow pace with officials from both countries offering generally positive assessments of the ongoing dialogue. But the serial bombing of Bombay commuter trains July 11, 2006, killed nearly 200 people and injured many hundreds more (Rao 2009: 40). With suspicions regarding the involvement of Pakistan based groups, New Delhi suspended talks with Islamabad. Actually, 7/11 train bombings were planned by ISI. So after this incident, Indian Government had strongly started to propagate against the Pakistani conspiracy to the world community. In January 2007, the then Minister of External Affairs, Mr. Pranab Mukherjee had paid a visit to Pakistan. He talked with his Pakistani counterpart, Khurshid Kurasi. The two ministers decided to maintain peace. India refused the Pakistani request to undertake a joint investigating into *Samjhauta Express* train (the train between Delhi to Lahore) attack which was held on early 2007. The two countries concluded an agreement to reduce the risk of accidental nuclear war. The ISI of Pakistan along with its sponsored terrorist group attacked in Mumbai in

November 2008. Pakistani national Ajmal Kasav was arrested by the Police after long fight. He was only alive terrorist. But Pakistan Government was not agreed to consider Ajmal as its citizen. India has so many proven documents about Pakistani involvement in Mumbai case.

Pakistan is using non-state actors like *Lashkar, Jaish-e-Mohammed* and *Harkat-ul-Muja-hiddeen* in what is known as sub-conventional war against India. The Inter-Services Intelligence (ISI) is busy in carrying out detestable operations against India on various fronts (Cohen 2005: 227). To weaken Indian economy it opened a new front in Nepal from where cheap false notes (printed in Pakistan) are pumped into India. A more normal India-Pakistan relationship could help India assume a place among the major Asian and even global powers. India needs to fully debate their relationship with Pakistan. The problem is that events may outrun India's capability to understand them (Biju 2000: 33). However, since the partition, both India and Pakistan have been looking to each other with mistrust, suspicion and fear. So many ups and downs have taken place in the interaction between both countries (Biju 2000: 129). In July, 2010, Indian Minister for External Affairs, S.M. Krishna had paid a visit to Islamabad. He talked to his Pakistani counterpart on Pak-sponsored terrorism. India's fundamental objective should be to stabilize our relations with Pakistan by political means, however long the effort may take. We hold take unilateral initiatives to encourage normal relations with Pakistan in the political, cultural, technological spheres (Vaughan 2006).

In 2003, Government of India announced her formal 'Nuclear Doctrine' which explicitly clarified India's nuclear capability as deterrent in nature and as a responsible nuclear power proclaimed the principle of 'No First Use' (NFU) as a basis of India's nuclear doctrine (Das 2015). The latest report by the Bulletin of Atomic Scientists highlights the future on nuclear weapons in this region. The report also claims that Pakistan had around 100 nuclear weapons (warheads) around 2011 and by now their nuclear arsenal has added approximately 20 more warheads. Within the next ten years their overall nuclear inventory could reach to 220 to 250 warheads (Lele 2015). In

April 2015, India has evacuated a few numbers of Pakistani nationals from Yemen; on the contrary, Pakistan also rescued a numbers of Indian citizens from Yemen. Both countries have shown their humanitarian diplomacy to each other. On April 29, 2015, Pakistani Prime Minister Nawaz Sharif has said, "Our desire for good neighbourly relations with India has not been reciprocal. India unilaterally called-off our bilateral dialogue process on a pretext" (*The Times of India* 2015).

Recently, K.P. Nayar has observed that, when Prime Minister Narendra Modi opted to engage Nawaz Sharif, his opposite number of from Pakistan, on the margins of the climate summit in Paris, two things became obvious. First, the positive: it is not in Modi's nature to give up on something beneficial that he has started and is keen to take forward. Second, the negative Modi, worryingly, is not in complete control of his foreign and security policies (Nayar 2015: 8). Modi wanted to break the ice in bilateral relations.

The activity of ISI is an irritating factor in Indo-Pak relations. ISI is recruiting a large number of youths as agents. On 30th December, 2015, three ISI agents have been arrested from Kolkata. These agents are alleged in keeping linkage with ISI and extremist groups of Pakistan. They are involved with illegal fake notes supply, arms trafficking and drug trafficking. ISI also recruited some Bangladeshi nationals to run its network in India. The bilateral peace talks have been failed to stop cross-border terrorism. On 2nd January 2016, Jaish-e-Mohammad, a Pakistani terrorist group has attacked on Pathankot (Punjab). In a pre-dawn attack, a group of heavily-armed Pakistani terrorists, suspected to belong to *Jaish-e-Mohammed* outfit, struck at an Air Force base in Pathankot in Punjab, leading to a fierce gun battle in which three security personnel were killed along with four attackers. The intrusion by a yet undetermined number of terrorists into the Air Force base at Pathankot began around 3 a.m. on 2nd January.

Indo-Pak Relations under Narendra Modi's Regime: Some Reflections

The exiting breakthrough of Indo-Pak relations under Modi's rule was started with Nawaz Sharif's present in Modi's

Oath ceremony (May, 2014) as the Prime Minister of India. In August 2014, around 800 incidents of ceasefire violations reported in the first year of Modi Government. Foreign Secretary-level talks called off in August 2014 after Pakistan High Commissioner Abdul Basit met Huriat leaders despite New Delhi's objections. In November, 2014, Modi and Sharif came face to face in Kathmandu at the SAARC Summit, but avoid any bilateral meeting. Even, on stage, two leaders seemed to avoid eye contact. As a part of another Modi initiative on neighborhood outreach, foreign secretary S. Jayshankar met his Pakistani counterpart Aizaz Ahmed Chaudhury as part of SAARC Yatra. In May, 2015, Modi visited Dhaka and made some critical remarks to Pakistan. Modi had called up Sharif on June 16 to extend Ramzan greetings and told him about a decision to release Pakistani fishermen in Indian jail. On July 10, 2015, a structured was held between India and Pakistan on the sidelines of Shanghai Cooperation Organization (SCO) in Ufa (Russia). The Ufa meeting decided on talks at NSA-levels on terrorism, but was finally aborted after Pakistan insisted on bringing Kashmir on table. Both have promised to maintain peace in border areas. But just after Ufa meeting Pakistan started to attack on India and a number of Indian soldiers were killed by Pakistani military. On 30th November, 2015, Modi and Sharif met in Paris on the occasion of climate change summit. A brisk handshake and an intense 160-second huddle following an unscripted encounter between Prime Minister Narendra Modi and his counterpart, Nawaz Sharif, at the Leaders' Lounge of climate change conference in Paris on 30th November, 2015 set off intense speculation of a possible thaw in India-Pakistan ties (*The Times of India* 2015: 1). Modi had paid a surprise visit to Lahore in last week of December, 2015 on the way back to New Delhi from Russia and Afghanistan visits. He wanted to establish a warm relationship with Nawaz Sharif's Government.

The US and China Factors on Indo-Pak Relations

The impact of international politics was vehemently affected to Indo-Pak relations. Pakistan is in the happy position of receiving generous arms aid from China as well as the USA. There is also a regular transfer of technology and material for nuclear weapon and missile programmes from China to Pakistan (Prakash 2011: 84). In early 1950s, the then American Vice President Nixon said, "America would be obliged to arm Pakistan and set up military bases on its territory." Immediately, the US President Eisenhower sent Nehru a letter which again "repeated the offer of American military aid to India" (Chopra 1985: 63). As a true Asian leader, Nehru saw to it that the American game of killing 'Asians against Asians' did not become successful. In 1954, Pakistan concluded a Mutual Defence Pact with the USA and joined to NATO, SEATO and SENTO. By this pact Pakistan had started to freely use of American arms. The process of militarization was started since then to use against India. American arms and military weapons used against India both in the Rann of Kutchh and Indo-Pak war of 1965. Similarly, 'Bilateral Cooperation Agreement' was signed between Pakistan and US in 1959, which was thrown into disuse for most of the time till Carter revived it to reaffirm American support to Pakistan against the eventuality of 'Soviet invasion' of that country is not quite an innocent document in the sense that it was meant against only communist aggression (Nayak 1991: 131).

In early 1970s, India's structural position became uneasy with the emergence of Pakistan-US-China nexus, but it countered by signing 'The treaty of friendship and cooperation' with the Soviet Union in August 1971. Its confidence buoyed, India took advantage of Pakistan's internal squabbles by intervening militarily (Basrur 2011). This treaty was perceived in light of potential threats of Pakistani aggression and sustained interest of the US in that country. Pakistan's increasing reliance on the USA and China was mainly responsible for the increasing Indo-Soviet understanding (Kaushik 1991: 114-15).

American hostility to India was unresistingly exploited by Pakistani leaders who are not known for fighting the cause of colonialism as India and invited superpower wrath. Filing to find a plaint India, the US as before did not stop at the strategy of encircling India in which Pakistan was the kingpin. A day before Mrs. Gandhi was killed; she had spelt out the danger of Indian security most forthrightly when she said that American arms supply to Pakistan was a matter of 'deep concern' (Nayak 1991: 144). Till 1990, the USA took an encirclement policy in the name of balance of power and after 1991 it transformer into double standard policy. The changing contours of Islamabad-New Delhi relations have also been affected for American double standard policy.

The American collaboration with the Pakistani ruling elites, military, bureaucratic, political it has become hard to differ between the interests of US policy-makers and these domestic elites. Most of Pak ministries have bilateral arrangements with the US. The commander of CENTCOM (US Central Command) makes regular trips to Pakistan. This has been extended after 9/11 incident. However, there is in fact, a growing discontent between the elites and the civil society which opposes the US role and presence. After signing of Defence Cooperation Agreement with the US, Pakistan gradually received a huge amount of arms aid from the US. During the 1982-90, Islamabad had received military hardware worth about US$ 2 billion from US. I think, US is equally responsible for it. Today, Pakistan is considered as a terrorist state. The US intelligences have sufficient evidence about Pakistan's terrorist activities. Washington is well-informed about the extremist activities of Islamist organizations and ISI-*Lashkar-e-Taiba-Taliban-al-Qaida* connections. Then, how the US is constantly supplying arms to Pakistan? The US has taken a dual policy about Pakistan. The US policy on South Asia, especially to Pakistan was mistakable from the very beginning. I think, American strategist could not understand South Asian pulse. The US already declared Pakistan as a terrorist state. During his visit to India in January 2015, US President Barrack Obama has strongly criticized the Pakistani involvement in Mumbai attack and cross-border terrorism. Actually, the US took a double slandered towards Pakistan. Due to its strategic interest the US administration is unable to takes such kind of bold steps.

In the name of development and cooperation, China has started to apply its expansionist policy in South Asia. Several developmental projects are already started by China in Pakistan. In Baluchistan province, China already opened up a numbers of manufactured products units. The Gadar port has been built up by China. According to Stephen Cohen, "The Chinese have been less restrained, and while no known treaty binds Pakistan and China together, Beijing has provided more military assistance to Pakistan than it has to any other state." Actually, Beijing has been supplying arms and military equipments to Islamabad to counterbalance India. The Chinese influence in Pakistan not only confined into military sector, but also extended in economic, technological and societal sectors. China has moderated its support for Pakistan's claims to Kashmir and gradually normalized its relationship with India. Cohen has rightly observed that, after 1988 New Delhi itself saw an opportunity to weaken the Beijing-Islamabad tie by moving closer to China and lately has been circumspect in its criticism of Chinese policies in Tibet and elsewhere.

According to the Asia Foundation Commission Task Force's report, while South Asia has become incrementally more important to the United States because of the opening of regional economics—particularly that of India—to the global economic order, American Security concerns in the region have intensified greatly. This report also stated, "specially, the United States should move beyond its recent offers to provide information about confidence-building measures (CBMs), and assume a more active role in ensuring that India and Pakistan do not stumble into accidental nuclear exchange" (*America's Role in Asia* 2001: 44). American expended security relationship is only possible if military relations with India and Pakistan are repaired. The USA should monitor on Pakistan, because of in Pakistan arm forces are likely to remain influential. The US strategic experts will have to consciously deal with India and Pakistan.

Some Positive Aspects in Bilateral Relations

There are some positive aspects in Indo-Pak Relations which are as follows:

In 1960, Indus Water Treaty was concluded in 1960 to resolve water distribution between two countries. Hitherto, the most irritating issue of Indo-Pak bilateral relations is 'Kashmir'.

Through the conclusion of Simla Agreement both countries tried to maintain peace in Kashmir border. The Simla Agreement signed by Prime Minister Indira Gandhi and President Zulfikar Ali Bhutto of Pakistan on 2nd July 1972 was much more than a peace treaty seeking to reverse the consequences of the 1971 war. It was a comprehensive blue print for good neighbourly relations between India and Pakistan. Under the Simla Agreement both countries undertook to abjure conflict and confrontation which had disrupted relations in the past, and to work towards the establishment of durable peace, friendship and cooperation. As a result of Simla Accord, the Line of Control (LoC) was delineated on 11 December 1972; war prisoners were returned after due process and future course of Indo-Pak bilateral relations were set to be through bilateral negotiations. Simla Agreement however, is only an end of a chapter and both India and Pakistan even after four decades of Simla Agreement are in the same position of conflict and no permanent peace solution is anywhere in the horizon.

In early 1980s, the military ruler of Pakistan, Zia-ul Haque gave a proposal to India to sign 'no war pact'. In 1982, he came to India and discussed with Mrs. Indira Gandhi about the future of bilateral relations. In 1988, the then Prime Minister of India visited in Pakistan and agreed to do three things (1) no country will attack to another's nuclear project, (2) both countries will jointly promote arts, sculptures, archeology, education, mass-media, sports, etc., (3) withdrawal of double taxation in aviation. In 1989, both countries were agreed to stop illegal arms trade, drug trafficking. In 1991, the then Prime Minister of India, Mr. Narashima Rao paid an official visit to Islamabad to enhance bilateral relations. During his visit he discussed on bilateral economic and cultural relations. Pakistan agreed to consider India as 'most favored nation' status. In April 1991, the foreign secretaries of two countries agreed to protect air space violence. In August, 1994, Pakistan gave a proposal to reduce nuclear arms jointly. In September, 1997, Prime Minister I.K. Gujral visited Pakistan and discussed with his counterpart, Mr. Nawaz Sharif on bilateral peace process. In February, 1999, Prime Minister Atal Behari Vajpayee paid a historic visit to

Pakistan and inaugurated Delhi-Lahore bus service. Through '*bus diplomacy*', Vajpayee wanted to implement his 'extended neighborhood' policy.

For the first time in the 57 years of conformation Pakistan ordered a unilateral ceasefire in November 2003. Perhaps the best gift the governments of India and Pakistan have given to their people on *Eid-ul-Fitar* 2003 is the declaration that their troops will observe ceasefire along the international border (from Madhopur to Sangam), Line of Control (LoC).

In January 2004, during the SAARC Summit in Islamabad both countries were agreed on several CBMs emphasizing people-to-people contact, such as—rail, road links, medical assistance by India to Pakistani children, visit by political and cultural delegations, release of prisoners and so on (Ghosh 2006: 237). In 2005, after the devastating earthquake in Pakistan, India had sent huge quantity of relief. New Delhi had given 22,600 US$ as relief. Apart from this, India also sent 25 tons relief goods to Pakistan. Indian cargo plane were also sent to earthquake areas with lifesavers medicine. Tents, plastic sheets, dry foods were also sent to Pakistan as humanitarian aid. In April 2005, Pak President Pervez Musharraf came to India and watch an India-Pakistan cricket match with the then Indian Prime Minister, Mr. Manmohan Singh at Firoz Shah Kotla Stadium in New Delhi. Both sides were willing to normalize their relations through 'cricket diplomacy'. A light of hope was shown in Indo-Pak trading relations just after implementation of SAFTA on 1st January 2006. On 2nd November 2011, Pakistan agreed in principle to grant 'Most Favored Nations' status to India with a view to liberalize trade between the two countries, disperse clouds of distrust, build confidence and bolster peace process. As a result India has been made a part of the Pak-Afghan Transit Trade Agreement (PATTA) (Mohapatra 2012: 20-21). There have been consisting efforts made from each side to increase bilateral trade while pashing out the negative list. The textile sector from both India and Pakistan are trying to work jointly. The proposed 'Iran-Pakistan-India gas pipeline project' (2005) has been pending due to some problems. It was a positive trilateral initiative towards energy security and economic engagement. Education and tourism are another two important areas where both can establish close ties. It is true, that Kashmir issue is almost irreconcilable. Apart from this, there are so many areas where both can rethink. There are so many factors in Indo-Pak complex relationship. The Kashmir issue is the key issue. To resolve Kashmir issue several peace talks have been held between the two sides through so many channels. The role of *Huriyat* leaders regarding the Kashmir issue is very much significant.

Some Reflections of Track II Diplomacy in Indo-Pak Engagement

Track II refers to attempts to avoid or deal with conflicts through non-governmental intermediaries with close links to the governmental policy-makers. It is undertaken by them generally at the instance of Track I diplomats to find a way out of difficult situations without feelings of loss of face on either side, without negative consequences if the diplomacy fails and without embarrassment if there is leakage to the media and the public. To succeed, Track II has to be discreet and unpublicised, with knowledge of it restricted to as few persons as possible. Since Track I officials or leaders are often at the rear of Track II players, unwise publicity could prove counter-productive and make positions even more rigid than they were before the efforts were undertaken (Raman 2003). Back-channel diplomacy is one of the effective diplomatic measures in normalization of bilateral relations. When frontline diplomacy becomes impossible, then back-channel diplomacy can be applied.

Some factors are essential for Track II diplomacy, such as, (1) there should be attempts to include stakeholders who are not necessarily part of any "clique". The exchanges can start by including more individuals not belonging to English-language media, especially those from the Hindi and Urdu media. While there are not many Punjabi publications in Pakistan, the Punjabi media in India has tried to play a positive role in improving bilateral relations. (2) Rather than having Track II exchanges at exotic locales or major cities like Delhi, Mumbai, Karachi, Lahore and Islamabad; dialogue in smaller towns which also have an interest and stake in peace, perhaps even more so due to their respective geographical location, could be advantageous. One would imagine that small towns such as Sargodha, Chiniot, Sukkur, Nowshera and Sibi in Pakistan; and Ludhiana, Faridabad, Ambala, Bhiwani, Hisar, Barabanki and Bhopal in India would be more representative of public opinion, rather than the cosmopolitan urban centres on either side of the border. It may also be helpful to choose locations where there have been large-scale migrations. (3) While those who make a contribution to improved relations should be included, there should be some sort of a rotation policy, where those who are not as committed are removed and newer faces are brought in, and the dialogue is expanded. There should be increased interaction between small business owners, trade unions, labor unions, lawyers from small towns, religious leaders from all communities and writers from the regional media. (4) Any such interaction should not be focused on a predetermined agenda. The idea is to let people meet and make up their own mind about whether they want peace and a relationship based on pragmatism and not emotion (www.thediplomat.com).

I think, through applying of Track II diplomacy, increasing cultural and economic relation in non-governmental level the bilateral cordial relation can be boost up. Regarding Pakistan India has taken a realist as well as idealist diplomacy. On the one hand, India is imposing pressure over Pakistan regarding terrorism and trying in increase bilateral, economic and technological relations on the other. In 2012, Pak President Asif Ali Jardari paid a visit to India and gave a signal to start a religious diplomacy. Indian Government also promised to Pakistan Government that it will simplify the visa processing for Pakistani pilgrims.

In 2015, The Jinnah Institute (Pakistan) has arranged a workshop, comprising of Pakistani and Indian scholars in Thailand. A Task force was formed on Clime Change. There are so many issues among two countries, which are vital for their existence. Environment and global warming is one of them. To protect environment 'green peace movement' can be started for awareness of both sides' people. Prof. Amitava Mattoo of Jawaharlal Nehru University was one of the members of Indian delegation team. They agreed that the multifaceted challenges of climate change on economies and communities in India and Pakistan warranted cooperation and concerted action by their governments in promoting a comprehensive and just global agreement.

Rob Asghar, a Pakistani American political writer and a journalist of *The Wall Street Journal* has shown how digital media can enhance 'citizen's diplomacy' or people to people contact. In the era of globalization, the digital media can highly effect on bilateral relations digital media serves as a luxurious tool and has entrusted power in citizen diplomacy entitled to citizens, who are in no way associated with governmental structures or power positions. The common man has always been considered a less important stakeholder in bringing about a change in antagonistic relations. But the nature of the media has acted as a catalyst in empowering citizens to build trust amongst each other, when both were long been fed with hatred and distrust through assertions of political and military superiority over the 'other'.

Conclusion

India has attempted several times for maintaining of peace with Pakistan. Through back channel diplomacy and Track II diplomacy India has tried its best for maintaining status quo in bilateral relations. Nalini Kant Jha mentioned few initiatives by India in this regard. As he said, India's repeated attempts to bring peace with Pakistan through Prime Minister, Atal Behari Vajpayee's bus journey to Lahore in 1999, his Ramjan peace initiative in Kashmir at the end of 2000, Agra Summit talks with Pakistan in 2001 and continued peace initiative in April 2003 despite provocative violence by Pakistan sponsored terrorists in Kashmir too illustrate India's emphasis on a peaceful settlement of disputes (Jha 2005: 24). Indo-Pak relations have marked hostility and rivalry. Like other postcolonial countries, India and Pakistan are also suffering from some basic problems, such as hunger, poverty, corruption, illiteracy, backwardness in industrial sectors, unemployment, etc. These are inter-related. Due to military competition both are spending a significant amount of money in military purpose. The issues like ethnic problem, security crisis, terrorism, religious fundamentalism, negative role of extra regional powers are barriers in bilateral relations. To maintain friendly relations with India Pakistan would emphasize on some issues: First, quickly implement few laws, through which terrorists and extremists can be arrested. The original culprits should have been punished at earliest. Second, act against banned groups that operate freely and against any groups and individuals calling for Jihad against India, invoking laws against incitement to violence. Third, Implement its plead to grant "most favored nations" status to India by end of 2012. Fourth, take urgent action against all militant groups and terrorist groups (*Asia Report* 2012: 1-4). A better understanding of Pakistan's own security concerns could help policy-makers in India frame a stable engagement strategy with its most important neighbour of the day. Pakistan's security strategy is built around a perceived existential threat from India. According to its narrative, since the birth of the two countries in 1947 India has been an aggressor on at least three occasions, dismembered it, humbled it militarily repeatedly, and built nuclear bombs that can wipe it off the map, has been subjecting Kashmiris to humiliation (Joseph 2016: 10). On the other hand, Pakistan viewed that 'Indo-centric' institution and that reality will not change in any significant way until Kashmir issue and water disputes are resolved. If a democratically stable Pakistan is India's best bet, then it is a long way off. Until Pakistan reaches that destination, what is India's best option? So far some 50,000 Pakistanis are estimated to have been killed in domestic terrorist strikes over the years. The situation can be transformed only if Pakistan can summon the political will to root out jihadist, and that means its military has to change. If Islamabad can genuinely help with catching those responsible for the Pathankot attack, instead of stalling on technicalities, it would be suggest that it is no longer differentiating between 'good' and 'bad' terrorist (*Deccan Chronicle* 2016: 8).

References

America's Role in Asia: American Views. (2001). *A Report of the Asia Foundation Commissioned Task Force on America's Role in Asia*, The Asian Foundation.

Asia Report (2012, May 3). International Crisis Group. Pakistan's Relations with India: Beyond Kashmir?

Basrur, Rajesh M. (2011). "India-Pakistan Relations," in Sumit Ganguly (ed.), *India's Foreign Policy: Retrospect and Prospect*. New Delhi: Oxford University Press.

Bhola, P.L. (1991). India's Perception and Response to Pakistan's Nuclear Programme. In Surendra Nath Kaushik and Rajan Mahan Ramakant (Eds.), *India and South Asia*. New Delhi: South Asian Publishers Pvt. Ltd.

Biju, M.R. (2000). *India's Foreign Policy towards a New Millennium*. New Delhi: National Publishing House.

Chopra, V.D. (1985). *Pentagon Shadow over India*. New Delhi: Patriot Publishers.

Chengappa, Bidanda M. (2004). *Pakistan: Islamization, Army and Foreign Policy*. New Delhi: A.P.H. Publishing Corporation.

Cohen, Stephen (2005). *Emerging Power: India*. New Delhi: Oxford University Press.

Das, P. (2015, July). Re-Examining India's Nuclear Doctrine. *ORF Issue Brief* (97).

Deccan Chronicle (2016, January 22). Editorial page.

Ghosh, Anjana (2006, January-December). Indo-Pak Relations 2005: Kashmir Solution? *The West Bengal Political Science Review*, Vol. IX (I & II).

International Institute of Strategic Studies (1999). *The Military Balance, 1999-2000*, Oxford: Oxford University Press.

Jha, D.C. (1972). *Indo-Pak Relations*. Patna: Bharati Bhawan.

Jha, Nalini Kant (2005, April). Peace and Security: Traditional Indian Perspective. *South Asia Politics*. New Delhi.

Joseph, Josy (2016, January 23). "Think Like the Neighbour". *The Hindu*, Editorial page.

Kaushik, Surendra Nath (1991). "India's Attitude and Policy towards Pakistan: Potential for Democratic Interaction". In Surendra Nath Kaushik and Other (eds.), *India and South Asia*. New Delhi: South Asian Publishers Pvt. Ltd.

Kronstadt, K. Alan (2007, December 19). *CRS Report for Congress*.

Lele, A. (2015, October 23). Why India must worry but not panic over Pakistan's nuclear cry. *Daily Opinion*. India Today Group.

Mohapatra, Anil Kumar (2012). "Gujral Doctrine and Foreign Policy of 'UPA-II': An Interface", *World Focus*, Annual Issue, December, 2012.

Nayak, Pandav (1991). "The US Factor in Indo-Pak Relations: Implications for Indian Security" in Surendra Nath Kaushik and Rajan Mahan Ramakant (eds), *India and South Asia*, New Delhi: South Asian Publishers Pvt. Ltd.

Nayar, K.P. (2015, December 2). "Narendra Modi is not in complete control of India's Foreign Policy." *The Telegraph*, Editorial page.

Nehru, Jawaharlal. *India's Foreign Policy: Selected Speeches, September 1946-April 1961*, The Publication Division, Ministry of Information and Broadcasting, New Delhi.

Paul, T.V. (Ed.) (2005). *The India-Pakistan Conflict: An Enduring Rivalry*. Cambridge: Cambridge University.

Paul, T.V. (2014). *The Warrior State: Pakistan in the Contemporary World*. Gurgaon: Random House India.

Prakash, Arun (2011). *The Rationable and Implications of India's Growing Maritime Power*. Woodrow Wilson International Center for Scholars.

Raman, B. (2003, August 18). Track II Diplomacy and Pakistan. *South Asian Analysis Group*, Paper no. 764.

Rao, Rama R. (2009, October). "Manmohan Singh's Faulty Pakistan Policy". *Indian Age*.

Riencourt, Amaury de (1982). "India and Pakistan in the Shadow of Afghanistan". *Foreign Affairs*, 81(2).

Saighal, Vinod (2012). *Restructuring South Asian Security*. New Delhi: Manas Publications.

Singh, M.P., and Kukreja, Veena (2005). "Peace Process between India and Pakistan", in their (Eds.), *Pakistan: Democracy, Development and Security Issues*. New Delhi: Sage Publications.

The Times of India (2015, April 30).

Vaughn, Bruce (2006, September 7). Bangladesh Background and US Relations. *CRS Report* (USA).

Web Sources

http://www.thediplomat.com

http://indianexpress.com/article/india/india-news-india/pathankot-air-force-base-terror-attack-punjab/#sthash.lv0gnppr.dpuf (Accessed on January 4, 2016).

15

Security Imperative in Contemporary India-Pakistan Relations: Terrorism as a Factor

Prosenjit Pal

Any analysis of India-Pakistan relations has to be analysed in the backdrop of the insolvability of the Kashmir issue which has clouded over other issues and aspects of the relation, due to which stability and convergences seems to be like meagre interruptions in between successive periods of instability and discord. The Kashmir issue has been a determinant of the level of relations since the Partition of the subcontinent in 1947 and still evades an amicable solution. The congenital animosity between these two frontline states has shaped the politico-economic dynamics of the South Asian region. As a result, the security imperative has been a predominant aspect in Indo-Pakistani ties and especially in the context of the threat of global terrorism in the post-9/11 world. The aspect of terrorism as a factor of security has been an important dimension in India-Pakistan relations, especially since the 1990s.

Security, as defined in Realist terms, generally, refers to the military dimension of the same. But, since the 1980s, various non-traditional dimensions of security have gained in prominence such as human security, economic, environmental, social security that has changed the discourse on security and put up questions concerning the comprehensiveness of the concept of security in IR. Yet, in the context of a global order marked by a structural power-based hierarchy of states, the military aspect of security dominates. Post-9/11, the outreaches of global terrorism seems to have been elevated to the ranks of the most crucial factor conditioning the security dilemma of the states and still evades a proper solution. Meagre use of military means, like The War on Terror (global coalition against terrorism), initiated by the USA following the 9/11 attacks, can only act as a temporary 'relief factor', but cannot dilute the roots of terror, or the factors that sustains the 'terror industry'.

The above may be a perfect backdrop in which one may embark on an analysis of the impact of terrorism in India-Pakistan relations as the most crucial factor conditioning the security imperative among the two frontline South Asian states. The dispute of Kashmir has a significant security dimension. The strategic context of the problem must be related to both domestic and external environments. Kashmir has been of great strategic importance to India and Pakistan as well as the great powers. Security of Kashmir is vital to the security of India. Nehru grasped the geo-strategic importance of Kashmir for Indian security thus: "Kashmir, because of her geographical position with her frontiers marching with three countries, namely, the Soviet Union, China and Afghanistan is intimately connected with the security and international contacts of India. Economically also Kashmir is intimately related to India" (Nehru 1961: 145). Since independence India has lost the western areas of Kashmir to Pakistan and the eastern areas of Aksai Chin to China. Pakistan too has viewed Kashmir as integral to her security. Accession of Jammu and Kashmir to India was considered as a threat to the security of Pakistan. Pakistan has linked the strategic importance of Kashmir with its national psyche on the dispute (Budania 2001: 92). In fact, this psycho-strategic imperative explains the interest and role of the Pakistani ruling elite in precipitating the Kashmir issue against India's unity and integrity (Budania 2001: 92). It may be argued that the Indo-Pakistani conflict over the issue of Kashmir has originated and continued because of the recognition of the psycho-strategic importance of Kashmir by both countries. For India, Kashmir has formed an important part in furthering its core national values of secularism. As such, the importance of Kashmir in India's security perceptions is based on the possible reverses it would inflict on communalism and also on Jinnah's two-nation theory (Budania 2001: 92). The Indian governments have faced a big task of evolving a new and mutually supportive post-independence relationship with Kashmir, vis-à-vis Pakistan's attempts at wresting Kashmir from India. India's security and threat perception arising out of the strategic importance of Kashmir must be evaluated in terms of not only a range of threats originating from Pakistan within the subcontinent but also from outside the region, as Pakistan has consistently internationalized the issue and rallied the support of China and USA in this context. Kashmir's strategic importance, therefore, is invariably linked to the Cold War geo-politics and the interests of external powers. For Pakistan, Kashmir has been an integral part of its 'unfinished nation-building process'. It has treated Kashmir issue as the 'core issue' and argues that 'solution' to the Kashmir issue should precede any progress in Indo-Pakistani peace process. Pakistan has always asserted that the question of Kashmir needs to be settled first, before any further progress of India-Pakistan talks on other issues can take place. Attempts at wresting Kashmir from India by using force, has been put up by Pakistan, as assertions in the process of exercising its right to self-determination-on behalf of the Muslim brethren of Kashmir who share ethnic, religious and cultural affinity with the demographic constituents of the Pakistani nation.

Initially Pakistan took recourse to declared wars in 1947, 1965 and 1971, to militarily wrest Kashmir from India. But as they failed to achieve their end, Pakistan took recourse to an alternative path of terrorism, insurgency, low intensity conflict and undeclared guerilla warfare, to slowly bleed Kashmir and seize it from India. In 1990, Pakistan initiated 'Operation Topac'—codename for these clandestine undeclared insurgency operations that brought terrorism to the corridors of 'The Valley of Peace', that gradually spread its tentacles and has assumed enormously lethal proportions, continuously acting as a deterring force in the path of development of any prospective peaceful relations among India and Pakistan. The process of engendering 'aman ki asha' has kept on stumbling whenever prospective silver linings were on the anvil. Pakistan has admitted to giving, what it calls, 'moral, diplomatic and political' support to militancy in Kashmir. In fact, its support goes beyond it. Pakistan has engineered militancy, given training and supplied weapons to militants in Kashmir, garnered support in this aspect from China and US, in total violation of the spirit of the Shimla Agreement. Pakistan has adopted the strategy of proxy war or low intensity conflict and terrorism, insurgency, after the futility of its war efforts in Kashmir by force. In these efforts the ISI has been deeply involved regarding the planning and implementation of these clandestine operations.

How Pakistan gradually became a 'breeding ground' of Islamic terrorism needs a critical analysis.

Pakistani State Structure and the Sustenance of 'the terror industry'

The nature of the postcolonial state in Pakistan, the bonapartist state apparatus, dominated by the military establishment, working in tandem with the Islamic fundamentalists, ISI has built up the infrastructure of what may be termed as 'the terror industry'—a breeding ground of terrorism. The military apparatus sustains itself chiefly on the basis of two factors—weak democratic apparatus and rising instability in Pakistani society and politics and its staunch anti-Indian sentiment through which it has been able to project itself as the only legitimate force for wresting Kashmir from India and winning it for the Pakistanis—something which no democratically elected government in Pakistan can possibly fail to instill using proper diplomatic means. Terrorism is another extended alternative aspect of its militaristic coercive attempts in this regard.

As to the nature of the state of Pakistan we may began by saying that it is a postcolonial, peripheral capitalist, draconian and relatively autonomous state (Cohen 2006: 124). In our attempt to clarify these adjectives attributed to the Pakistani state, we can do no better than quote in extensor, Hamza Alavi, an acknowledged expert on Pakistan's political economy. He writes, "...that there is a widespread tendency on the part of the regimes in peripheral capitalist societies, such as Pakistan, to acquire an authoritarian character and to proliferate military dictatorships. It is not the subordinate classes alone which have to confront the state as an alien force. The economically classes too have to contend which it as such; the administrative arm of the state is deployed against them even while upholding their fundamental interests. Unlike the advanced capitalist countries where the state has developed in the wake of a single dominant class, and the state institutions and powers have developed in keeping with the needs and demands of that class, this is not quite the case in peripheral capitalist countries" (Alavi 1979: 38).

In a nutshell it maybe contended that the army in Pakistan has all along maintained its overarching role as it has zealously maintained its autonomy within the framework of the relatively autonomous Pakistani state. As a "state" within a state it has been consistently concerning a lion's share of Pakistan's national budget as it has cornered numerous other benefits (Ghosh 2009: 36).

One needs to analyse the role of Pakistan's ubiquitous Inter Services Intelligence (ISI). In a sense, if the army in Pakistan is an egg, then the ISI is its yolk. Created way back in 1948 by a British army officer major general William Cawthorne (then Pakistan's Deputy Chief of Staff) the ISI was supposed to tone up Pakistan's military intelligence. Trained by British American and French intelligence agencies the ISI has evolved considerably overtime. Consider two things. First, an assumption of power in October, 1958, Ayub Khan (the then military rules and first Pakistani commander-in-chief) gave the ISI three tasks: (a) to safeguard Pakistan's interest, (b) to monitor political opposition, and (c) to sustain military rule in Pakistan. Hence the primacy of the ISI, for its role embodies both external and internal intelligence, plus much more (Ghosh 2009: 37). That "much more" is supposed to be subsumed by our second point: during the Afghan crisis Pakistan was so-called the "frontline state" and an ally of America in the fight against the Soviet forces that intruded into Afghanistan in 1979. And the ISI was the frontline agency of the "frontline state" to handle the Afghan operations. In this connection one analyst writes: by 1984, three years after serious money began to flow from Washington, the United States was supporting the Afghan rebels with at least $200 million annually, almost all of it handed over to the ISI (Ghosh 2009: 36). The ISI "insisted" that it would itself maintain contact with Mujaheedins in Afghanistan and that no Americans (the CIA included), would cross the Afghanistan border from Pakistan. Another fact issuing from all this was that the CIA or any other organizations did not have "any clear or tight oversight of what the ISI (and by extension that Pakistani military government) was doing with the money or the arms" (Ghosh 2009: 36). From late 1980s the ISI launched "a much more assertive strategy to destabilize Jammu and Kashmir" (Ghosh 2009: 36). Its strategy included, inter alia, creation of military organizations that could become "vehicles" for the ISI and such militant organizations included Lashkar-e-Toiba (created in 1990), Harkat-ul-Ansar (formed in 1993) and Jaish-e-Mahammed (formed in 1994) (Ghosh 2009: 38). Hence the terror industry built up from 1979 onwards was outsourced for carrying out anti-Indian operations in Kashmir as well.

The 'ground realities' we have referred to just above pertains to Pakistan's congenital anti-Indian approach. But probably more important as to the crucial relevance of anti-Indians in Pakistan's identity formation is how Pakistan has sought to rise successive generations of Pakistanis. We mean the type of mindset, the psyche the Pakistani people should have (and what the state in Pakistan should do about it) vis-à-vis India. It is here that Pakistan's negative attitude towards India has been playing a positive role in shaping the contours of the Pakistani psyche. And in this type of education in Pakistan has been playing an exceedingly crucial role. We are speaking of the products of Madaris (plural of Madrassah) (Ghosh 2009: 47). Of course; there is considerable difference of opinion as to the number of Madaris in Pakistan or as to the number of students thereof. Various estimates of the number of Madaris or students studying therein vary widely. No wonder Pakistan is steeped in Jihadi culture (Ghosh 2009: 47). But one thing is clear that the same represent the breeding grounds of Islamic Terrorism in Pakistan to be used against India to wrest Kashmir from Indian control. In this context General Zia-ul Haq's military regime in Pakistan from 1977-85, coincided with the recognition of Pakistan as USA's frontline state in its anti-Soviet operations in Afghanistan. Zia's Islamization and Militarization programmes further weakened the socio-political system of Pakistan and in turn bolstered the strength of the military apparatus as well as its conjunct-terror and fundamentalist apparatuses. USA's overt and covert military support to Pakistan (since 1954) and China's aiding of Pakistan's nuclearization, boosted further the military and its allied establishments and also aided the process of its stepping up the anti-Indian rhetoric especially over Kashmir. In trying to harness Islam to legitimize and bolster his rule Zia actively cultivated radical Islamist groups and parties. He did substantially Islamize the army and the elements from Jamat-i-Islami became highly active. One upshot of this "frontline" role was that from Al Qaeda's perspective was surpassed only by "Taliban" Afghanistan "as an ally". Again, the huge money and huge catches of weapons that the ISI used and the Mujaheedins who graduated from Afghan operations—battle hardened and fired by islamist zeal-made for the palpable shift of Pakistan's India policy: shift from the policy of Jung (war) to Jihad (Ghosh 2009: 41).

Now the ISI had at its disposal a grand strategy especially vis-à-vis India: "from late 1980s Pakistan had began to step up support for separatist for separatist militants fighting for the independence of Jammu and Kashmir from India. The pertinent elements of this plan were four-fold: (a) to divert arms and ammunitions from the Afghan conflict—including many of those siphoned off during the Afghan war by the ISI-and use the weapons to empower favored Jammu and Kashmir separatist groups; (b) to expand the member of Madaris and the training camps inside Pakistan administered Kashmir to boost the number of trained, indoctrinated fighters who could be infiltrated into Indian controlled territory; (c) to transit Afghan and international muslim fighters from the Afghan conflict to the new pan Islamist holy war in Jammu and Kashmir; and (d) the creation of new militant organizations that could become the vehicles for ISI control of separatist insurgency (Ghosh 2009: 42).

Terror as an Instrument of State Policy (1971)

As the Bangladesh liberation struggle gathered momentum and Islamabad became convinced that the movement had gained the sympathy of India to its cause, Pakistan's Intelligence Bureau (IB) prepared a plan and presented it to President Yahya Khan, seeking his approval for flagging off a campaign of destabilization of the state of Punjab in India. This was supposed to be Pakistan's response to India's perceived involvement in Bangladesh. The plan was to mobilize the unemployed, disaffected and the criminal elements among the Sikh community in India and sections of the rich and the well-off non-resident Sikhs living abroad, enticing them with the promise of an independent State of Khalistan which Pakistan would help create (Banerjee 2006: 22).

The call for the creation of a sovereign State of Khalistan thus, took the form of an intelligence agency-directed revivalist movement. It was envisaged as a terror campaign to be conducted against the Indian State. A critical component of this plan was the lure of money, which included involving the participants into the hugely lucrative drug trade. Drug-trafficking was supposed to generate a major part of the funding needs of the campaign. Bank robberies and extortion rackets constituted the other sources of funding. The operational part of the terror plan included recruiting young volunteers, training them in sub-conventional warfare in secret training camps mostly located within military cantonments, fabricating explosive devices, providing them with arms supplies and communication gadgetry, ex-filtrating them out of India and then infiltrating them back into the country and so on. The objective was to create mayhem, murder and chaos on a large scale, making Punjab ungovernable (Banerjee 2006: 23).

In order to keep the leading activists, many aspiring leadership roles, happy and satisfied, a cluster of terror outfits was created. The proliferation of these terrorist organizations created panic in the hearts of the security community in India. Later, taken over by the ISI during the rule of General Zia, the Khalistani terror campaign became the first formal non-

Islamic milestone in the use of terror as a part of Pakistan's state policy. The march of events, littered with mounting murders and massacres, forced the Government of India to launch the operation Blue Star within the Golden Temple complex in Amritsar. Sant Jarnail Singh Bhindranwale, the terror leader, holed up in *Akal Takht* within the temple complex died fighting the Indian Army (Banerjee 2006: 23). It was followed by the assassination in 1984 of Indira Gandhi by her Sikh bodyguards, which on its own was an earth-shaking event. The ISI saw in these events remarkable success of its Khalistan operations. It was perceived as its finest hour.

The Kargil War

The Kargil adventure planned and executed in 1999 across the LoC by General Pervez Musharraf when he was the Chief of Army Staff under PM Mian Nawaz Sharif, had a subtle nuclear dimension to it. The India-Pakistan bonhomie centering around the Islamabad Declaration in January 1999 was disrupted due to the same. Its other aim was to grab land clandestinely under the cover of the nuclear umbrella. Pakistan had tested its nuclear bombs in 1998 followed by a declaration that Islamabad would build and maintain a minimum nuclear deterrent against India and will be ready to use it on a 'first use' formula, if and when the need arose. The Kargil infiltration took place within a year after the nuclear tests. Apparently, the Army had calculated that India would refrain from taking counter-measures to repossess the territory against a nuclear State that Pakistan now was. The Kargil war has been analysed as an extended spill-over effect of the simmering levels of low intensity conflicts, insurgency and proxy war carried out under Pakistani supervision in the Kashmir valley.

Pakistan perceived that New Delhi would rather lose territory than run the gauntlet of a possible nuclear stand-off. Kargil would then be presented to the nation as a great victory of the Pakistan Army and a fitting revenge against the enemy.

The prospect of a nuclear war breaking out over the Kashmir issue threatened global stability and security. It caused great nervousness in the international community. US President

Bill Clinton had warned the world of a looming nuclear catastrophe if a full-scale India-Pakistan war broke out. He was basing his warnings on Pakistani threats of dire consequences if India responded militarily. As it turned out, the threats were empty and carried no substance (Banerjee 2006: 25). The Indian military response, however, was overwhelming and no real nuclear threat was posed by Islamabad. Kargil, thus, became a test case about defining the phrase minimum credible nuclear deterrence. Pakistan found it to its regret that the minimum deterrence was not enough at the time of Kargil. The misadventure ended in a humiliation for the Pakistan Army losing to India every inch of the territory it had occupied illegally and clandestinely.

Sensing that the Kargil border war was taking a dangerous turn, PM Nawaz Sharif flew to Washington seeking American intervention. He signed a joint declaration issued on 4 July 1999 with President Clinton, wherein Pakistan was asked to withdraw its troops behind the LoC. The US stipulated that "Pakistan must observe the sanctity of the LoC" which, as it turned out, became a significant input towards the evolution of a framework for a final solution of the Kashmir problem.

General Musharraf had code-named his clandestine but disastrous Kargil operations as Operation Badr. What was the significance of the timing of the invasion? They were as follows:

The Indian security forces were making significant progress in flushing out terrorists and the efforts by Pakistan to destabilize Jammu and Kashmir and cutting it off from India, made no progress. It was time that this situation was reversed. The Pakistan Army believed that the Indians would not be able to mount a coordinated large-scale surprise attack after its troops had entrenched themselves on the top of the strategic heights of the Himalayas. Pakistan feared that the international community may support a settlement of the Kashmir 'dispute' on the basis of the LoC. Therefore, it was necessary to push the LoC to a more favorable position by moving it eastwards. The involvement of the Pakistani army in Kargil was proved.

Hijack of Indian Airlines Flight and Its Impact

The dramatic hijacking to Kandahar in the Taliban ruled Afghanistan of the Indian Airlines Flight IC-814 on 24 December 1999 scheduled to fly from Kathmandu to New Delhi proved one thing above everything else; Pakistan was actively escalating covert violence and terrorist action against Indian targets, not only in Jammu and Kashmir but also wherever vulnerable targets were available. The direct involvement of Pakistan in the hijacking became evident when an under-cover ISI officer named Mohammad Arshad Cheema, First Secretary (Consular) in the Pakistan Embassy in Kathmandu, went out to meet and pass last-minute instructions to the hijackers in the Tribhuban airport just before departure. Amir of *Harkat-ul-Ansar,* Fazlur Rahman Khalil was in constant touch with the hijackers. The other points of contact for the hijackers and the Pakistani handlers were the Mumbai-based ISI operatives who were put under arrest. Among the 36 prisoners held under charges of terrorism whose release the hijackers were demanding, 33 were Pakistanis. One of whom was Maulana Masood Azhar, who later founded the *Jais'i-e-Mohammad,* a Pakistan-based terror organization closely linked to the *al-Qaeda.*

After taking a circuitous route landing first in Amritsar, then in Lahore, followed by Dubai, IC-814 finally landed in Kandahar. The Government of India was not willing to risk the lives of the hostages and decided to accept the hijackers' demand. The plane and the hostages were released on 31 December 1999. Terrorist leader Maulana Masood Azhar, a native of Bahawalpur, is now roaming freely in Pakistan, directing terror outrages in India without let or hindrance.

Terror Attack on Indian Parliament

The intention of the terror attack on the Indian Parliament on 13 December 2001 was to wipe out the entire political leadership of India in one go. But the terrorists failed to achieve their objective, thanks to the quick action taken by the security forces killing all the militants. New Delhi militarily responded to the terror attacks, by deploying about

800,000 troops along the LoC (Operation Parakram) and the international border but refrained from crossing them. It was a sure sign that the much-vaunted minimum nuclear deterrence was now established. New Delhi was not prepared to take chances. It, however, claimed bravely that coercive diplomacy through troop deployment had fully achieved the desired result without waging a war.

The level of terrorist violence, however, refused to subside after the withdrawal of the Indian troops, proving vacuity of the Indian claims. The breakup of the Soviet Union had created an entirely new situation for Pakistan. The world was now left with only one superpower, the US—Pakistan's traditional friend and ally. It was time for rejoicing for the top brass of the Pakistan Army. Yet, there was deep concern over what should be done with the large numbers of unemployed *Islamic Mujahideen,* the veterans of the Afghan war. They could turn their US-supplied weapons on Islamabad if they were not paid their wages or found new jobs to keep them busy. The military found a novel answer to this strategic threat. It decided *to* open two warfronts, one on the western front across the Durand Line and the other on the eastern front across the LoC in Kashmir (Banerjee 2006: 31).

Afghanistan under Pakistan's control was expected to serve two purposes. In the event of a future war with India the vast stretches of land in Afghanistan would serve as a valuable military asset beyond the range of fire of the Indians. In the long run the country could be absorbed into Pakistan which would transform the nation with its extended territorial domain into a vast and influential country. The Taliban, it must not be forgotten, merely served as the human shield of the Pakistan Army's Afghanistan military campaign. General Aslam Baig, who had served as the Chief of Army Staff came up with a dedicated military doctrine for India. In the proxy war that was launched against India around 1989, Pakistan would "carry war into the enemy territory". It meant the opening of indoctrination centres for new recruits *of Mujahideen* and setting up of training camps on the Pakistani soil, followed by infiltration of heavily armed and well-funded terror gangs into Kashmir and elsewhere and creates mayhem, death and destruction. The ensuing war would be a war of a thousand cuts that would bleed India into submission (Banerjee 2006: 31).

Pakistan's two-front military engagement developed interesting characteristics. When the insurgency was intensified on the Kashmir front, there was lull on the Afghan front. Similarly, when there was movement on the Afghan front, Kashmir remained quiet. The planning and deployment were so calibrated, meticulous and detailed that these Islamic warriors hardly had the opportunity to create trouble for Pakistan. Pakistan's proxy war on both the fronts is a continuing process with no end in sight; its strategic goals have remained unchanged to this (Ganguly 1986: 57).

The 26/11 terror attacks in Mumbai in 2008 by suspected Pakistan-backed terrorists of Lashkar-e Toiba again exposed the Pak-engineered terror threat that hangs on India. One hundred sixty-five people were killed, the Taj heritage hotel was held hostage for several hours and it changed the face of urban terrorism—terrorism now had come closer to the common people home, instead of simply specific targets. Nine terrorists were killed and the 10th one Ajmal Kasab was captured and hanged in September 2008. David Coleman Hedley, a Pakistan-origin American agent who became a Lashkar-e Toiba operative and conducted surveillance for the Mumbai attacks has revealed the involvement of the ISI, How Lashkar commander Zakiur Rehman Lakhvi and Lashkar Chief Hafiz Saeed plotted the attacks and the prior training of the militants in areas under Pakistani control (*The Telegraph* Feb. 9, 2016).

Terror Attacks in Pathankot and Its Implications

In early hours of January 2, 2016 terrorists attacked the Indian Air Force base in Pathankot, killing seven Indian soldiers. Timely retaliation by Indian forces resulted in all six terrorists killed, preventing the greater devastation that could have occurred if the terrorists had been able to reach the high-value strategic assets they were targeting.

Media reports in the wake of the attack suggested that the terrorists received clandestine support from Pakistan. *India*

Today has claimed that "the brazen attack was carried out on the behest of Pakistani's intelligence agency Inter-Services Intelligence (ISI)". Other reports have suspected the involvement of Pakistan-based Jaish-e-Muhammad. *The Hindustan Times* and other Indian newspapers have reported that phone calls made by the terrorists were intercepted, and were made to Bahawalpur in Pakistan, the hometown of Jaish chief Maulana Masood Azhar (Biswal 2016, The Diplomat online edition).

Experts in India feel that the heavily armed terrorists would not have been able to carry out the attack without the full knowledge and support of the Pakistani military and the ISI. G. Parthasarathy, former Indian High Commissioner to Pakistan, said on an NDTV programme that it would be naïve to believe the argument that the attackers were rogue elements or non-state actors (Biswal 2016, The Diplomat online edition).

In fact, while welcoming Prime Minister Narendra Modi's surprise visit to Lahore, many security experts and former diplomats had cautioned India to be ready to deal with an adverse situation like the Kargil War, which took place following the Lahore Summit of 1999. At the same time, there was apprehension among the Indian strategic community that the Pakistani Army would not have taken kindly to Modi's oblique reference to Pakistan as a sponsor of terrorism in Afghanistan in his address to the Afghan parliament on December 25. The fears may well have been justified, given Pathankot and the subsequent attack on the Indian consulate in the city of Mazar-i-Sharif. At any rate, the incidents refute any belief that the Pakistani military is supporting Prime Minister Nawaz Sarif in his endeavor to improve ties with India.

Only an investigation by the National Investigating Agency will enable India to conclusively establish the identity of the terrorists and ascertain the role of the Pakistani military and ISI. But what is clear from the Pathankot attack is the fact that the terrorists had two main aims. The first was to destroy MiG-21, Mi-25, Mi-35, and other military hardware, while the second was to derail the peace process, which received a boost with Modi's surprise stopover in Lahore (Biswal 2016, The Diplomat online edition).

While the Indian forces neutralized the terrorists before they could reach their target area, the Indian Government has taken care in dealing with the attack, trying to ensure that it does not cast a cloud over the peace process, especially given that a meeting of foreign secretaries is scheduled in mid-January. This is evident from the fact that New Delhi has been cautious about naming Pakistan with regard to this terrorist attack. Commenting on the attack, Modi said, "Today, enemies of humanity who can't see India progress tried to strike at our strategic area, a prominent airbase at the Pathankot" (Biswal 2016, The Diplomat online edition).

Meanwhile, in an unprecedented move, the Pakistani Government condemned the attack, and offered its cooperation to India. In a brief press statement, Pakistan's Foreign Office said India and Pakistan will continue with a "sustained dialogue process". A spokesperson went on to say that, "In line with Pakistan's commitment to effectively counter and eradicate terrorism, the government is in touch with the Indian Government and in working on the leaders provided by it." Yesterday, NDTV reported that Pakistani authorities have carried out raids in relation to the attack, leading to some arrests, and has formed a joint investigation team. These are welcome steps (Biswal 2016, The Diplomat online edition).

Understandably, the Pathankot airbase attack has put the Indian Government in a difficult situation, especially at a time when Modi is ready to travel miles to forge a durable peace with Pakistan. In fact, the attack has given opponents the opportunity to criticize Modi's overtures towards Pakistan. However, it is equally true that New Delhi has very limited options as far its relations with Islamabad are concerned. It is only through talks that India and Pakistan will be able to move towards building a peaceful environment in South Asia. The renewed dialogue process provides India with an opportunity to place all the evidence relating to the Pathankot attack before Pakistan and ask it to show its commitment to fighting terrorism (Bhaumik 2016, *The Times of India*).

Recent reports have showcased that there could have been a 26/9 or even a 26/10 in 2008 but it was foiled. A recent US intelligence report also has allayed fears that Pakistan's nearly 113 nuclear arsenals can be misused in case of a regime-change in Pakistan. If the military-Islamic Fundamentalist-ISI-terror establishment wrests control of Pak polity from civilian hands, threats can loom large about a possible 'first-use' of nuclear weapons, shedding aside the logic of nuclear deterrence and ushering in the fears of a nuclear holocaust in South Asia. The dangers of nuclear terrorism in South Asia, having its roots in Pakistan, also cannot be ruled out. Although the Nawaz Sharif-led Government has pledged not to let the Pakistani soil to be used by the terrorists, yet the 'terror industry' seems to have gone out of control and is virtually self-sustaining. Ideological rationality and sophisticated technology has imparted a new lethal face to the sources of terror outsourced from Pakistan. Although Pakistan aided the Abottabad operation with US forces in killing Osama bin Laden, with operational secrecy being its cornerstone, yet the Pak-sponsored terrorism with its ideological rationality based on the Kashmir issue and the doctrinal romanticism of Islam still seems to sustain the terrorist mindset in the youths who are forming a part of this India-centred terrorist operations having ethno-nationalist logic in their minds—one of liberating entire Indian part of Kashmir. Pakistan-engineered freedom movement in Kashmir continues to take the form of terrorist attacks meted out on the Indian side of the border.

The terror industry in Pakistan has assumed autonomous proportions and seems to be beyond civilian control. The Bonapartist state structure under the control of the military establishment, co-opting with the Islamic Fundamentalists and ISI network continues to breed terrorism which is now hurting Pakistan as well. The rhetoric of Anti-Indianism, ideological indoctrinations of the same which are carried out in the Islamic Madrasas in Pakistan, seems to work as a lifeline for the 'terror industry'. Terrorism has been resorted to derail any concerted attempts at restoring the India-Pakistan peace process, which can go a long way to sustain the Bonapartist-military state apparatus and its allied terror industry and Islamic fundamentalist establishments in Pakistan who tend to survive on the anti-Indian rhetoric.

A proactive foreign policy stance, offensive force projection capability and pre-emptive security and intelligence management strategies, adept intelligence sharing, maintenance of operational secrecy, are of utmost requirement for India to tackle the menacing face of Pak-sponsored terrorism. It should use both soft and hard diplomatic tactics—on the one hand, India should step up the composite peace process and dialogues with the civilian-democratic establishment of Pakistan, but at the same time be vigilant about any disruptive moves by the non-civilian army and Islamic Fundamentalist establishments in Pakistan.

If one dwells into the realm of IR Theory to explain the security dynamics in India-Pakistan relations, one may harp on the Realist-Neo-Realist chord by analyzing that Kashmir is an undeniable aspect of power struggle between the two states of India and Pakistan in an anarchical world order where there is no overarching authority and the pressures of the global hierarchical systemic order acting as a constraint on both the states. Structural constraints like nuclear proliferation across the globe and USA and China's support to Pakistan's militarization (in February 2016 US President Obama has pledged to sell fighter aircraft to Pakistan despite his earlier assurance to India to stop military aid to Pakistan) and nuclearization process imbued India to tread the nuclear path, setting off a nuclear arms race in South Asia. Terrorism as an aspect of Pakistan's India-centric policy is aimed at indirectly boosting Pakistan's power potential in an alternative yet negative way, vis-à-vis India in 'the battle over Kashmir'. But the Realist-positivist school of IR theory somewhat fails to provide any solution to the same, although explaining how the same is being sustained. If one turns to the so-called 'emancipatory' research projections of the Post-Positivist Constructivist paradigm, one can explain how the ideas, values, interests of leaders on both sides of the border are at least attempting to dilute the discordant spirit bolstered by cross-border terrorism from Pakistan, vis-à-vis alternative pressures from the 'terror industry' that are working to derail the same. Modi and Sharif's recent initiatives at initiating a composite dialogue process and bring back Indo-Pakistan ties. Somewhat back on the track can be highlighted, although the Pathankot terror attack has been acting as a vehement constraining force on the same. Yet a question remains—can any theory of IR really theoretically address the questions of causes of terrorism in India-Pakistan relations and suggest any measures to root out the same? The constructivist logic of "anarchy is what the states make of it" may not be able to research further on the same yet out of its theoretical folding emerges the notions of identities, interests, norms, values, cultural norms, human factors, which can be used for further theoretical research in the context of the deep-seated cultural factors, factors of exclusion, disillusionment, identity crisis of the minorities—a people-centric approach that can be utilized to dilute the causes that grow and sustain terrorism, the terrorist mindset and the terror-industry. Meagre Realist advocacy of military means cannot be a long-term solution to the problem of terrorism, since it cannot remove the real causes of terrorism. Hence, there remains a further scope of research in the theoretical field of IR in this aspect which can also be useful in the context of terrorism as a prime security imperative in the context of India-Pakistan relations.

References

Alavi, Hamza (1979). "The State in Post-Colonial Societies: Pakistan and Bangladesh" in Harry Goulborne (Ed.), *Politics and the State in the Third World*. London: Macmillan.

Banerjee, Sashanka S. (2006). *India's Security Dilemmas: Pakistan and Bangladesh*. USA: Anthem Press.

Bhaumik, Subir (2016, January 5). Countering Pathankot. *The Times of India*.

Biswal, Sumit (2016). The Pathankot Attacks and the Future of India-Pakistan Relations. From http://thediplomat.com/2016/01/the-pathankot-airbase-attack-and-the-future-of-india-pakistan-relations/ (Accessed on February 18, 2016).

Budania, Rajpal (2001). *India's National Security Dilemma: The Pakistan Factor and India's Policy Response*. New Delhi: Indus Publishing Company.

Cohen, Stephen Phillip. (2006). *The Idea of Pakistan*. New Delhi: OUP.

Ganguly, Sumit (1986). *The Origin of the War in South Asia: Indo-Pakistani Conflicts Since 1947*. London: Westview Press.

Ghosh, Sekhar Chandra (2009). "Pakistan: State Society Interface and Islamist Terrorism" in Radharaman Chakraborty and Iman Kalyan Lahiri (Eds.), *The Challenge of Terrorism*. New Delhi: Academic Excellence.

Karindalam, Aniruddha (2016). "Trust Deficit". *The Week*, January 10, 2016.

Nehru, Jawaharlal (1961). *India's Foreign Policy: Selected Speeches, September 1946-April 1961*. New Delhi: The Publications Division, Ministry of Information and Broadcasting, Government of India.

The Times of India, Kolkata Edition, January 3, 2016.

The Telegraph, Kolkata Edition, January 3, 2016.

The Telegraph, Kolkata Edition, February 9, 2016.

16

India and Bangladesh: Can the Asymmetry in Bilateral Relations be Overcome?

Purusottam Bhattacharya

I

As the second decade of the 21st century reaches its midpoint, South Asia finds itself in a paradox. With a population of 1.5 billion, nearly one-sixth of humanity, it offers great prospects for a deeply co-operative regional order while the reality is it is one of the least-integrated areas of the world. South Asia is a compact unit with a naturally demarcated geographical space, enjoying a broad cultural unity and a wide range of intra-regional economic complementarities. Yet the level of political, economic, social, security and cultural co-operation that prevails is much less than what is desirable.

As the largest and the most dominant country, India attracts the maximum attention among the eight States in the region. With its location in the middle of South Asia, India shares land and maritime borders with all the other countries of the region with the exception of Afghanistan. The Indo-centric nature of the region has been a source of discord between India and its South Asian neighbours for the past seven decades. The size, resources and capabilities of India have given rise to an asymmetry which has caused feelings of insecurity among the smaller states of the region. Besides India also has contentious issues at stake which characterize, to a considerable extent, its bilateral relations with its neighbours. A somewhat dominant presence in a less than contented neighbourhood also gives India a rather negative image in the wider world which is not conducive to New Delhi's aspirations to play a major role in international affairs in the decades to come.

II

It is in this context, the recent improvement in India's relations with its important eastern neighbour Bangladesh assumes considerable significance in creating an ambience of good neighbourliness in the region. As is well-known, India's relations with Dhaka have undergone many ups and downs since the emergence of Bangladesh as an independent state in 1971 (Jacques 2000). After the assassination of Mujibur Rahman, the founding father of Bangladesh, in August 1975, the relationship has generally been strained with the exception of the period 1996-2001 when an Awami League Government led by Sheikh Hasina Wajed, daughter of Mujibur Rahman was in power. Geopolitical factors have contributed to a power asymmetry between India and her smaller neighbours including Bangladesh which has complicated India's bilateral relationships in the South Asian region. In the eyes of the smaller states, India's intentions are suspect; as a Bangladeshi commentator puts it, after 1971 Indian strategists evolved "the South Asian version of the Monroe doctrine, wherein India views the entire region as a single strategic unit and herself as the sole custodian of security and stability in the region" (Sabur 1992: 159).

Geopolitics has been a major factor in conditioning India-Bangladesh relations. Bangladesh is often referred to as 'India-locked' because 90 per cent of its border is shared with India. Its access to the Bay of Bengal is also problematic due to a robust naval presence of India. On the other hand, India's North-East is 'Bangladesh-locked' prompting India to seek transit rights through Bangladesh in order to "open up the region to trade and economic activity, and in particular, to bring it closer both physically and psychologically to the rest of the country" (Majumdar 2014: 329; Murshid 2011: 50).

The irritants which have bedeviled India-Bangladesh relations over the years comprise long-standing issues like illegal migration, sharing of water of 54 common rivers, energy resources, access to seaports, maritime and land border disputes, presence of anti-social and anti-national elements in both countries. Any improvements in India-Bangladesh relations depend considerably on the resolution or at least partial progress in the above-mentioned contested areas (Dasgupta 2010). It is therefore natural that the overwhelming electoral victory of the Awami League (AL) led by Sheikh Hasina Wajed in the general elections in Bangladesh in December 2008 generated all round hopes of an improvement in India-Bangladesh relations since historically ties have been better when the AL was in power in Dhaka.

The climate of bilateral relations between New Delhi and Dhaka indeed has witnessed a distinct improvement since the installation of the Awami League Government in January 2009. This has been considerably facilitated by the better security-related co-operation between the two countries in recent times. India's security concerns vis-à-vis Bangladesh related to the sanctuaries enjoyed by indigenous Indian ethnic terrorist organisations such as the ULFA of Assam; the trans-border terrorist groups such as the Muslim Liberation Tigers of Assam (MULTA), the Independent Liberation Army of Assam (ILAA), and the Peoples United Liberation Front (PULF); the activities from Bangladesh territory of pro-al-Qaeda organisations of Pakistani origin supported by the ISI such as the LET, HUJI and the Harkat-ul-Mujahideen (HUM); gun running into India's North-East from and through Bangladesh; the unchecked illegal migration from Bangladesh into Assam and West Bengal; the flow of funds from Wahabi charity organisations in Saudi Arabia to the Bangladesh-India region; and the ISI's alleged use of Bangladesh and Nepal for pumping counterfeit currency into India and so on (Raman, H.B.).

While this has been the adverse security scenario so far as India is concerned for years the Government of Sheikh Hasina has taken many positive steps during the last seven years. Indian security agencies have been able to capture Arabinda Rajkhowa of the ULFA because of the co-operation of the Bangladesh authorities; investigation and prosecution of elements which were indulging in gun running under the previous BNP-Jamaat Government led by Begum Khalida Zia has been possible; an alleged plot by the LET to attack the Indian and US diplomatic missions in Dhaka was neutralized; pressure was applied by the Bangladesh authorities against one or two Indian Mujahideen elements living in Bangladesh territory which forced them to cross over into India and fall into the hands of the Indian security forces.[1]

One of the blunt realities of India-Bangladesh relations is the existence in Bangladesh of a strong anti-India lobby which comprises the Bangladesh Nationalist Party (BNP) founded by the late President Zia-ur-Rahman and currently led by his widow and two-time Prime Minister Begum Khalida Zia and the Jamat-e-Islami (JEI). This lobby views any friendly gestures on the part of Bangladesh towards India as a sell-out of Bangladesh's interests. Consequently, any attempts on the part of the Awami League to adopt a more positive attitude towards India during its tenures have been portrayed by the BNP and the JEI as a betrayal of Bangladesh's interests.

Therefore, Sheikh Hasina has been obliged to take a more cautious approach to Bangladesh-India relations during her present tenure. Hasina decided to visit India only after having been in office for a full one year so as not to give the impression that the Indian ties were being given any special consideration. The visit which took place during 10-13 January, 2010 was however a high point of the relationship in the last seven years. The Bangladesh Prime Minister was accompanied by a 123-member delegation that included Ministers of Foreign Affairs and Water Resources, advisers and a 50-member strong business contingent. The visit, was very successful and gave both countries a historic opportunity to build a new and forward looking relationship. During the course of the visit, Sheikh Hasina was conferred the prestigious Indira Gandhi Prize for Peace, Disarmament and Development for 2009 by the Government of India as a mark of recognition of her as a mass leader and statesman. A number of agreements and an MoU were also signed during the visit on mutual legal assistance in criminal matters, transfer of sentenced persons and combating international terrorism, organised crime and illegal drug trafficking, co-operation in power sector and a cultural exchange programme. The prime ministers of the two countries agreed to put in place a comprehensive framework of co-operation for development of the two countries on their mutually shared vision for the future. A Joint Communique issued during the visit outlined various initiatives which included India's announcement of a line of credit of US$ 1 billion for a range of projects pertaining to railway sector, procurement of buses and dredging of rivers (High Commission of India).

III

While the campaign for general elections was underway during April-May 2014, the prospect of the advent of Narendra Modi-led National Democratic Alliance Government in New Delhi was being viewed with apprehension and anxiety in India's neighbourhood, especially in Bangladesh and Pakistan. In the words of a veteran Indian journalist, interest in the Indian elections in Bangladesh was so intense that people knew the minutest details of the poll campaign as they watched India's television channels which are readily available in that country. People in Bangladesh were indignant about Narendra Modi's remarks about Bangladeshi illegal migrants in India. There was anxiety about the advent of a right wing Hindu nationalist government in India which would raise tensions between New Delhi and her neighbours, especially Muslim countries like Pakistan and Bangladesh.

The anxieties and apprehensions were however set to rest, at least for the time being, with the initiatives taken by the Modi Government in ushering in a new positive neighbourhood policy. In a masterful stroke in diplomacy, Narendra Modi invited all the eight leaders of the SAARC nations to his swearing in ceremony in New Delhi on 26 May 2014. He followed it up with his first personal foreign visit to Bhutan. The importance attached to Bangladesh was also soon made clear when the newly appointed Minister for External Affairs Sushma Swaraj visited Dhaka, the first such stand alone visit by the concerned Minister. Narendra Modi himself visited Bangladesh in June 2015 when the much touted Land Boundary Agreement (LBA) which was hanging fire for a long time was signed.

It may also be noted that these high profile visits by the leaders of the NDA Government had been preceded by similar visits by important functionaries of the previous United Progressive Alliance (UPA) Government led by the Congress Mr. Pranab Mukherjee, then Minister for External Affairs, visited Bangladesh in February 2009 and two agreements on trade and bilateral investment promotion and protection were signed. Mr. Somnath Chatterjee, the then Speaker of the Lok Sabha, visited Dhaka in the same month to address the Members of Bangladesh Parliament at the opening ceremony of 'Parliamentary Orientation Programme for 9th Jatiya Sangsad'. The Indian Prime Minister Dr Manmohan Singh made a high profile visit to Dhaka in September 2011. These and other high level visits have strengthened the bilateral relations between the two countries (Transcripts of Press Conferences).

No doubt the very notable improvements in India's relations with Bangladesh during the tenure of Sheikh Hasina have created a more positive ambience in the region, though as mentioned earlier there are elements in Bangladesh led by the BNP and the JEI who are not favourably disposed towards India. It should also be noted in this context that the attitude of many Indian political leaders, business magnates and strategic thinkers towards Bangladesh almost borders on disdain and apathy. To quote the former Foreign Secretary of India, Muchkund Dubey, "Very few of these people either understand the dynamics of the domestic politics of Bangladesh or have grasped the full import of Indo-Bangladesh relations." India has to realize that dealing with Bangladesh is a larger strategic issue and not just a commercial one. As noted earlier Bangladesh is located in a region geopolitically crucial to India. The North-East of the country is a disturbed zone with borders with China and Myanmar. It is also the pathway to integration of India's economy with those of the South East and East Asian countries whose markets are among the most important ones in the world for India's manufactured products. A friendly relation with Bangladesh is therefore an imperative and not a charity for New Delhi.

As also noted earlier there are high profile issues like river water sharing, final settlement of the land boundary and killing of Bangladeshis (mostly petty smugglers) by the BSF.

Discussions have been going on the first two issues and, as will be noted later in this paper, a solution to the boundary dispute has finally emerged in the year of 2015. So far as the water sharing issue is concerned, Bangladesh needs and wants free flow of river water for sheer existence. Any restrictions on river water flows can result in large arid zones in Bangladesh. A lot of discord occurred between the two countries on the issue of sharing of the waters of the principal river, Ganga, which flows through India and Bangladesh. After nearly two decades of tussle, an accord was reached in 1996 during Sheikh Hasina's first government which has a duration of 30 years, i.e. till 2026. However, the sharing of the waters of the river Tista is again, like the Ganga, proving to be contentious. The Tista originates in Sikkim and flows through North Bengal before entering Bangladesh where it merges with the Brahmaputra. A treaty on the sharing of the waters of this river was drawn up prior to the visit of Dr Manmohan Singh to Dhaka where it was to be signed in September 2011. In the draft treaty, India and Bangladesh were allocated 39 per cent and 36 per cent of the water flow, respectively. However, the West Bengal Chief Minister Mamata Banerjee refused to accept the draft treaty on the ground that the volume of water in the Tista was not adequate enough to allow for sharing. The proposed treaty would have hurt the interests of farmers in North Bengal, a sensitive issue with electoral repercussions for the Trinamul Government in West Bengal. On the other hand, Bangladesh proposes to undertake irrigation projects on the assumption that adequate waters from the Tista would be available.

The issue is taken very seriously by both Bangladesh and West Bengal. As a result, a solution is proving to be illusory. During Modi's trip to Dhaka in June 2015, Mamata Banerjee accompanied him and the Land Boundary Agreement was signed with Banerjee's consent. However, the Tista water sharing agreement was not part of the agenda and therefore remains unresolved. Modi has initiated a dialogue with Banerjee to settle the issue. However, in poll-bound West Bengal any settlement that appears to hurt the interests of North Bengal would be electorally damaging for Banerjee. On the other hand,

Bangladesh views the Indian stand with Mamata Banerjee calling the shots as yet another instance of Indian insensitivity towards the vital interests of Dhaka.

The Land Boundary Agreement has been the single most important achievement in India-Bangladesh relations in recent times. The border demarcated by the British at the time of partition was done at a hurry; consequently the international boundary between India and the then East Pakistan became a source of dispute. Apart from the problem of unsatisfactory demarcation of the boundary arose the unique phenomenon of 111 Indian enclaves in East Pakistan (subsequently Bangladesh) and 51 East Pakistani (subsequently Bangladesh) enclaves in India. It created a bizarre situation with the inhabitants of the respective enclaves becoming stateless and deprived of basic rights of life and living enjoyed by the citizens of a state. The 1974 Indira-Mujib agreement intended the transfer of these enclaves but it did not happen due to various reasons. Though the LBA was finally approved during the tenure of the UPA Government, the Indian Parliament passed the necessary constitutional amendment only after the Modi Government came to power. The LBA was signed by the two countries during Modi's Dhaka visit in June 2015 whereby India handed over a total of 17160 acres covering 111 enclaves to Bangladesh whereas in return India received 7110 acres comprising 51 enclaves. The exchange of population started after the agreement came into effect on 31 July 2015.

Environmental issues introduce yet another challenge in India-Bangladesh relations. It is now widely accepted that as a result of global warming sea levels would rise submerging low-lying areas and displacing a large number of people in a few decades from now. R.D. Kaplan feels that such environmental changes would trigger an anarchy which would be precipitated by growing population, disease and other degradations such as rising sea levels in critical overcrowded regions such as the Nile Delta and Bangladesh prompting mass migrations and inciting group conflicts. Environmental predictions suggest that as a result of global warming a rise in sea level may encompass around 20 to 25 per cent of the country's land in the next twenty to thirty years. The consequent displacement of population can only send the environmental refugees to India.

Another area where India needs to show greater generosity to Bangladesh is trade. For years the trade balance has been hugely in India's favour. In fiscal year 2008-09, Bangladesh's imports from India were US$ 2.841 billion and exports to India were US$ 276.58 million. Total bilateral trade in FY 2008-09 stood at US$ 3.117 billion. India needs to buy more from Bangladesh to redress as much of the trade imbalance as possible. India has already agreed to address removal of tariff and non-tariff barriers and port restrictions and facilitate movement of containerized cargo by rail and water. India's initiative to provide duty-free access to SAARC LDCs to the Indian market and reduction of the number of items from India's negative list that are of direct interest to Bangladesh are developments in the right direction (High Commission of India). On the whole it has to be borne in mind that India's foreign exchange earnings from trade in goods and services with Bangladesh are more than $ 10 billion annually and there are potentialities for doubling this earning in the near future.

It is pertinent to mention here that India is aware of the developmental needs of Bangladesh. In this context, India has made unilateral gestures to Bangladesh in several areas of bilateral relationship in recent times. Some of these gestures include allowing Bangladesh to export eight million pieces of readymade garments to India duty-free, lifting the ban on foreign direct investment (FDI) from Bangladesh, duty-free access to several items, pruning the sensitive list for promoting exports from Bangladesh to India which is to be noted in the context of Indian decision to allow a large number of items duty-free from the least developed countries in the SAARC area. More initiatives have been taken in recent times to improve the trade infrastructure of Bangladesh including land customs stations and to develop road, rail and riverine routes to facilitate greater economic engagement between the two countries. Notable in this context is also the Indian help extended after natural disasters such as the cyclone of November 2007 (Transcripts of Press Conferences).

India has been a major partner in Bangladesh's economic development. Areas which come within the purview of such co-operation include railway infrastructure, transportation, dredging, power grid inter-connectivity, human resource development and, as mentioned earlier, investment and trade. Mention may also be made here of the Indian decision to provide Bangladesh transit facilities to Nepal and Bhutan. The extension of $ 1 billion line of credit which was announced during the visit of the Bangladesh Prime Minister to India in January 2010 was implemented in August 2010. This is the largest ever credit given by India to any country. It can be a veritable stepping stone for a shared destiny (Transcripts of Press Conferences).

The issue of the so-called illegal Bangladeshi migrants in India is a huge irritant in bilateral relations. The porous border facilitates easy movement of people across. Domestic turmoil, pressure of population on limited land space and lack of economic and employment opportunities encourage people to look for greener pastures. There is a widespread perception in India, especially the states bordering on Bangladesh, that illegal migration from Bangladesh into India is a reality notwithstanding strenuous denials by successive regimes in Dhaka. The fear in India is that these migrants are not only taking away jobs from Indians but are also posing security threats as smugglers and radical Islamist terrorists may sneak into India in the guise of refugees. However, any attempt on the part of the Modi Government to expel the so-called illegal migrants will be fraught with constitutional and legal complications as it will be extremely difficult to establish the distinction between Bangladeshi Muslims and Indian Muslims. The actual numbers of migrants from Bangladesh is also a subject of debate among experts. Many political experts argue that such a potentially damaging issue should not be brought into the ambit of bilateral ties.

IV

In conclusion, it needs to be reiterated that the principal strategic challenge for New Delhi and Dhaka is to manage the geographic interdependence. In the words of C. Raja Mohan, "It is only recently that both sides have recognized that they need the other to make progress on a whole range of issues, from internal security to water resource management and economic modernistation" (Mohan 2015: 47). The logic of interdependence also calls for cooperation in the fight against terrorism and extremism in both countries. While reciprocity is a necessary part of the diplomatic game India must recognize that as the larger country with greater resources at its command it should be more generous to Bangladesh in its quest for development and greater prosperity. India is in a position to extend more help to the Bangladesh economy to develop to the extent it can engage its growing population at home. Such help can be extended on water conservancy and agriculture as well. As explained in the long run a developed Bangladesh economy will only help India itself.

The BSF needs to exercise greater restraint on the border. Between January 2009 and February 2010, it killed 93 Bangladeshis on the border. These killings are regularly reported on the Bangladeshi media which gives India a bad profile among the people of that country and is an easy fodder for India baiters.

India also needs to give greater access to Bangladeshi films and television. Till now Indian producers have received greater favour. The importance of the cultural issue must be better understood in India. The cultural issue was a major factor in the break with Pakistan and Bangladeshi emotions and sentiments in this regard must be appreciated in India.

What I am arguing here is that Bangladesh must be given greater quarters by India in its own interest. That is not to suggest that it should be a one sided affair. Both sides need to benefit from the relationship. However, as already argued, as the bigger and the stronger partner India can afford to be more magnanimous. The anti-India lobby in Bangladesh will be neutralized once the people of that country realize the benefits of the India connection. It is necessary to appreciate that Sheikh Hasina and her government which will be in office till the end of 2018 are fighting against heavy odds. India needs to support them in their struggle. However pragmatic diplomacy also recognizes the need to deal with whatever regime is in power in a country at a given point in time. Therefore, India should not keep all its eggs in the basket of the Hasina administration. As noted earlier India's foreign policy establishment also needs to take Bangladesh more seriously and deal with it with greater sensitivity and tact. So far as Bangladesh is concerned it also needs to realize that geopolitical reality dictates that the asymmetry between India and itself cannot be overcome but needs to be wisely negotiated. In the words of two Bangladeshi scholars S.A. Khan and A.K. Azad, "while as the most powerful and resourceful actor India is expected to show concessionary and flexible attitude towards its smaller neighbours, there has also been a growing realization among the smaller countries that the costs of conflict with India would be higher than the costs of co-operation." Bangladesh needs to cultivate links with the main political parties in India. Bilateral diplomacy has to be accompanied by people to people exchanges. Establishing a long-term good relationship is in the best interest of both the countries prisoners of geography as they are; it will also go a long way in creating an ambience of good neighbourliness in the South Asian region. It will be a significant step in establishing peace and security in South Asia.[2,3]

Notes

1. The recent success in this regard was the handing over of the much wanted and notorious Anup Chetia by the Bangladesh authorities to India.
2. In recent times there has been a greater appreciation in Bangladesh of the efforts India has been making in normalising India-Bangladesh relations. General H.M. Ershad, former military ruler of Bangladesh, during a recent visit to India, acknowledged that Delhi now treats Dhaka as equal partners and it is a happy sign. However he also pointed out that sharing of river waters remains the most important issue between the two countries. Bangladesh, being the lower riparian state, expects that India will not do anything which will harm its interests. General Ershad thinks that India is aware of Bangladesh's sentiments in this regard and is acting appropriately. Interview with General H.M. Ershad, *The Statesman*, 13 November 2010.
3. ———, "Some Thoughts on the Foreign Policy of the New Government", *Mainstream*, May 31, 2014.

References

Bhandari, Prakash (2015). "Navigating the woes of Distribution". In *The Statesman*, 23 August.

Dasgupta, Siddhartha (2010). "India-Bangladesh Ties: New Challenges for Distant Neighbours" in Raj Kumar Kothari (ed.), *India's Foreign Policy in the New Millennium*. Academic Excellence: New Delhi.

Dubey, Muchkund (2011). "Indo-Bangladesh Relations—Failure of Leadership on the Indian Side". In *Mainstream*, September 17.

High Commission of India, Dhaka (n.d.). *India-Bangladesh Relations*. From pharmexcil.org/components/com_mtree/attachment.php?link_id

Jacques, Kathryn (2000). *Bangladesh, India and Pakistan: International Relations and Regional Tensions in South Asia*. New York: St. Martin's Press.

Kaplan, R.D. (1994). "The Coming Anarchy". In *The Atlantic*.

Khan, S.A. and Azad, A.K. (1999). "Confidence Building Measures in South Asia-Bangladesh Perspective". In Dipankar Banerjee (ed.), *Cofidence Building Measures in South Asia*. Regional Centre for Strategic Studies: Colombo.

Majumdar, Anindya Jyoti (2014). "Making Sense of India-Bangladesh Relations". In *India Quarterly*, 70(4).

Mohan, C. Raja (2015). *Modi's World: Expanding India's Sphere of Influence*. New Delhi: Harpers Collins.

Murshid, K.A.S. (2011). "Transit and Transhipment: Strategic Considerations for Bangladesh and India". In *Economic and Political Weekly*, XLVI (17), 23 April.

Raman, B. (n.d.). "India and Bangladesh-Security Related Issues", *Occasional Papers from the South Asia Analysis Group*. From www.southasiananalysis.org

Sabur, A.K.M. Abdus (1992). "Bangladesh—India Relations: An Overview". In Bertram Bastiampillai (ed.), *India and Her South Asian Neighbours*. Bandarnaike Centre for International Studies: Colombo.

Thakar, Milind (2010). "Indo-Bangladesh Relations: The Puzzle of Weak Ties". In Sumit Ganguly (ed.), *India's Foreign Policy: Retrospect and Prospect*. New Delhi: Oxford University Press.

Transcripts of Press Conferences/statements/Q&As. From http://mea.gov.in

17

Emerging Trends in India-Nepal Relations: Select Issues

Budh Bahadur Lama

Introduction

India-Nepal relations are 'distinctive' for many reasons ranging from geographical proximity to close cultural ties, and wide institutional and social relationships. Socio-cultural, political, economic and geographical factors along with the common bond of a shared religion have had a great impact on their bilateral relations. The two sovereign states—India and Nepal are generally guided by their national interests that includes social, cultural, geo-political and economic concerns. In spite of some turbulence in the past, India-Nepal relations have remained close, stable and mutually beneficial to each other. However, some internal and external factors are responsible for creating disturbances in their bilateral ties which could be seen in the recent movements launched by the Madhesi groups against the newly drafted constitution of Nepal in Terai regions. People from Terai understand the new constitution of Nepal in a different way which has no provisions incorporated to secure the autonomy and representation of Madhesi groups exclusively in various political institutions in their own country. As a result roads are blocked and no flows of goods from India to Nepal for which people in hills have been suffering for their basic necessities.

In the era of globalisation and a multi-polar world order, it is assumed that actions taken place in a particular state can have trans-national consequences in the present world. Therefore, no single country has the capacity to deal with challenges without the support and cooperation of other countries. India is also equally involved in the spheres of globalised influences. India therefore believes that all its neighbours whether big or small are crucial for its economic growth and stability and security interests. Like any other country in the world, India's foreign policy is also rooted in its national ethos which supports the processes of national development and transformation through the persistence of the country's national interests. Foreign policy of India ensures its security, promotes its socio-economic development, and maintains the country's strategic autonomy and working towards a more just global order. It also has a strong multilateral stand working closely as partner in international bodies to tackle contemporary global challenges such as terrorism, climate change, sustainable development, energy and food security and the others. In addition, India seeks reforms in the structural set up of international institutions to reflect the global reality of contemporary world and to clarify a probable role for India. At the same time, India's priority has been to "ensure a peaceful, secure and stable neighbourhood" (Annual Report 2010-11) through cooperation and by making its neighbours stakeholders in India's growth by linking them to the larger Indian economy. In most of the occasions, India has attempted invariably to bring all its neighbours into a common platform called South Asian Association for Regional Cooperation (SAARC) to face the challenges that affect regionally or globally.

Dr. Karan Singh calls South Asia as "a microcosm of a multicultural world" (Singh 2015)[1] which means building of the cultural unity of South Asia in the context of music, dance, painting, literature and sculptures as a part of its shared legacy. He believes that colonialism had shattered the deep socio-cultural and economic links of the South Asian countries in the past. Dr. Singh asserts that the region should pick up the threads and try to reconnect economically, politically and socially. Here he cites a classic example of such initiatives taken by India and Bangladesh like the recent border agreement between them.

However, misunderstandings arise despite of best intentions that are exercised by some analysts in different countries to criticize India for its alleged 'hegemonic' intentions. Nepal is an important neighbour of India and occupies special magnitude in its foreign policy because of the geographic, historical, cultural and economic linkages for centuries. The India-Nepal relationship is determined more by geography and history than any other concerns. These two countries share an open border and unrestricted movement of people, which is unique in Asia. The open border is a symbol of their deep trust and friendship. However, there are certain issues that influence the nature of bilateral relations between India and Nepal and cause a misunderstanding between them. It is obvious that the issues of influence may gradually turn into perhaps a clash of understanding between the two countries. Such a clash may destroy their historical relations. To avoid any kind of misunderstandings, both the countries must pay attention to the emerging trends in their bilateral relations so that they may restructure and develop a flexible pattern for their friendly relations based on their national and global interests. Here my paper is an attempt to discuss the emerging trends in India-Nepal relations with a special focus on the select issues.

Politicisation of Peace Treaty

It is claimed that India-Nepal relationship has been established since time immemorial. No one can challenge the reality that India and Nepal have successfully built up their bilateral relations even before the treaties and agreements signed. It can be said that these treaties and agreements signed by the two independent nations have been further strengthened their bilateral ties. One of the most important treaties is the Treaty of Peace and Friendship signed by India and Nepal in 1950. The Treaty recognises sovereignty, territorial integrity, and independence of both the nations. Article 2 of the 1950 Treaty contains some mutual obligations by stating that the "two governments hereby undertake to inform each other of any serious friction or misunderstanding with any neighbouring state likely to cause any breach in the friendly relations subsisting between the two governments". According to Article 5, "the

Government of Nepal shall be free to import, from or through the territory of India, arms, ammunition or warlike material and equipment necessary for the security of Nepal. The procedure for giving effect to this arrangement shall be worked out by the two Governments acting in consultation." Article 6 states that "each Government undertakes, in token of the neighbourly friendship between India and Nepal, to give to the nationals of the other, in its territory, national treatment with regard to participation in industrial and economic development of such territory and to the grant of concessions and contracts relating to such development". Similarly, Article 7 refers to the reciprocal privileges to be granted to the nationals of both countries. The letter exchanged with the treaty, which was kept as a secret document until 1959, further explains the necessity of mutual consultation by stipulating that: "Neither government shall tolerate any threat to the security of the other by a foreign aggressor and to deal with any such threat, the two Governments shall consult with each other and devise effective countermeasures" (Baral 1992: 815-29). An agreement was signed by the two governments in January 1965 "under which New Delhi agreed to underwrite as far as possible the entire requirements of the Nepalese army. American and British assistance would be sought only when India was not in a position to supply the necessary equipment" (Rose 1971: 273).[2] Even in such a case, Nepal could import arms from those countries only in coordination with India, thus restricting Nepal's independence in acquiring arms from the United States and the United Kingdom (Baral 1992: 815-29).

However, the 1950 Treaty has different reasons to become a disturbing concern in Nepal and the demand for its abrogation has frequently attributed in election manifestos of different political parties. It had been observed that the Rana regime broke within six months of signing it. Either directly or indirectly the following regimes in Nepal have been expressing their reservations on the 1950 Treaty. Nepalese leaders thought that the 1950 Treaty represented Indian hegemonic attitude in terms of bilateral relations. The 1950 Treaty is one-sided and undemocratic in nature that carries out India's vested interest in Nepal. In various occasions, the Nepalese leaders have raised their voices against the Treaty being discriminatory in nature. So they want restructuring of the 1950 Treaty which will serve the interest of Nepal in the bilateral relations with India. But the political leaders of Nepal have failed to come out with the consensus of people both from the Hills and Terais in this regard.

In Nepal, people of Terai have strong connections with people across the border in India and they are very much inclined to India than Nepal and want the continuation of the 1950 Treaty. One of the important reasons behind it is that this Treaty grants resident status to the citizens of both countries. So many Nepalese citizens who have entered into India for different purposes like taking up government jobs, farming, etc. have enjoyed the resident status from the very beginning. In due course of time, they have been settled down in different parts of India. Even though Nepal does not respond on this section of the 1950 Treaty which has really enabled many Nepalese citizens to take up government jobs in India. They have been treated equally without any discrimination on the basis of caste, gender, religion, etc. in Indian territories. Many of them have been enrolled in voter list and enjoy the political rights including right to vote. Some of them are having citizenship of both India and Nepal which is illegal. It has been frequently reported that the Nepalese citizens are privileged to access all rights in both the nations.

However, Indian Gorkhas have expressed their dissatisfaction to the privileges facilitated by the 1950 Treaty to Nepalese citizens in India. Indian Gorkhas (Bharatiya Gorkhas) are Indian citizens of Nepali ethnicity who speak Nepali language incorporated as one of the eighteen languages in the Eighth schedule of the Constitution of India in August 1992. They are resident of Gorkhaland region of India and scattered all over the country, with a large concentration of population in Northeast India. The term 'Indian Gorkha' is used to distinguish between Indian citizens who identify themselves as Gorkhas and the citizen of Nepal who prefer are being referred to as Nepalese. In the introduction to the book *Gorkhas Imagined* (2009), Prem Poddar comments about the Gurkhas in Nepal versus the Gorkhas in India: "the word 'Gorkha' as a self-descriptive term and has gained currency as a marker of difference for Nepali-speaking Indian Gorkha living in India as opposed to the Gurkhas in Nepal".

The perception of Indian Gorkha carries some kind of negative remarks in this context and since 1980s they have been trying to abrogate the 1950 Treaty. Indian Gorkha thinks that the 1950 Treaty has raised fingers on their constitutional rights in India. They have been labelled as 'Made in Nepal' instead of 'Made in India'. It is happened due to massive presence of Nepalese citizens in India. It has been observed that Government of India has failed to keep the record of Nepalese citizens residing permanently in India. Despite this, there are healthy amount of seasonal migrants coming from Nepal and entering into India for jobs and the others. This has created confusion in the minds of other Indians that Indian Gorkhas are originally from Nepal and their demand for separate state within Indian federation is considered as unconstitutional. Indian Gorkha raises their voice at regular interval for 'Gorkhaland' a separate state in Indian federation as 'their constitutional rights' which they want to have it. But their demand for a separate state is not yet fulfilled. So they consider themselves underprivileged and 'homeless' Indians within their own country and the label that is 'Made in Nepal' continues to be a brand for Indian Gorkhas in India. This is how the 1950 Treaty has successfully created two different Nepali ethnic groups in India—Indian Gorkha and Nepalese.

Eventually, Nepal has passed much legislation to dilute the original spirit of the 1950 Treaty. The leaders at the local level in Nepal have politicised the 1950 Treaty to serve their political interest by inculcating the anti-India sentiments in the minds of Nepalese citizens. The 40 demands of the Communist Party of Nepal (Maoist) in 1995 also focused on the 1950 Treaty and produced intense anti-India feelings during the People's War. For the period of the constitutional monarchy, the Nepalese Foreign Minister Kamal Thapa of the royalist Rashtriya Prajatantra Party (RPP) visited India in August 1998 made some proposition to revise the 1950 Treaty. Manifesto of the Communist Party of Nepal (Maoist)[3] for Constituent Assembly (CA) elections in 2008 incorporates the promises to abrogate the Treaty and to sustain equal distance between India and China. The Communist Party of Nepal (Unified Marxist-Leninist, UML) also assured to reconsider 'all unequal Treaties', whereas the Nepali Congress remained silent on the subject (Overwhelming Support for Maoist Proposal 2008). When India expressed its willingness to amend the Treaty, there has been no political consensus in Nepal over the matter and no alternative or specific proposal has been given by Nepal regarding the provisions they want to revise (Nayak 2014). The politicisation of this Treaty is also obvious from the fact that no political party of Nepal wants to abrogate it.[4]

With a continuous assertion of Nepalese Maoists on revision of the Treaty, India and Nepal agreed to form a high-level committee headed by their foreign secretaries to review the Treaty and to suggest possible modifications in 2008. In May 2008, former Indian Ambassador to Nepal, Deb Mukherjee stated that the demand for the revision of the Treaty has been raised several times in the past and we [India] have said, fair enough, renegotiate or restructure. In fact, Clause 10 of the Treaty clearly says it can be abrogated by either side on a year's notice. And I remember that during the Foreign Secretary-level talks in 2001, we had reminded the Nepali delegation of the clause and said, why don't you do it? We should be prepared to discuss all options (Nepal to Delhi 2008).

India's former Foreign Secretary Shyam Saran also dismissed the contention of Prachanda that the Treaty was an 'unequal pact', and pointed out that under the pact "Nepali citizens enjoy special privileges in India" (India ready to...). India has told Nepal it is ready to revise the 1950 India-Nepal Friendship Treaty. Prime Minister Narendra Modi, first bilateral visit by an Indian PM to Nepal in 17 years, told his counterpart Sushil Koirala that he wanted to see it completed in his tenure. Nepal has been asked to send a team to negotiate this with India as soon as possible. By putting this out on the table at the start of his engagement with Nepal, Modi has made it clear he will not accept popular Nepali gripe about this Treaty. Nepal has used the "unequalness" of the Treaty as a stick against India over the years. But despite repeated Indian requests for revision, Nepal has shied away from the actual negotiations. "The India-Nepal treaty is unequal in its treatment of Indian citizens in Nepal, which India has never complained about," said Jayant Prasad, former Ambassador to Nepal (Bagchi 2014). While Nepali citizens get national treatment here, the same is not applicable to Indians in Nepal. Some Indian thinkers have developed different perspectives on the relevance of the 1950 Treaty in the present global security scenario. Former Indian Ambassador to Nepal, K.V. Rajan (2008) has observed that "the relevance of the Treaty for India's security in the present context is limited and uncertain due to growing terrorist activities in South Asia and the other parts of the globe" (Rajan 2008).

Despite the fact that the Treaty not only addresses mutual security concerns of both countries but also covers other socio-cultural and economic issues. It has been seen that people have criticised more the 1950 Treaty than the Treaty itself. However, both countries have at regular intervals recognized each other's importance and value and have also portrayed the relationship as 'special' on a variety of events. For instance, Maoist leader and former Prime Minister Baburam Bhattarai stated that "Practically, we are more closely linked with India, with an open border and closer economic ties. As a result we have maximum exchanges with India and maximum troubles too, which sometimes creates misunderstanding" (Nepal won't jeopardise...). Hence, keeping in mind the dynamism of geopolitics in the contemporary world, both India and Nepal should develop a serious thought on the 1950 Treaty issue and must build a consensus to revise it for the benefits of people of both nations.

Strategic Importance of Nepal for India

The notion of 'Big Brother' is very much relevant in the context of bilateral relations between India and Nepal. India as a big brother of Nepal always extends its cares and guidance and assistance in various fields in the interest of Nepal and India. Nepal also prefers India to China in making a better flow of goods, ideas, and people and of course transportation and communication for its economic growth and stability. Nepal is aware of having the maximum economic, socio-cultural and political developments possible by making cordial relations with India. There is no doubt that the expected development of Nepal would be possible due to open border that represents a deep trust of both India and Nepal.

Nepal being a landlocked country surrounded by two Asian giants—India and China, always keeps hands open for the assistance and maintains a balanced relations between India and China. Nepal frequently uses 'China Card' to have soft threat to India in order to have extra-privileges from India. No doubt India has its strategic interests in Nepal since 1950. Jawaharlal Nehru in December 1950 said: "From time immemorial, the Himalayas have provided us with a magnificent frontier.... We cannot allow that barrier to be penetrated because it is also the principal barrier to India" (Nehru 1961: 436). Therefore, "the political instability and adverse security situation in Nepal has been a cause of deep concern to India" (Annual Report 2005-06: 13). India believes that the Himalayas are the natural frontiers which will not allow Chinese militants to have illegal enter easily into Indian territories.

However, due to technological advancement, mass destruction weapons, and globalisation and of course the improvement in India-China relations, the Himalayas as a natural frontier have become less relevant in recent years. The Chinese have also broken the Indian belief of the Himalayas as a natural barrier by extending the Qinghai-Tibet railway line till Lhasa. Beijing plans to extend it to Nepal in the near future and later further into the South Asian hinterland (Li 2009: 81). China has realised that South Asia would be the best business hub for Chinese products which can flow easily through Nepal via Tibet Autonomous Regions (TAR). For this China is always ready to tie with Nepal. Similarly, Nepal also wants to become a transit point in post-monarchical phase between China and India in order to benefit from the economic growth taking place in its neighbourhood. So the growing Nepal-China relations may have a negative impact on India-Nepal relations especially in their strategic equations.

Moreover, Nepal will undoubtedly continue to be of strategic importance for India due to various reasons. Nepal is the only country in South Asia whose citizens are privileged like an Indian in India. The Treaty of Peace and Friendship (1950) guarantees provisions to both the nationalists for free movement, settling down and carrying out business freely both in Indian as well as in Nepalese territories. It is also to be noted that Nepal has topographical parallel with the northern borders of India. As a result, India's heartland will be in danger to Chinese attacks during any kind of conflict situation. Despite this, the old trade route between Kathmandu and Tibet via Kerung is the new Silk Road. Traditionally used by yak caravans bartering salt for rice, the route has been upgraded to an 18 km highway connecting Syabrubesi to Rasuwagadhi. That road is already connected to Kathmandu and to the Prithvi Highway, making it an alternative to the Kodari access to Tibet (Sthapit 2011).

According to Nepal Government sources, technically, the Syabrubesi-Rasuwagadhi road is "more reliable than the Kodari Highway" (*Republica Kathmandu News* 2009). However, the Syabrubesi-Rasuwagadhi highway and Araniko were blocked due to the damage caused by the earthquake, hampering trade with China. Even then China had assured Nepal that China will provide support for restoration and re-opening of Araniko and Syabrubesi-Rasuwagadhi Highways as priority projects (Nepal Army with...). Once these roads are opened, Nepal will be able to transport gas and petroleum products from China through this route (Pandey 2010: 130). So Nepal will have some more space to bargain with India. India at the same time must pay attention towards Nepal's inclination to China for its security concerns and economic growth. Undoubtedly, India has built up substantial military protection all along the India-China border but it remains in danger by the side of Nepal's border with China. In addition, given the Chinese security build-up in Tibet over the last 15 years, India's susceptibility has increased even further. China has immensely improved the roads connectivity and military infrastructure on its side of the border in Tibet. It is reported that China has set up 23 airfields in TAR (Tibet Autonomous Region), exclusively for military purposes very recently. This has become a key concern for India. Even if India has upgraded its physical and air protection by adding to its existing strength, it is still unable to match the Chinese preparations. Therefore, Nepal's valleys are more important than its mountains for defending Indian territory in case of any warfare (Mihaly 2002: 172). Since the Chinese interest in South Asia has increased for the expansion of its trade and commerce, China will try to make further investments in strategic locations in Nepal. India being a closed country to Nepal believes that Nepal will always abide by the UN principles and will not allow any third country to attack India through its territory. Similarly, Nepal, as a small neighbour of China would like to maintain its close relationship with India as a restraint for any potential Chinese aggression (Nayak 2014).

Madhesi Protest and India's Stand

Nepal is topographically divided into three areas—Mountains, Hills and Madhes. Madhes consists of 22 districts which refer to 'Madhya-desh', a region also known as 'Terai' all of which share their borders with Northern India. The inhabitants of Madhes are called 'Madhesi', who are the original dwellers of Madhes. Many Madhesis are of Indian origin and so they have strong socio-cultural linkages across the border. Since long, Madhesis have been suffering from a sense of discrimination and deprivation. They also feel exploited and discriminated by the upper caste Pahadi migrant communities. The residents of hill are called 'Pahadi' (hill people). Pahadis have migrated not only to urban but also to rural areas of Madhes for their easier life. As a result the Madhesi population constitutes nearly one-third of the Nepali population which includes Hindi-speaking Indian Madhesis. Indian Madhesis were excluded from citizenship certificates under the Citizenship Act of 1964, due to which they could neither acquire land ownership nor could get jobs in government sectors. However, the Citizenship Law was amended in November 2006 which refers to the provisions for acquiring the citizenship by people born in Nepal before 1990 and residing there permanently. It has also been alleged that many Madhesis and Dalits are deprived of acquiring the citizenship in Nepal.

The Pahadis of Nepal understand that India has been in support of the demand for federalism raised by the Madhesis in Nepal. They also think that India has been constantly encouraging the demand for 'One Madhes One Pradesh' made by Madhesis in Terai regions. Many Nepalese have viewed that the demand of Madhesis is an attempt backed by India to bifurcate Nepal into two different regions based on Madhesis and Pahadis. According to Dr. Nihar Nayak, "the perception gained currency in the early 2000s as India was attempting to carry out special development programmes in the underdeveloped and neglected Terai region to prevent Nepalese Maoist from gaining influence there, given the strategic linkages with Indian Maoists". Since then most of the development projects funded by India had been carried out in Terai regions only. Dr. Nayak says that after Constituent Assembly election, India reportedly used this constituency to promote its interests in Nepal. It is alleged that India had attempted to use Madhesi parliamentarians to keep the Maoists out of power.

In recent scenario, India has reacted strongly to Nepal's new constitution. Professor S.D. Muni says that in India's official statements issued on the subject, the promulgation of the new Constitution has just been 'noted' not welcomed. Nepal has been urged to resolve differences "through dialogue in an atmosphere free from violence and intimidation" so as to "enable broad based ownership and acceptance". Dr. Muni further says that India has its reasons to be upset with the way Nepali leaders have gone about the constitution-making process. Three of them are obvious and openly stated. First, the constitution as promulgated is not inclusive. It ignores the aspirations and sensitivities of the Madhesis, the Janjatis (tribal groups), Dalits and women. This is contrary to the spirit of the Jan Andolan-II that created a vision of New Nepal and against the assurances given by the late Girija Prasad Koirala as Prime Minister in 2007 during the Madhes agitation. Dr. Muni also says that leaders of the major political parties belonging to the dominant hill social groups have ignored the wishes of the marginalised groups in the new constitution. The marginalised groups are accordingly agitating against the bulldozing of the constitutional process. The use of force by the government to suppress the agitation has resulted in the loss of more than 40 lives, with many more injured. Life has come to a standstill in nearly 20 of the 22 Terai districts of Nepal.

To Dr. Muni, India had been encouraging Nepali leaders to draft an inclusive and democratic constitution. In Prime Minister Narendra Modi's address to the Constituent Assembly in August 2014, Modi had hoped that Nepal's new constitution would be like a bouquet of flowers representing the different shades of Nepal's communities, regions and opinions—and reflecting a broad national consensus. His address had been universally acclaimed in Nepal. He underlined the same theme during his second visit to Kathmandu during the SAARC summit in November last year.

Dr. Muni says that some prominent Nepali leaders like Sher Bahadur Deuba of the Nepali Congress, Madhav Nepal of the Communist Party of Nepal—United Marxist Leninist (UML) and Prachanda of the United Communist Party of Nepal—Maoists, were invited for consultations to New Delhi to make them appreciate India's concerns. All of them endorsed these concerns and assured India that marginalised groups would be accommodated. But there were no signs of this being done. The External Affairs Minister of India Sushma Swaraj in a statement on September 14, 2015, recalled "the encouraging voices…from Nepalese leaders" that "the Constitution will carry along all regions and sections". She expressed India's concern "over the ongoing protests and strife in several parts of Nepal" and urged "continuing flexibility on the part of all the political forces so that all outstanding issues are addressed through dialogue and widest possible agreement, in an atmosphere free from violence". The new constitution has sharply polarised Nepal along ethnic and regional lines. This polarisation will keep Nepal unstable and turbulent, which is not at all in India's long-term interests.

Conclusion

Here a proverb *it is easy to make friendship but difficult to maintain it,* becomes quite relevant in the context of India-Nepal relations. Their bilateral relations are not a just one or two-day efforts to have a strong tie or bond. Since it is a relation of time immemorial which has a thread of deep trust and belief, shows greater prospects in coming days if they continue their unique relations. Both India and Nepal can set up as an example of deep trust and non-violence in today's world where terrorism prevails and makes the lives of people and their economy unsecured. India needs to bring some flexibility in its approach towards the development of Nepal. Nepal a sovereign state always tries to prosper its economic growth and development for which it may try to develop better relations with China. However, Nepal is not in a position to avail all its necessities from China so easily like availing from India. So Nepal knows its limitations and always try keep good relations with both the giant Asian countries—India and China.

It is also reported that many Nepalese youths have targeted to go gulf countries in order to find out jobs and opportunities instead of going to India. So the number of the seasonal migrants from Nepal and Nepalese youths coming to India has gradually decreased. This trend blurs their bilateral relations in the international scenario. Nepal's political system is still under experimentation so it has to face both internal and external challenges like Madhesi protest, etc.

Notes

1. Dr. Karan Singh, Member of Indian Parliament, Rajya Sabha, delivered the Keynote Address at the inaugural session of the two-day 9th South Asia Conference on "Culture as a Factor in Regional Cooperation in South Asia", organised by the Institute for Defence Studies and Analyses (IDSA) on November 26-27, 2015.
2. A full text of the "secret" document is in *The Statesman* (New Delhi), May 27, 1989.
3. Overwhelming support for Maoist proposal (2008, March 15-31). *The Red Star*, a CPN (Maoist) publication, Kathmandu, I(6). The manifesto also promised to bring necessary changes in managing and controlling of Nepal-India border, initiation to conclude encroachment of Nepalese land at India border, end of Gorkha recruitment centre, etc.
4. Article 10 of the Treaty of Peace and Friendship between the Government of India and the Government of Nepal was signed

on 31 July 1950, says "This Treaty shall remain in force until it is terminated by either party by giving one year's notice."

References

Annual Report 2010-2011. (2010-11). Introduction and Synopsis section. *Ministry of External Affairs, Government of India*. From http://mea.gov.in/Uploads/PublicationDocs/45_Annual-Report-2010-2011.pdf

Annual Report 2005-06. *Ministry of External Affairs*, Government of India.

Article entitled *'India's Nepal Policy Needs Caution, Not Grandstanding'* by S.D. Muni at (http://thewire.in/2015/09/23/indias-nepal-policy-needs-caution-not-grandstanding-11430 (Accessed on February 05, 2016).

Bagchi, Indrani (2014, August 4). India ready to revise 1950 friendship treaty with Nepal. *The Times of India*. From http://timesofindia.indiatimes.com/india/India-ready-to-revise-1950-friendship-treaty-with-Nepal/articleshow/39577338.cms?gclid=CNuuhrbp3coCFQ8eaAody1cKzQ (Accessed on February 04, 2016).

Baral, Lok Raj (1992, September). India-Nepal Relations: Continuity and Change. *Asian Survey*, 32(9): 815-29, Published by University of California Press. From Stable URL: http://www.jstor.org/stable/2645073 (Accessed on January 16, 2016).

India ready to renegotiate 1950 treaty with Nepal (2008, May 6). *One India News*. From http://news.oneindia.in/2008/05/06/india-ready-to-renegotiate-1950-treaty-with-nepal-1210072316.html (Accessed on February 04, 2015).

Li, Zhang (2009, October). To manage conflict in South Asia: China's stakes, perceptions and inputs. *Asia Paper*, Institute for Security and Development Policy, Stockholm. 81.

Mihaly, Eugene Bramer (2002). Foreign Aid and Politics in Nepal: A Case Study. Himal Books, Kathmandu.

Nayak, Nihar R. (2014). *Strategic Himalayas Republican Nepal and External Powers*. New Delhi. Institute for Defence Studies and Analysis.

Nehru, Jawaharlal (1961). *India's Foreign Policy: Selected Speeches, September 1946–April 1961*. New Delhi: Ministry of Information and Broadcasting, Government of India. 436.

Nepal Army with China Troops to reopen north trade points (2015, July 25). *Nepal Mountain News*, Kathmandu. From http://www.nepalmountainnews.com/cms/2015/07/25/nepal-army-with-china-troops-to-reopen-north-trade-points/ (Accessed on February 01, 2016).

Nepal to Delhi: Junk sentiment and special ties (2008, May 3). *The Telegraph*, Kolkata.

Nepal won't jeopardise any genuine Indian interest (2011, September 3). Former Nepal Prime Minister Baburam Bhattarai's interview to Prashant Jha, *The Hindu*. From http://www.thehindu.com/opinion/interview/article2419048.ece (Accessed on January 06, 2015).

Overwhelming Support for Maoist Proposal (2008, March 15-31). *The Red Star*, a CPN (Maoist) publication, Kathmandu, I(6).

Pandey, Nishchal Nath (2010). *New Nepal: The Fault Lines*. London: Sage Publications.

Rajan, K.V. (2008, May 3). Should the 1950 treaty be scrapped? *The Hindu*. From http://www.thehindu.com/2008/05/03/stories/2008050352481000.htm (Accessed on January 06, 2015).

Rose, Leo E. (1971). *Nepal: Strategy for Survival*. Bombay: Oxford University Press.

Singh, Karan's Keynote Speech (2015, November 26-27) in 9th South Asia Conference on *Culture as a Factor in Regional Cooperation in South Asia* organised by the Institute for Defence Studies and Analyses (IDSA), access at http://www.idsa.in/sac/speakers.html

Sthapit, P. (2011). The New Silk Road. Kathmandu, *Nepal: Nepali Time*, Issue 577.

Tulsi Sitaula, Joint-Secretary and Chief of Construction Department, Ministry of Physical Planning and Works, Government of Nepal, interview to *Republica* on 30 December 2009, Kathmandu, at http://www.myrepublica.com/portal/index.php?action=news_details&news_id=13437 (accessed on 26 January 2016).

18

India and Myanmar: Implications of New Democratic Forces' Victory in 2015 Elections for New Delhi

B.N. Mehrish

The spirit of democracy is in the air in Myanmar. India's relations with its neighbour are crucial for both foreign policy and domestic security reasons. A terrible security dilemma faced the P.V. Narasimha Rao Government in the early 1990s. Kashmir was in flames and the Naga rebels were running rampant. India's efforts to stabilise the Northeast with the help of Myanmar combined with the economic benefits of trade and transport links across the Indo-Myanmar border and the Northeast is an important determinants in its policy towards Myanmar. The Look East policy has largely focused on a stretch running from Bangkok to Jakarta. One gap has been second largest Southeast Asian nation. More importantly, Myanmar is the only with a land border with India.

China and India, two of Myanmar's giant neighbours, as for long have showered the military junta with investments, aid and sale of armaments. China's active support is not surprising at all as it has its own record of suppressing democratic movements at home.

India has also helped the military junta with arms and training. The "idealist" phase of India's foreign policy approach to Myanmar dates from when Indian Prime Minister Jawaharlal Nehru and his counterpart, U Nu, were close friends and decided policies based on trust and cooperation. After U Nu's ouster in a military coup in 1962, successive India governments opposed the dictatorship on principle. With the coming of the P.V. Narasimha Rao Government in 1991, India wagged its tail all along. The "pragmatic" phase of Indian foreign policy towards Myanmar since the early 1990s meant throwing principles out of the window and doing anything required to further Indian strategic and economic interests. India also perceived need to counter, "Chinese influence" in Myanmar (Sagar 2007: 4027).

India needs a stable and self-confident Myanmar that can keep China at bay. Events in Myanmar took a significant turn on September 5, 2007, when 500 monks marched through the streets of Pakhokku in Central Rangoon's Magwe division. On September 22, 2007 hundreds of monks reached in front of the house where Aung San Suu Kyi had been under house arrest for more than 15 years. As expected the military junta cracked down the march for the restoration of democracy. A large number of monks were shot dead and many more injured. Not surprisingly, pressure mounted on international community to tighten sanctions, with the UN Security Council demanded that junta should show restraint. China and Russia opposed sanctions. The Association of South East Asian Nations (ASEAN) had been unable to persuade the Myanmar generals for a political dialogue with Suu Kyi, the leader of the democratic movement. ASEAN asked India and China to do something constructive. The US and European Union also called for further sanctions and urged China and India to intervene and facilitate dialogue between military rulers and pro-democracy groups. But the junta did not care for the world opinion. The UN envoy Ibrahim Gambari had to wait for three days before he could meet with Senior General of Myanmar, Than Shwe.

India like its Asian neighbours has made investments in Myanmar. Apart from economic ties, Myanmar is also "an important list of the strategic jigsaw" for both India and China. Since China is and will remain India's key competitor in the race for Asian supremacy, India has to maintain good relations with Myanmar to contain China in South East Asia (Jha 2007: 47-48; Sundaraman 2009: 11; Chaudhuri 2012: 19). India will need to restore its image among pro-democracy activists in Myanmar. India's past policy has been seen by Aung San Suu Kyi as "opportunistic". Her most recent biographer, Peter Popham has observed Suu Kyi learnt the Indian way of "passionate, long-winded and often ferocious discussion". Ex-Indian foreign secretary and Ambassador to Myanmar Shyam Saran described her relations with India as "strongly sentimental—almost familial". David Mathieson of Human Rights Watch said "There is surprisingly little mention of India among democracy circiles." Through the uneven course of Myanmar's politics, Aung San Suu Kyi has remained as unbending as ever. Suu Kyi's politicial story is of "sudden challenge, the mass acclaim, the tireless campaigning, and the nation-wide crescent of support" (Popham 2012).

Aung San Suu Kyi greets supporters after the inauguration of a branch of her National League for Democracy in Yangon. Suu Kyi's mother was appointed Burmese Ambassador to India and Nepal in 1960 and Aung San Suu Kyi followed her there. She studied at the Convent of Jesus and Mary School, New Delhi, and graduated from Lady Shri Ram College in New Delhi with a degree in politics in 1964. In this time, she became interested in Gandhi's philosophy of non-violence. In the 1980s, India was a supporter of Suu Kyi's fight against the country military. In the 1990s, the situation changed as Kashmir was in flames and the Naga rebels were running rampant. The government didn't have enough soldiers to suppress both. India's solution was to ask the Burmese military to deny the Nagas safe haven in return for India turning its back on Suu Kyi. Helping Myanmar achieve a sustainable democratic order would be step towards stabilising India's Northeast. India has an advantage in Suu Kyi, whose intellectual influences are dominated by India's greats including Mahatma Gandhi and Rabindranath Tagore. Healing the rift with Suu Kyi is now a pressing requirement of the PM's visit. Suu Kyi, being the daughter of the father of independent Burma and with a high sense of moral vigour adopted non-violence in revolt against the military junta like Mahatma Gandhi, Rabindranath Tagore and even Rammohan Roy. A devout Buddhist, Suu Kyi knew that violent revolution would taint her country more.

Winds of Change in Myanmar

On her first engagement in 20 years, democracy leader Suu Kyi told international community to avoid 'reckless optimism' over changes in Myanmar. Speaking at a gathering of leaders of World Economic Forum in Bangkok (June 1, 2012) she warned China and the United States against turning Myanmar into a "battling ground" as they vie for influence over the strategically important country (*Hindustan Times* 2012: 17). The European Union (EU), the United States and Canada favoured easing of sanctions imposed over the past 20 years on the military regime. Prompting the change and a series of reforms implemented by the nominally civilian government that took power in 2011 and censorship eased, legalized trade union and released hundred of political prisoners.

In recent years, Chinese companies have invested in infrastructure and natural gas to timber and precious gems. The India Company Kirloskar—pump makers' Vice-President Shipra Tripathi also visited Myanmar and led a trade delegation in connection with a pilot project (Burke 2012: 19). Myanmar announced a ceasefire in January 2012 with the most prominent rebel group—the Karen National Union. The defiant stance of the Karen leadership appeared to be a significant setback for the government's efforts to end the grinding civil conflicts that have divided Myanmar for decades. Reconciliation with many armed ethnic groups has been one of the conditions that the United States and other Western countries have put on Myanmar before economic sanctions are lifted (Fuller 2012: 19).

India's Equation and Links with Myanmar

Myanmar's military regime had assured India it will act against Northeast insurgents and anti-India groups on its territory. This assurance was given to Prime Minister Manmohan Singh during his state visit to Nawpyitaw. The Naga hard line fugitives fled and hidden themselves in north Myanmar. Former Indian Foreign Secretary Ranjan Mathai during the visit of Manmohan Singh personally raised the issue and Myanmar's President Thein Sein gave an assurance that North eastern insurgents and anti-Indian groups would not be allowed to operate on Myanmar soil. He also stated that this will necessitate "intelligence sharing" between India and Myanmar. The military to military relations will be long and continuing process and help India develop a "a more nuanced view of the Tatmadan, the Burmese name for Myanmar's armed forces (Chaudhuri 2012: 17).

Prime Minister Singh promised to install a 16-foot sanstone replica of the Sarnath Buddha, reminding Myanmar that it is the home of India's dominant religion (Chaudhuri 2012: 17). Indian officials insisted China was not "a factor behind the visit of Manmohan Singh. But state-owned Chinese newspaper, *Glopal Times* observed Singh had gone because India had been "edged out" of Myanmar by China and the United States (Chaudhuri 2012: 17).

India is to catch up with other nations that are building infrastructural links to Nyapyitaw. Prime Minister Manmohan Singh handed over an invitation to Aung San Suu Kyi to give Jawaharlal Nehru Memorial Lecture in India. Singh also said that Suu Kyi would "play a defining role" in the national reconciliation process launched by Myanmar President Thien Sien. Myanmar has not yet completed a transition to free and fair elections that is due in 2015 but freedom of press is allowed, exactly 50 years after army generals took over in a coup in 1962 (Nayar 2012: 40-42).

Aung San Suu Kyi took the oath in Parliament after her historic journey from political prisoner to parliamentarian on May 2, 2012, opposed to wording in the oath, Suu Kyi and her partymen of National League for Democracy. As a parliamentary minority, the Suu Kyi-led opposition will have little power to change the constitution which allots 25% of assembly seats to unelected military appointees.

Myanmar can be India's gateway and it has to catch up with other nations. Prime Minister Manmohan Singh in his visit sought to make up for 15 years of stunted relations with Myanmar. India is making efforts to side up the security issues that once dominated India's Myanmar policy. India has committed to a 2016 deadline for completing the stretch of the Trilateral Highway running from India's Northeast, across Myanmar to the Thai border.

The Sittwe multimodal transport corridor will run from the Myanmar port of Sittwe to Aizawl in Mizoram. This corridor will be a big gain for India on several levels. One, it would give another means to supply Mizoram and Manipur in case Northeast insurgents ever block National Highway 45 again. Two, it would open up the areas of southwest Myanmar and Mizoram and Manipur to trade and development. It goes through the poorest and least developed parts of both Myanmar and India. The most ambitious and geopolitically significant project is this highway running from India to Vietnam. Conceived as a three-nation project by India under the Mekong Ganga cooperation agreement in 2004, it now includes Cambodia and Vietnam. The most difficult parts to build will be in India and Myanmar, two countries with poor infrastructure traditions. A target date for the bilateral section of 2016 has been set.

As part of a broader strategic vision of being the economic hub of the South Asian periphery, India has built ICPs at Wagah and is building one on the Myanmar border in Moreh. The biggest barrier is not tariff but infrastructure bottlenecks. Negotiating trade facilitation agreements are difficult anywhere. India itself does not have a great record and Myanmar is no better. Bilateral trade agreement only covers 40 items, compared to the thousands in most such deals. Further in the future is a plan to develop the southern Myanmar port of Dawei. This would allow shipments from the Indian Ocean to find easy access to Thailand and Southeast Asia, avoiding the much longer route via the Malacca Straits. Thailand is more enthusiastic than Myanmar about this project. Myanmar's extreme south is isolated from its northern mainland. Dawei was notably absent from the 46-point joint statement on this trip.

Myanmar's Nuclear Trail: India's Reactions

Two Myanmar defectors who escaped to Thailand claimed Myanmar's military regime is trying to acquire a nuclear bomb in the next five years, "and building a secret nuclear reactor and a plutonium-extraction centre with North Korean help" (Chaudhuri 2009: 1). The motives for Myanmar, a poor and isolated military dictatorship to go nuclear remain unclear. Some believe its junta considered nuclear weapons as a guarantee against a US attack and wanted to tackle Western pressure over democratic rights. An Indian defence ministry source, speaking anonymously said a Myanmar N-test could change "the balance of power in Asia...a matter of concern not just for India but the entire international community". Hillary Clinton, former Secretary of State also expressed the view that N-abled Myanmar "triggers domino effect in Southeast Asia, Bangladesh". India also has been worried about a Pakistan-Myanmar N-alliance is 2007. Myanmar and Russia signed deal for a civilian nuclear centre. The United States asked India to bring down a plane that flew from North Korea to Myanmar and was heading to Pakistan (Chaudhuri 2009: 1).

Conclusion

In conclusion, India has enhanced its influence in every major capitals in East and Southeast Asia. The tide is turning after Prime Minister Manmohan Singh's visit in October 2011. Stronger India-Myanmar ties could counter China. When President Thein Sein took office in March 2011, he suspended the $ 3.6 billion Chinese-funded Myitsone Dam project which was to send 90% of power generated to Yunnan Province in China for the next 50 years. To be sure, Myanmar is of strategic importance to India because it is positioned above the Andaman Sea, which leads into the shipping checkpoint of the Malacca straits. Committed to democracy, India has now joined with the west to break the authoritarian nexus and reduce Myanmar's reliance on China. Myanmar President Thein Sein in his address to 67th Session of the UN General Assembly affirmed that foreign policy of Myanmar valued peaceful settlement of disputes will bring an end to long-standing ethnic conflicts and democratise the political process.

The results of Myanmar's polls may set the stage of more conflict between the military and the democratic forces (Bhaumik 2015). Myanmar's President Thein Sein vowed peaceful power shift. Handling the equation between the new democratic forces and the army in Myanmar is going to be tricky (Hazarika 2015). Suu Kyi has won by the massive mandate which reflects

References

Bhaumik, Subir. "Of the people, by the generals". In *Hindustan Times* (New Delhi); November 6, 2015.

Burke, Jason. "MNCs enter Myanmar's door". In *Hindustan Times* (New Delhi); February 5, 2012.

Chaudhuri, Pramit Pal. "India no inspiration for democracy" Reuters and AFP reposted in *Hindustan Times* (New Delhi); May 27, 2012.

———. "Singh makeup to Myanmar". In *Hindustan Times* (New Delhi); May 29, 2012.

———. "Myanmar close to N-bomb". Quoted from *Sydney Morning Herald's* report in *Hindustan Times* (New Delhi); August 2, 2009.

Fuller, Thomas. "The ceasefire that wasn't—or May Be It was". In *Hindustan Times* (New Delhi); February 5, 2012.

Hazarika, Sanjoy. "For Suu Kyi, the real battle has just begun". In *Hindustan Times* (New Delhi); November 17, 2015.

Hindustan Times (New Delhi); May 5, 2012 and June 2, 2012.

India Today; November 23, 2015.

Jha, Nalini Kant. "Dealing with Junta of Myanmar: Need for a Cautious Indian Approach". In *South Asia Politics*, Vol. 6, No. 7; November 2007.

Nayar, Dhiraj. "Out of the General's Shadow". In *India Today*; June 11, 2012.

Popham, Peter. *The Lady and the Peacock: The Life of Aung San Suu Kyi* (2012). Ranton House.

Sagar, Satya. "Glopal Mypocrisy on Myanmar". In *Economic and Political Weekly*; October 6, 2007.

Sundaraman, Shankari. "India must talk rights, not realpolitik, with Burma". In *The Asian Age*; May 26, 2009.

The Week; December 13, 2015.

